Bahá'u'lláh, the West, and the Birth of Modernity

An Essay on the Awakening of Humanity

By the same author

Between the Menorah and the Cross: Jesus, the Jews, and the
    Battle for the Early Church
The Logic of the Apocalypse

Bahá'u'lláh, the West, and the Birth of Modernity

An Essay on the Awakening of Humanity

Stephen Beebe

GR

GEORGE RONALD • OXFORD

George Ronald, Publisher
Oxford
www.grbooks.com

A catalogue record for this book is available from the British Library

ISBN 978-0-85398-629-4

Cover design: René Steiner, Steinergraphics.com

Contents

Prologue

The year 2017 of the Gregorian calendar marked the two hundredth anniversary of the birth of One who will become known to history as He is currently recognized by some six million followers throughout the world: as the Manifestation of God Who appeared to establish a unique and climactic period in the evolution of human society, which is to say, its stage of maturity, indissoluble unity, and peace.

Mírzá Ḥusayn-'Alí, later to be known as Bahá'u'lláh, the Glory of God, was born in Tehran, capital of Persia on 12 November 1817. Son of a one-time minister of the Shah, He spent His childhood, youth and early manhood in comfort and ease as a member of the Persian nobility, while dedicating most of His time to philanthropic and charitable works. Even in this period He was noted for His knowledge of the Qur'án and of Islamic traditions, though He had no formal education in these, but His life changed dramatically when in 1844 He accepted unreservedly a twenty-five-year-old merchant from Shiraz, Siyyid 'Alí-Muḥammad, as the expected Messiah of Shí'ih Islam. That Youth took the title of the Báb, signifying the Gate – a name by which He is universally known today.

Thus began a period of spiritual upheaval in Iran, but this had been in gestation for more than half a century. Messianic fervour had been building since the end of the 18th century and throughout the first decades of the 19th century. From an obscure island of the kingdom of Bahrain, a Muslim saint known as <u>Shaykh</u> Aḥmad-i-Aḥsá'í set forth as inspired by God to purify <u>Shí</u>'ih Islam from the superstitions and dogmas into which it had fallen. Sensing the near advent of the Promised One, <u>Shaykh</u> Aḥmad and his youthful successor, Siyyid Kázim of Rasht, taught that the signs of that appearance and indeed many of the widely accepted doctrines of Islam were not to be understood literally but were symbolic of inner spiritual realities. Inciting the ire of orthodox clergy, these two luminaries were but the first rays of light of that Sun of Truth that would burst upon the world at mid-century.

Confronting the combined opposition of clergy and state, the Báb's ministry was short, eventful and dramatic, ending with His martyrdom in 1850 in a public square in the city of Tabriz in Persian Azerbaijan. An estimated twenty thousand of His followers would likewise be sacrificed in one of the crudest examples of religious persecution in history. Yet His Mission, far from being limited to establishing His own independent Message, was no less than to announce the near arrival of One Whom He proclaimed to be far greater than Himself, One Whom He designated as 'Him Who God will make manifest'.

As one of the most prominent of the followers of the Báb, Bahá'u'lláh was arrested and imprisoned, and suffered attempts on His life. Placed in a dungeon in the heart of Tehran, it was there that He experienced that to which only His own words can do justice.

> During the days I lay in the prison of Ṭihrán, though the galling weight of the chains and the stench-filled air allowed Me but little sleep, still in those infrequent moments of slumber I felt as if something flowed from the crown of My head over My breast, even as a mighty torrent that precipitateth

itself upon the earth from the summit of a lofty mountain. Every limb of My body would, as a result, be set afire. At such moments My tongue recited what no man could bear to hear.[1]

One night, in a dream, these exalted words were heard on every side: 'Verily, We shall render Thee victorious by Thyself and by Thy Pen. Grieve Thou not for that which hath befallen Thee, neither be Thou afraid, for Thou art in safety. Erelong will God raise up the treasures of the earth – men who will aid Thee through Thyself and through Thy Name, wherewith God hath revived the hearts of such as have recognized Him.'[2]

I was but a man like others, asleep upon My couch, when lo, the breezes of the All-Glorious were wafted over Me, and taught Me the knowledge of all that hath been. This thing is not from Me, but from One Who is Almighty and All-Knowing.[3]

Thanks to the intervention of the consul of Russia, He whose advent the Báb had prepared was spared martyrdom but instead, Bahá'u'lláh was exiled from His native Iran, never to return. His belongings pillaged, He and His immediate family travelled in the dead of winter through the mountains of western Iran to Baghdad, a regional capital of the Ottoman Empire on the banks of the Tigris River. It was here and after a lapse of a full decade that Bahá'u'lláh would reveal to His closest associates the secret that He had guarded within His heart, that He was that One to Whom the Báb had referred as the Promised One of all ages. Still, the enemies of the young Faith never rested, and as a result of their machinations Bahá'u'lláh was to suffer another three exiles, first to Constantinople (modern Istanbul), then to the remote city of Adrianople on the western frontier of the Ottoman Empire.

Thus did Bahá'u'lláh reside for five years on the European continent, the only Manifestation of God of whom we have record to have trod the soil of Europe. From Adrianople He directed His weighty epistles to the leaders of East and West – epistles in which He berated the kings for their arrogance and their militarism, in which He adjured them to be united in search of peace and to address the needs of the poor in their midst, in which He commented on the forms of government that were then evolving, in which He warned them of the inexorable transformations that were sweeping across the world and that would overtake them and their regimes.

In a final exile that purposed to distance Him from any possible interaction with friend or follower, He was sent to the dismal and fetid penal colony of Akka on the Mediterranean coast of Palestine. Bahá'u'lláh's sufferings reached their climax in Akka, as local officials poisoned the populace against One who was stigmatized as the 'god of the Persians', and within the prison barracks where His youngest son yielded up his life after a fatal fall through a skylight. But such was not to be His fate forever. Progressively gaining the respect of local dignitaries, and through the efforts of His eldest Son, 'Abdu'l-Bahá, conditions within the city evolved to a state of house arrest in gradually improving accommodations. Eventually He would be permitted to live outside the city where He received pilgrims who travelled from the East. In this period the famous English orientalist Edward Granville Browne would attain His presence.

Upon the Ascension of Bahá'u'lláh, 'Abdu'l-Bahá assumed the role of Successor and authorized Interpreter of the Writings of the Faith, as stipulated in the Testament of Bahá'u'lláh, a document that established His Covenant whereby the legitimate authority in the Faith is maintained, first in the person of 'Abdu'l-Bahá, then in His grandson Shoghi Effendi, and today in the Universal House of Justice, a body elected from among the

Bahá'ís of the world and that promotes the development of the Bahá'í community in accord with the teachings of Bahá'u'lláh.

It was under the guidance of 'Abdu'l-Bahá that the teachings of Bahá'u'lláh were spread to the West, a process that was greatly augmented by a three-year journey between 1911 and 1913, with extended stays in Europe and the United States. Speaking to literally hundreds of organizations, special interest groups and religious congregations, many of His talks during that time were social commentaries reflecting the needs of an increasingly globalized society. Offered at a time when the modern era was settling into the mold that we know today, these reflections continue to be relevant as the world seeks to deal with the crises that appear at every turn. This essay attempts to extend those reflections of 'Abdu'l-Bahá, both backwards into the birth of the modern era, and forward into our own times, as a complement to those epistles of Bahá'u'lláh set in their own historical context.

It is expected that most readers will be relatively familiar with the origins of the Bahá'í Faith that are outlined here. However, for the reader who is not familiar with this history, this brief overview is no more than the scantiest of summaries so as to set the context for this study. It is hoped that anyone who seriously wishes to understand this context will refer to one of the far better accounts of this divine drama.

As to the historical content of this current study bearing on those countries and their kings who were addressed by Bahá'u'lláh, I have refrained from extensive referencing for that information of a general nature, but typically have limited references to specific and telling points of interest. Nonetheless, it is proper to recognize the authors of those historical accounts that were particularly useful in developing this treatise: Dr Kenneth Bartlett of the University of Toronto; Dr William Cook, State University of New York, Geneseo; Dr Suzanne Desan of the University of Wisconsin; Dr Allen Guelzo, Gettysburg College; and Dr Alan Charles Kors, University of Pennsylvania. Dr David Zarefsky of Northwestern University and Dr Robert Weiner of Lafayette College, Pennsylvania graciously responded to my questions, and I owe special thanks to the latter who set me on this path of study.

1

Why Europe?

Why Europe?

Why not India? . . . or China? . . . or Africa?

Why were the majority of the epistles that Bahá'u'lláh addressed to kings and rulers directed to sovereigns of countries that He had never visited, who had not participated in persecuting His followers, and who were largely uninformed of the history and tenets of a nascent religion? Why did He take such an active interest in lands and cultures that were apparently so foreign to His immediate surroundings and context? Why did these potentates merit some of His weightiest Tablets? Why did Bahá'u'lláh focus so much attention on Europe, which seemed to be so far off-centre of the unfolding history of His Faith?

Of course, the crowned heads of Europe were not the only ones to be addressed by Bahá'u'lláh, and He did indeed write epistles to Middle Eastern monarchs and ministers of state but in a very different tone from that in which He addressed those of the West. His condemnation of the Sultan of Turkey was in the vein of his oppressive role in persecuting the young Faith, and in his opposition to His own Person. His Tablet to the Shah of Iran recounts the intense and widespread suffering of the innocent followers of the Lord of the Age. These monarchs brought upon themselves the well-earned chastisement that Bahá'u'lláh meted out to them in ample measure.

So again, why Europe? . . . and why sovereigns with no previous contact with the Faith? For while 'epoch-making counsels and warnings [were] collectively addressed by the Báb and Bahá'u'lláh to the sovereigns of the earth', these were 'more particularly directed to the kings of Christendom'.[1] It is clear that 'those mighty ones of the earth who had either so sorely maltreated Him, or deliberately withheld from Him their succor'[2] bore a burden of guilt either for sins of commission or omission:

'Twenty years have passed, O kings!' He, addressing the kings of Christendom, at the height of His mission, has written, 'during which We have, each day, tasted the agony of a fresh tribulation. No one of them that were before Us hath endured the things We have endured. Would that ye could perceive it! They that rose up against Us have put Us to death, have shed Our blood, have plundered Our property, and violated Our honour. Though aware of most of Our afflictions, ye, nevertheless, have failed to stay the hand of the aggressor. For is it not your clear duty to restrain the tyranny of the oppressor, and to deal equitably with your subjects, that your high sense of justice may be fully demonstrated to all mankind?'[3]

Yet the situation of the sovereigns of Europe was particular, as the visible heads of a continent which had set the cultural, economic and political standards for lands far beyond their own borders.

The 19th century has been called the century of Europe, and by mid-century when Bahá'u'lláh made His epoch-making proclamation to the kings, Europe was well on the way to dominating the world scene. However, the roots of this domination can be found as long as four centuries earlier. Europe had initiated its world-embracing role largely as a group of competing commercial powers seeking hegemony in lucrative trade with the Far East. The New Testament hints at the delicacies of the East with the frankincense and myrrh that were presented as gifts to the new-born Saviour, but it was the spice trade in particular that motivated European journeys of discovery and conquest. Vigorous commerce in spices was by no means new. It had functioned by land and sea routes for centuries, and even before the 15th century it was dominated in the Mediterranean by the Venetians. However, with the rise of Islam, and as Turkey and Egypt sought to exact profit from the trade through their territories, European merchants sought other routes free from monopolies of the Muslim States. Motivations for exploration were initially commercial and often led by private concerns with government mandates, but eventually these were supported by military might which grew into political power.

Iberia would take the lead in extending European influence, pushing both to the East and to the West. The drive to the East was led by tiny Portugal, perched on the western extreme of continental Europe and facing the unknown vastness of the Atlantic. Portugal's explorations in the early to mid-15th century led it gradually down the coast of Africa, establishing trading posts along the way, and eventually rounding the Cape of Good Hope in 1488 to enter the Indian Ocean. This was a landmark in opening the trade with the East, breaking the monopoly of the Ottoman Turks and stimulating competition from other European powers. Still, the Portuguese would dominate the spice trade for the better part of a century through naval power. Remnants of its trading empire persisted into the 20th century with its colonies of Goa in India, Macau in China, East Timor, as well as its African colonies, Angola, Mozambique, Guinea-Bissau and Cabo Verde. It extended its influence to the western hemisphere when its ships strayed from their standard routes and landed in what is modern-day Brazil in 1500.

The Dutch were the second power to expand aggressively

into the spice trade of the Indian Ocean, establishing a far-flung commercial network of trading enclaves that virtually encircled the globe in the early 1600s. Becoming a world power in the first half of the 17th century, the Dutch had a significant presence in the Caribbean and northern South America (in modern Suriname), in Brazil, in Africa in South Africa, Ghana and Angola, in Ceylon (modern Sri Lanka), among other sites, eventually displacing the Portuguese in southern Asia and elsewhere. The participation of the Dutch in the Indian Ocean spice trade through their East India Company led them to establish a power base in Java from which they exercised control over the far-flung islands that would become Indonesia, and which they would dominate well into the 20th century.

In the same period the British initiated their commercial forays into the East with the establishment of their own East India Company in 1600. It grew gradually as a commercial enterprise throughout the 17th century, and in the 18th century Britain came to dominate in India, excluding the French who were its main competitor. James Cook's explorations in the late 1700s led to the establishment of several British colonies on the Australian continent, with this influence expanding in the Pacific region in the 19th century. The Napoleonic Wars in Europe motivated a more aggressive role in other parts of the world, as the British consolidated their place in India and took Cape Town from the Dutch, eventually to be a beachhead for the British conquest of southern Africa. China was likewise submitted to the commercial interests of the Europeans, powerless to resist their superior military might.

European domination of the western hemisphere paralleled the process in the East and led to colonial domination even more rapidly. As the Portuguese monopolized the Indian Ocean trade, Spain set its face westward in the late 15th and early 16th centuries, hoping to bypass the Portuguese-dominated route around the cape of Africa. The 'discovery' of the Americas by Columbus was an effort to find a direct westerly route to the spice-rich East. The Spanish would exercise power only gradually after the voyages of Columbus, first in Mexico with the conquest of the Aztecs, and later with the brutal and treacherous subjugation of the Incan Empire by the Pizarro brothers. Soon the Spanish would be extracting huge quantities of silver to finance projects on the home front in Europe. Spain would gradually dominate the interior of an area much larger than all of Europe, from California to Tierra del Fuego.

Just as Portugal's success attracted other trading enterprises in the East, Spain's experience stimulated a rush among European powers to establish beachheads in the 'New World'. As in the East, competition among European powers intensified during the 17th century. In spite of repeated early attempts, the French presence was only consolidated in this period, and Great Britain established itself in the North American continent in 1607 in Jamestown, fully a century later than the Spanish, while the Dutch established a colony in upstate New York in 1614, famously purchasing Manhattan in 1626 from the natives for a few pounds of trinkets. The eastern seaboard of North America lacked the mineral wealth that the Spanish possessions enjoyed but here the wealth lay in abundant furs, timber and farmland. France became the great competitor in the forests of Canada and in the future United States. Competition was especially intense in the Caribbean islands, where sugar production dominated the economy and which would become an important component of European wealth. Britain, France, Spain and the Netherlands all maintained a colonial presence in the Caribbean, and short of open warfare, piracy became a sort of guerrilla conflict on the open seas.

Thus, by the time Bahá'u'lláh proclaimed His Faith to the crowned heads, Europe had subjected the ancient civilizations of the East to its military might in service to commercial interests, soon to be transformed into imperial or colonial dominion. In the West where the European powers had conquered and sub-jugated empires and diverse peoples from Alaska to Tierra del Fuego, those vast lands would be lost to the descendants of those conquerors who had enriched Europe. By that time European culture, language and political systems were firmly established. Only the interior of Africa remained to come under the dominion of Europe, and that would soon occur in the late 19th century.

However, by the mid-18th century, the major European powers on a world level had been reduced to two or three, while others had stagnated and simply sought to maintain the status quo. Spain had been in decline for many decades but still maintained a vast colonial empire, most of which would be lost during and after the Napoleonic Wars. Portugal main-tained its colonial presence in Brazil and scattered outposts but was in no position to challenge other players. The Dutch were holding on with ups and downs but would soon suffer severe reverses in the Napoleonic Wars. Russia's international presence was largely on its borders or in far-off Alaska, while Prussia (the future core of a pan-German State) was scarcely on the ascend-ant in central Europe under the Hohenzollern king Frederick the Great. Austria had never had a truly world presence except through its extended Hapsburg dynasty, but was maintaining its extensive empire of eastern Europe and the Balkans, dominat-ing a plethora of ethnic groups, facing off against the Ottoman Empire, and with influence in Italy. After nearly three centu-ries of intense international competition, two major players now competed for hegemony in the western hemisphere and in the East in India: Great Britain and France. Indeed, much of the history of the late 18th century would evolve around the competition between these two superpowers, and of these two, Britain would emerge the stronger.

France nominally had a vast empire in North America, from Newfoundland west along the St Lawrence River, and westward from the Mississippi in what would come to be called the Louisiana Purchase (briefly ceded to Spain in the settlement of the Seven Years' War in 1762 and later recovered). However, France had never truly colonized Canada in a way that was comparable to the English settlements in its thirteen colonies or the Spanish in Latin America, and relatively few French had actually established themselves in Canada. Rather, the French presence existed as trading posts that extracted goods and especially furs for shipment to Europe, but the French influence was perpetuated in modern Quebec and in place names around the north-central United States. The French presence and economic interest were much greater in the Caribbean where sugar and coffee were produced, and which contributed significantly to its economy. The islands were its jewels and its wealth, and were sustained almost exclusively by slave labour. Saint-Domingue (future Haiti) was the largest of these possessions. Still, back home on the continent France continued to bask in the glory of the court of Louis XIV, a reign that had opened the 18th century and that had set the pace for European culture. Throughout the century French remained the lingua franca of diplomacy across the continent. Paris was the intellectual capital of Europe, illumined with the brilliance of Voltaire and Rousseau. Setbacks in the East and West still had not dimmed the lustre of its earlier preeminence, rooted in the medieval social system and focused on the crown.

Britain was France's great rival, and in North America Britain wrested Canada from France in the Seven Years' War ending in 1763. In the East likewise, Britain and France played a cat and mouse game in India that was focused on trade, but Britain turned commercial skirmishing into an opportunity to gain the political upper hand, and by the end of the century France was effectively excluded from the sub-continent. Britain's major setback came with the loss of its North American colonies who earned their independence with the support of France. Thus, the 18th century would draw to a close with these two giants still facing off, but with Britain holding the upper hand and France smarting from recent setbacks. Such was the scene on the eve of the most eventful century that Europe would ever experience.

And when, at the end of that transformative period known to historians as the 'long 19th century' – from the start of the French Revolution in 1789 to the First World War – 'Abdu'l-Bahá initiated His historic missionary journeys throughout the West, He chose to give His first public address in London, at the heart of the British Empire which had expanded dramatically in the interim. Britain was now the undisputed leader on the world scene and the master of the most widespread empire in history – the result of centuries-long power struggles, and the fruit of its industrial prowess and its naval might. London was the focal point of the empire, at the centre of which stood 'Abdu'l-Bahá. In that first public address in the West in 1911, He declared that this is a 'new cycle of human power'.[4]

A careful observer might well have noted that the changes that Europe had experienced throughout the previous century were a reflection of that power, albeit still in its infancy. Such new power was implicit in the words of Bahá'u'lláh when He said that God had taken power away from two groups in this age: kings and ecclesiastics. Implicitly this left a vacuum that would need to be filled by new powers in a century that witnessed the dawn of the age of maturity of mankind – powers that must eventually serve the Divine Plan of God.

The 19th century saw the emergence of two new powers, that of technology and that of the emerging social classes, and in particular the masses of humanity. These would confront the resistance of ancient social and economic patterns, like massive tectonic plates smashing into each other, inevitably creating tensions that would find release in occasional tremors of social disorder, strikes or coups, or in the case of Russia where the ancient powers resisted more tenaciously, with a massive earthquake that would reverberate throughout the rest of the world. These tectonic plates would change the entire landscape, raising up new mountains of political power, economic hegemony, and urban lifestyles.

Science had been gathering momentum since the 17th century through the efforts of minds such as Newton, Boyle and Descartes. One would expect that technology would be born of science but in fact most early technology grew out of the efforts of workmen with little or no formal training – men whom we would call 'tinkerers'. Their inventions would fuel the Industrial Revolution and economic growth, but would also provide horrific new tools of war. New sorts of energy were created to drive factories which would employ migrants from rural areas. The Industrial Revolution would also encourage urbanization and would have social implications that were even more important than its economic or technical impacts.

Regarding the masses and their new-found energies, even the Báb hinted at this when He refused the offer of Manúchihr Khán, governor of Isfahan, to promote His Cause, because God had ordained that 'Through the poor and lowly of this land, by the blood which these shall have shed in His path, will the omnipotent Sovereign ensure the preservation and consolidate the foundation of His Cause.'⁵ The Báb foresaw that the so-called 'common people' would be the source of spiritual and social transformation, reflecting this nascent power. Popular power would not be limited to the Cause of God but would be expressed in all fields of human endeavour. It would advance by fits and starts in the 19th century, interacting with both old and new models of authority.

However, the masses laboured under severe restrictions

imposed by the cultural and political milieu in which they lived, which limited their possibilities either to participate in public life or to acquaint themselves with the Message of Bahá'u'lláh that was shaping the age:

> It would be no exaggeration to say that in most of the countries of the European and Asiatic continents absolutism, on the one hand, and complete subservience to ecclesiastical hierarchies, on the other, were still the outstanding features of the political and religious life of the masses. These, dominated and shackled, were robbed of the necessary freedom that would enable them to either appraise the claims and merits of the Message proffered to them, or to embrace unreservedly its truth.[6]

A heavy burden of guilt rests upon those who intervened between the Manifestations of God and the masses who hungered for the food of the spirit, and who would suffer the consequences of that forced separation.

In those very years that <u>Shaykh</u> Aḥmad arose in the East to stir Islam from its lethargy and to initiate a spiritual transformation, in the West the French were immersed in one of the first society-wide experiments in social transformation, carried out consciously, systematically and with much heated debate, and testing models in the exercise of popular power. Indeed, the French Revolution would become a microcosm of the 19th century, encapsulating in two brief and intense decades many of the changes, conflicts and challenges that the rest of Europe would confront up to the First World War. The patterns of the French Revolution would be repeated in other parts of Europe throughout the length of the 19th century and within an overall context of tension between the forces of change and the forces of conservative reaction. Such a pattern began with idealism born of the Enlightenment – idealism that would at first fuel enthusiastic optimism among the masses but, still in its infancy and immature, then would falter and turn violent as the forces of the old regime would cast roadblocks in the path of popular power. Progress toward public participation of the masses would be evidenced by an extension of the voting franchise to an ever wider citizenry, but both in France and later in other countries the development and maturation of popular power would be distracted by the emergence of new dictatorial authority. Napoleon Bonaparte in France, and subsequently the neo-absolutist monarchs in other countries, would manipulate the masses, at times through outright oppression, and at times through nationalism which simultaneously would create a firmer sense of nationhood. The pattern would culminate in the militarization of societies and would eventually result in disastrous military defeat. Throughout this evolutionary process, the Church would be one of the biggest losers, ceding its privileged position to the State.

When Bahá'u'lláh was born in 1817, the French Revolution had only recently come to an end with the defeat of Napoleon Bonaparte, while the revolutionary experience in the rest of Europe was in its earliest stages. Its course would be contemporary with events in the history of the Faith, and Bahá'u'lláh would direct His gaze toward that transformational process and comment upon it. Thus when Bahá'u'lláh directed His epistles to the crowned heads of Europe, He was addressing those who held in their hands the destinies of their subjects, and beyond them the destinies of far-flung empires, and who had the opportunity to contribute positively to their development: 'The instruments which are essential to the immediate protection, the security and assurance of the human race have been entrusted to the hands, and lie in the grasp, of the governors of human society.'[7] As a prelude to the individual epistles that He

would soon transmit to them, He addressed them jointly in the
Súriy-i-Mulúk (Tablet to the Kings) with a severe judgement.

> O kings of Christendom! Heard ye not the saying of Jesus, the
> Spirit of God, 'I go away, and come again unto you'? Where-
> fore, then, did ye fail, when He did come again unto you in
> the clouds of heaven, to draw nigh unto Him, that ye might
> behold His face, and be of them that attained His Presence?
> . . . Ye have, by reason of your failure, hindered the breath of
> God from being wafted over you, and have withheld from
> your souls the sweetness of its fragrance. Ye continue roving
> with delight in the valley of your corrupt desires. By God!
> Ye, and all ye possess, shall pass away. Ye shall, most certainly,
> return to God, and shall be called to account for your doings
> in the presence of Him Who shall gather together the entire
> creation. [8]

Bahá'u'lláh and later 'Abdu'l-Bahá would critique the civilization for which the kings and rulers had willingly sacrificed
millions of lives and for which they claimed moral superiority.
While recognizing its benefits and great advances in science and
forms of government, Bahá'u'lláh was uncompromisingly stern
in His judgement of western civilization in its negative aspects:

> Consider the peoples of the West. Witness how, in their pur-
> suit of that which is vain and trivial, they have sacrificed, and
> are still sacrificing, countless lives for the sake of its establish-
> ment and promotion.[9]

> Consider the civilization of the West, how it hath agitated
> and alarmed the peoples of the world.[10]

> When the eyes of the people of the East were captivated by

the arts and wonders of the West, they roved distraught in the wilderness of material causes, oblivious of the One Who is the Causer of Causes, and the Sustainer thereof . . .'[11]

The civilization, so often vaunted by the learned exponents of arts and sciences, will, if allowed to overleap the bounds of moderation, bring great evil upon men. Thus warneth you He Who is the All-Knowing. If carried to excess, civilization will prove as prolific a source of evil as it had been of goodness when kept within the restraints of moderation.[12]

Indeed, Europe and European peoples around the planet had contributed more than their share to science and technology, but also to create 'a world that has lost its bearings, in which the bright flame of religion is fast dying out, in which the forces of a blatant nationalism and racialism have usurped the rights and prerogatives of God Himself, in which a flagrant secularism – the direct offspring of irreligion – has raised its triumphant head and is protruding its ugly features . . .'[13] And as to those kings who headed up those civilizations, who promoted both its progressive ends and its aggressive designs, and who 'held unchallengeable sway over the multitudes of their subjects, their relation to the Faith of Bahá'u'lláh constitutes one of the most illuminating episodes in the history of the Heroic and Formative Ages of that Faith'.[14] Above and beyond Bahá'u'lláh's general and many-faceted calls to the peoples of the world, these cannot compare to 'that peculiar pregnancy which direct and specific messages, voiced by the Manifestation of God and directed to the world's Chief Magistrates in His day, must possess'.[15]

Still, we shall see that those epistles sometimes bore a significance beyond the immediate circumstances of the monarchs to whom they were apparently addressed. Some of the Tablets credit a monarch with events that fall outside of the reign of that monarch, but rather in the time of a predecessor. Occasionally they can be understood as applying to an entire dynastic line of a royal house, to a tradition of that dynasty, or perhaps even to a system of government represented by that monarch. Such instances will be mentioned in the course of this study.

God had launched a 'new cycle of human power' and it could not be turned back, and it would magnify those forces of civilization that been in gestation for centuries. But the course of that newfound power would depend on mankind's response to the Divine Call. Western civilization had agitated the world, but mankind would have a unique opportunity to direct the forces of civilization toward greater good, or . . . toward even greater evil. We will seek to trace the development of the process of transformation in light of the epistles of Bahá'u'lláh, the principles that He outlined for the age of maturity of mankind, and the analysis offered by 'Abdu'l-Bahá, His Successor and appointed Interpreter. In particular, we will focus this study on the empowerment of the masses, with its ups and downs, its successes and failures, and its disastrous frustrations. For this empowerment – specifically spiritual empowerment – is a central theme in the Mission of the Faith of Bahá'u'lláh. It is a theme that emerges with greater dynamism with the advance of the 21st century. With this we seek to identify the forces of popular empowerment that were influenced by the crowned heads of the period and that led to the present era, and to understand the significance of the current efforts of the Bahá'í community in spiritual empowerment, as a response to and fulfilment of the processes that were born in the long 19th century.

2

The Enlightenment

Even as the kings of Europe were extending their influence over Asia, the Americas and eventually Africa, changes in age-old manners of thinking were gestating at home on the continent. Conceived in the 16th and 17th centuries, and taking their embryonic form in the attitudes and mindsets of the 18th century, these would bear fruit in the revolutions, social movements, economic makeovers and cultural changes of the 19th century. The radical upheavals of the 19th century would be the product of much earlier transformations that wrought fundamental changes in the way Europeans viewed the world, first in the realm of religion, later with regard to the physical environment, and then in social relations. These tectonic shifts occurred in virtually all areas of human intellectual endeavour and in ways that seemingly different currents of thought interacted to revolutionize Europe.

Prior to the 16th century, erudition was essentially in the hands of clergy, and there was little or no distinction between religion and science or 'natural philosophy', which was considered to be an extension of the study of God's will as expressed in the creation. Astronomy was the highest form of science, since the heavens were a manifestation of God's majesty, vast and unchanging, and raised far above the imperfect and transient world of man. The science of earthly phenomena was considered far inferior to astronomy which was one step away from divine revelation. Just as the Bible held eternal truths through revelations received from ancient times, such that truth was the domain of past sages and prophets, so too did the scientific teachings of the Greeks enjoy the same aura of ancient authority. Thus, in both religion and science, the truth lay in the past, and erudition consisted of explaining current observations or theories in relation to established authority.

How did Europeans undergo a radical transformation in their mode of thinking, from conforming submissively to the unshakeable truths of the ancient authorities, to uncovering truth through study and research? How did Europe shift from backward-looking thinking derived from long-accepted theorems, to forward-looking rational thought, extracting principles from multiple observations of phenomena to unveil the secrets of nature and the universe? This complex story of intellectual history is summarized here as a prelude to reflections on events and social transformations that made the 19th century an inflection point in human history.

Religion

The first rumblings of change came precisely in religion – that fundamental bastion of authority and unquestioned truth. For more than a millennium the Papacy had held unswerving sway over kings and paupers alike, with power to dethrone dynasties or control potentates under threat of excommunication. For those who accepted the logic of its authority derived from Jesus Christ through the succession of popes from Peter, its power was absolute and formidable. The crack in its seamless wall of power and a major upheaval in the realm of religion grew out of the Reformation as the drama of Martin Luther unfolded, starting in 1517 when he nailed his ninety-five theses on the door of his local church in northern Germany. Minor German princelings flocked to his cause as they saw the opportunity to seize church lands and feed their coffers, such that the Protestant cause rapidly took on a political dimension. John Calvin generated a parallel movement in Switzerland later in that same century, and the door was open to widespread undermining of the centralized authority of the Pope and the Catholic Church. While Lutheranism gained a stronghold among the Germanic principalities and in Scandinavia, Calvinism and its offshoots spread across the Low Countries, and established itself as Presbyterianism in Scotland and among dissenting Puritans in England. In France the Calvinist Huguenots threatened to become the majority at one time, so dynamic was the movement.

Religious wars between Christians marred much of the 16th century, as the Spanish crown bankrupted itself in defence of Catholicism. Where the Protestant cause had flowered, conflict followed in the Netherlands, France, the German states and with the famous attack on England by the Spanish Armada. Religious fratricide reached its peak in the 17th century in the Thirty Years War (1618–1648) that gutted northern Europe, leaving an estimated third of the population dead in some areas, and finally ending in a stalemate between Catholic and Protestant Europe.

Beyond the tragic loss of life and treasure over nearly a century and a half, the central pillar of authority in Europe and its greatest unifying force – the Catholic Church – was shaken forever. The Church had been practically synonymous with Europe, but now diversity of opinion and doctrine displaced the omnipotent authority of Rome. If the authority of the Church was brought into doubt, what area of human endeavour could be immune to questioning?

Science

Parallel to the challenges to the authority of the Church were challenges to other time-honoured standards of truth about the material world. The pillar of the old world view in the intellectual sphere was respect for the authority of Aristotle and other ancient Greek and Roman writers. All earthly matter was assumed to be composed of four essential elements or essences: air, earth, fire and water, while the heavens (the fifth essence) were composed of concentric spheres that defined the orbits of the stars and other planets, and with the earth at the centre. To the extent that science is the study of cause and effect, Aristotle classified causes of phenomena in a hierarchy of four levels: the material cause or the 'what' of matter; the formative cause or the 'shape' of matter; the efficient cause or the force that creates the form; and the final cause or the 'why' or purpose. In the Middle Ages scholars (the creators of 'scholasticism') would use the ancients and especially Aristotle as the unquestioned reference point for knowledge, together with the Bible. In Christian theology the final cause would be the equivalent of the Will of God – the ultimate and all-satisfying explanation of natural phenomena as opposed to exploring the physical laws inherent in creation. While the Bahá'í Writings do see God as the ultimate cause of all creation, and nature as the expression of God's Will, science does not stop there but identifies the underlying principles of phenomena, and man, 'by his understanding or intellect, has been able to gain control of and adapt some of those natural laws to his own needs'.[1] Increasingly in the 16th century, time-honoured concepts of scholasticism were gradually questioned, challenged and finally discarded in a process that opened the modern era.

One such example that has filtered into popular folklore and that is familiar to the modern public is the confrontation between Galileo (1564–1642) and the Church over the nature of the universe. Galileo argued in favour of a heliocentric or sun-centred universe, while the official position of the Church was that of a system with the earth at the centre – an inheritance of the 2nd-century Greek astronomer Ptolemais. That story is representative of a significant shift in perspective involving philosophy and natural science but is merely the tip of the iceberg.

The authority of the ancients was made operative through the deductive method – deductive in the sense of deducing conclusions from a prior and accepted truth. In the example cited above of the earth-centred universe, an elaborate and complicated astronomical system was *deduced* to explain the movement of the planets, under the assumption of the Ptolemaic system that all celestial bodies revolved around the earth. In the deductive method all observations of astronomical reality were adapted to and interpreted in light of this prior assumption. In contrast, an English contemporary of Galileo, Francis Bacon (1561–1626) is credited with promoting the inductive scientific method based on distilling truths from measurable, systematic and repeatable observations about reality, positing principles to explain observations, and testing these newly posited truths through consciously designed experiments. In the inductive method, general principles were not the point of departure but were derived from observations as a result of investigation.

While Bacon is credited with articulating this approach to the generation of knowledge, many others in this age of burgeoning intellectual curiosity contributed to evolving concepts about the very nature and process of knowledge. This period saw ample discussion about the character of the human mind in its quest for knowledge. Descartes (1596–1650) in his trademark statement 'I think, therefore I am' sought to find an unassailable point of departure for knowledge that was independent of the ancients and that could counter a tendency toward sterile scepticism, while his contemporary Thomas Hobbes (1588–1679), an early materialist, discounted Descartes' claim to have demonstrated a non-material thinking being, arguing that matter might also have such capacity to think.

In particular, John Locke (1632–1704) put forth a theory of knowledge as derived from the senses, each experience contributing to the cumulative compilation of small bits of data into wider and greater ideas. Sight, hearing, touch – all were channels through which facts flowed into the mind where they were compiled in an ever-growing database and where they were subject to the power of reflection. Under the assumption that all knowledge is derived from experience, the social and physical environments would take on importance as conditioning those opportunities for experience. Locke's perspective on the acquisition of knowledge through the senses was a theoretical complement to the practical method of Bacon, and turned the attention about the generation of knowledge toward the gathering of information through systematic observation and analysis.

Still, these debates might have been restricted to an intellectual elite, except for a far more remarkable milestone when Isaac Newton (1642–1727) described the gravitational relations between planets as a product of their masses and inversely proportional to the square of the distance between them: $(m_1 \times m_2)/d^2$. Newton was not the first to describe astronomical phenomena quantitatively. Kepler and others had made other remarkable discoveries long before. But compared to other science of the age, describing the gravitational forces of the heavenly bodies was like the contrast between a family portrait and Michelangelo's painting on the ceiling of the Sistine Chapel. Both Newton and Michelangelo inspired awe, transcending the mundane and opening a vision on the world of God. Newton's discovery, beyond being a stroke of genius, caught the imagination of both the intelligentsia and the public, and gained the admiration of his own generation and all since then. Apart from his extraordinary mental capacity, what set Newton apart from others was his impact on the public appreciation for the power of scientific investigation. More than any other individual, Newton validated the power of the intellect and put science on the public agenda.

Newton himself was deeply religious in his attitude toward God. He understood the mathematical description of gravity that held the planets in their orbits as the Will of God writ large upon the universe. This iconic discovery is representative of what would become the foundation of a major current of thought about religion – that God's plan could be read through reason from the book of nature. Others would extend this premise to say that reason was as good or even superior an avenue to understanding God's plan as was revealed religion, which is to say, the Bible.

Social relations

As the emphasis on reading God's Will in nature through reason was popularized by the findings of Newton, the intellectual curiosity of Europeans extended to reflections on the nature of human beings – asking themselves 'What makes man tick?' as if searching after the Newtonian equation that explained the inner life of man. Even prior to Newton, Hobbes identified two vital forces, pain and pleasure. In a dog-eat-dog world in which the masses of society still lived on the edge of hunger or were decimated by epidemics, the actions of man were seen to be driven by attempts to evade or lessen pain, and to increase pleasure or *happiness*. Just as God had made the universe to be a vast tablet upon which He had inscribed His Will, this essential nature of man was likewise a reflection of God's handiwork.

The avoidance of suffering and the search after pleasure were therefore part of mankind's divine inheritance. Whereas in traditional church doctrine the search after pleasure had been seen as the cause of perdition, it now was justified as being part of God's plan. Furthermore, the purpose of society and the role of government were now defined as facilitating these two essential instincts of minimizing pain and maximizing happiness. Herein was the basis of the social contract whereby society deposited authority in its rulers to deal with these two basic needs of humanity. In the political realm the age saw thinkers of various inclinations who suggested different approaches to the theory of social contract that defined the purpose of government.

England in the 17th century was an especially fertile field for speculating about theory of government, since the English had gone through an entire generation of political turmoil. England's tradition of political rights dated back to the Magna Carta in 1215, but a new round of crises emerged in the 1600s. Ascending to the throne in 1625 as the Thirty Years War raged on the continent, King Charles I still believed in the divine right of kings and clashed with Parliament over taxation and issues of religion, the king being viewed as too sympathetic to Catholicism. His reign led to a period of political chaos and civil war, resulting in his overthrow and decapitation in 1649, the parliamentary dictatorship of Oliver Cromwell, the restoration of the monarchy and subsequent overthrow of James II, and finally the imposition of William of Orange as king in the 'Glorious Revolution' in 1688 – glorious insomuch as the 'people' had chosen their ruler in a bloodless coup to function in a constitutional monarchy. These upheavals and the rapid-fire evolution of experiments in the government of England generated multiple theories and perspectives heavily coloured by perceived abuses of the crown, and that were attempts to correct or preempt such abuses.

Like other political theorists of the age, Hobbes expounded the concept of the social contract, but he believed that the common good was best served by a strong central authority that would quash any expression of the baser and aggressive instincts of man – perhaps a response to the factionalism that was tearing England apart in that period. John Locke was younger than Hobbes but lived in the same chaotic period. In addition to his reflections on knowledge and mind, Locke was also a political theorist and like Hobbes, he posited that governments must arise from the consent of the governed. Additionally, he proposed that if government failed in its essential mission, the populace had the right to throw off its government and establish another, as indeed occurred during his lifetime in the Glorious Revolution. Both the political theories and the emergence of a stable constitutional monarchy would influence others far beyond the British Isles. Nearly a century later Jefferson would repeat this principle of Locke in the American Declaration of Independence:

> That whenever any Form of Government becomes destructive of these ends, it is the Right of the People to alter or to abolish it, and to institute new Government, laying its foundation on such principles and organizing its powers in such form, as to them shall seem most likely to effect their Safety and Happiness.

Among the French, Montesquieu (1689–1755) was an admirer of the English system and is remembered for the concept of a balance of powers – indeed, an idea that dated to antiquity – whereby the sharing of power among the executive, legislative and judicial branches of government denied any single branch the opportunity to dominate. His life is fixed firmly within the age of the French Enlightenment, when the debate around the optimal form of government was building to a head. Voltaire would be another admirer of the British system, and American revolutionaries would refer to those theories of Locke and Montesquieu in their own process of constructing a system of government.

Such were the reflections of the philosophers of the late 17th and early 18th centuries that would serve as the seeds of revolutions, and subsequently of an age of rapid social change. Hobbes, Locke and Montesquieu are some of the best-known names among political theorists of the period, but they were hardly the only ones. To the contrary, intellectual ferment about forms of government was dynamic and occupied the attention of many creative minds, even as absolute monarchy was the standard form of government – the inheritance of the medieval period.

The resulting 18th century

In brief, at the close of the 17th century and as the 18th century dawned the stage was set for an accelerated debate in these three areas of human endeavour: religion, science and government. History knows this period of intellectual ferment as the *Enlightenment* – a movement that drew much energy from the scientific investigations of the previous century, as the rational approach of Galileo, Descartes and Newton set the tone for opening new vistas of intellectual pursuit. The intellectual liberation of the 17th century (and the opposition to it!) was in large part the domain of an intellectual elite, but as the 18th century dawned, this increasingly became a movement that extended this new-found intellectual freedom into new audiences, and into the salons where the educated aristocracy met to debate, questioning not only ways to view physical phenomena, but also social and political structures. A diverse intellectual movement, its admirers included absolutist monarchs such as Maria Theresa and Joseph of Austria, Frederick the Great of Prussia, and Catherine the Great of Russia who were attracted by its modernizing tendencies but not, obviously, by its egalitarian principles.

At the core of the Enlightenment was a conviction that reason was the central, primary and often the only reliable criterion of knowledge. Newton's spectacular discovery of the laws of gravitation raised the prospects of understanding all phenomena if the power of reason was brought to bear. Science and knowledge gained an unprecedented respect. In France a massive encyclopedia was published in seventeen volumes, purporting to set forth for all times the state of knowledge and putting it at the service of society. Linked to the optimism about the power of the intellect was a burgeoning faith in the possibility of progress – the potential to overcome pain and promote happiness for the whole of society, for example, through vaccination to prevent smallpox – a cause championed by Voltaire and opposed by the Church and the medical profession.

In contrast and considered to be in opposition to reason, religion was often viewed as being founded upon superstition and ignorance. The miracles of the Bible were dismissed as incoherent and illogical, and as evidence of the questionable nature of traditional religion. Critical analysis of the Biblical text including linguistic analysis pointed out inconsistencies, and led to conclusions that the Bible was literature based on folk tales accumulated over centuries. Furthermore, and especially in France, the Church was its own worst enemy, being the refuge of idle younger sons of the aristocracy who were denied rights of inheritance and who sought a life of ease and comfort in a monastic life. The corruption of the Church, its accumulation of wealth, its taxes in the form of tithes, all made the church hierarchy an easy mark for criticism that was inevitably directed toward its Divine Message as well, through increasing scepticism. In France Voltaire was the most vocal and acrid critic of the Church.

Deism was a common alternative to traditional religion among the Enlightenment thinkers – a view that God created the world and then left it to run its course with little or no additional intervention. Deism viewed revealed religion as recorded in the Bible with scepticism, often seeking to read the Will of God in nature. In this case 'God' might be synonymous with 'natural law' as the impersonal driving force behind phenomena, a view that went hand in hand with the growing sense that science could explain natural law and the origin of all existence. Deism chose to focus on the ethical and social aspects of religion, and was generally dismissive of its mystical elements and of the divinity of Christ. And although in a minority, atheists were also making themselves heard. This is not to suggest that traditional religion based on faith had passed into oblivion, or that it took the challenge of the Enlightenment lying down. On the contrary, the 18th century saw widespread revivalism, often of a Calvinist strain, that swept across both Europe and the English colonies of America. However, the intellectual classes that sought to give new direction to society were typically of a more 'enlightened' mindset.

The understanding of the 'natural' order was extended to social relations whereby 'natural rights' (or human rights) were interpreted as the birthright of each human being, these rights being derived from the needs inherent in the human condition to seek happiness and avoid pain. Thomas Jefferson expressed this concept in the American Declaration of Independence in 1776 where he wrote 'that all men are created equal, that they are endowed by their Creator with certain unalienable Rights, that among these are Life, Liberty and the pursuit of Happiness'. Here the principle of egalitarianism or equality before the law is explicit as a banner of the Enlightenment. The possession of property was another of these essential natural rights, and its protection was an essential condition for the stability of society. Utility became the watchword of social structures which were to be judged on the basis of their effectiveness in serving the reduction of suffering, the increase of happiness, and the protection of property.

Such were the forces of intellectual and social ferment that would produce the 19th century. Standards of public responsibility of rulers that developed over the 17th and 18th centuries would lead both the intelligentsia and the masses to judge governments harshly, and to find them deficient in their duty to govern in accord with the needs of the population. While the British had resolved many of their own questions and had arrived at a stable constitutional monarchy in 1688, the American colonies of the British crown were not convinced and felt marginalized, and France remained in the grips of a monarchy that – if not possessing all the vigour of the absolutism of Louis XIV at the turn of the century – still sought to exercise substantial power, while France in general suffered under the medieval system of Church, nobles and peasantry. Austria and Prussia enjoyed firmly established dynasties, Russia represented the extreme of absolutism, while the plethora of German and Italian principalities stood in the way of any central government at all. Revolutions would emerge from intense frustrations and anger with the perceived tyranny of monarchs, first in the thirteen English colonies of North America, then in France, and finally across Europe.

Natural rights – so sacred to the Enlightenment and so fundamental to a just society – would be structured into experiments with republican government, and these would eventually result in the liberal democracy of the middle classes that would prevail in the western world. Political rights would be linked to economic freedom and to a free-wheeling capitalism manifested through the Industrial Revolution. Modernity would gradually extend beyond the political realm and would transform social relations, education and the role of women.

The thirst for knowledge and the intellectual revolution of the Enlightenment stirred curiosity on all fronts. Science would continue to gain ground as the first fruit of reason and the ultimate criterion of truth, making ever more significant contributions to knowledge and human well-being, but would also influence fundamental attitudes about life. After Newton's discovery inspired widespread sensation at the power of science at the level of the heavens, Darwin would have an equally powerful effect at the level of human biology. Each offered his results as the objective conclusions of careful observation and analysis, but in the hands of others their results would have an impact on the wider public in general. The discovery of one renewed a sense of awe at God's handiwork, the findings of the other cast doubts on the very concept of what it means to be human.

Religion would be caught off guard and would be put on the defensive under the onslaught of such challenges as it had never before witnessed. Subject to scepticism and the challenges of reason, confronted with accusations of corruption and superstition, and faced with alternative explanations for the origin of creation and the human species, religion would be slow to reinvent itself. The Catholic Church in particular would suffer setbacks, many of them of its own making.

Let us turn our attention to the year 1789 that historians often take as the point of departure for the 19th century – the so-called 'long 19th century' that would end with the butchery of the First World War. These 125 years would witness changes in Europe that would reverberate throughout the entire world, and would establish the directions of modernity.

3

The French Revolution

For many historians the 19th century actually started in 1789, and would last until 1914 – a period of 125 years that is known as the 'long 19th century'. It started with unbridled optimism, and ended in the most complete savagery that would leave mankind's confidence shaken at the depths of its own depravity. Nonetheless, these years were the bookends of a period of social change unsurpassed in the history of mankind – an era of unequalled promise and potential that challenged age-old social structures and customs and the assumptions that supported them. And it began with the French Revolution, occurring at the intersection of two contrary and incompatible social realities: the maturation of Enlightenment thought, especially in the writings of Voltaire and Rousseau; and the moral and financial bankruptcy of the French feudal system.

Paris was a hotbed of Enlightenment thought, and Voltaire was France's most prolific writer. Exiled from Paris for most of his adult life for insulting a senior aristocrat, he was also the most acrid of all critics of the Church and its corrupt clerical structure, and beyond the Church, of anything that reeked of superstition. Still, he was the foremost advocate of toleration, and defended the principle of religious freedom to the benefit of Protestants and Jews. Voltaire is associated with Deism and is considered one of its principal spokesmen.

Rousseau famously initiated his work, *The Social Contract*, stating, 'Man is born free, and everywhere he is in chains.' While not the creator of the term 'noble savage', he is credited with popularizing the concept and expanding on the idea that man in the 'natural state' is superior, whereas civilization has corrupted man. Liberty is at the core of much of his discourse, and he is remembered for his reflections on government and the social contract derived from a joint agreement whereby the members of society would mutually forfeit a degree of their personal freedom for the purpose of living in a social context. Legitimacy of a government grows out of the power granted to that government by the people. Such principles flew in the face of traditional concepts of kingship still held by the Bourbon monarchs, which viewed the crown to be endowed by Divine Providence with its authority.

Although some crowned heads of Europe in the 18th century such as Frederick of Prussia subscribed in theory to ideas of progress as proposed in the Enlightenment, in essence such ideas as were discussed and debated in salons of academics and intellectuals were incompatible with the traditional social structures of Europe, and especially France. So corrupt was the French *ancien régime* that it was a ready target for critics and thinkers. In stark contrast to the egalitarianism engendered by the Enlightenment, the French social structure was organized in three tiers or 'estates' with the Catholic Church in the First Estate, and the nobility in the Second. These two social classes enjoyed extensive privileges including exemption from taxes, and the right to exact payment (or tithes in the case of the Church) from the commoners of the Third Estate. In addition, in a society that was largely agricultural, these two estates also owned most of the land. Indeed, the distinction between the Church and the nobility was blurred by the fact that many younger sons of the nobility, bereft of the full rights of inheritance, would take refuge in church positions that afforded them comfort, prestige, an assured income, and a life of leisure. The king obviously pertained to the Second Estate, yet there were also independent interests between the king and the lesser nobility such as in the need to finance the State, from which the nobles were exempt. The Third Estate in turn was, simply put, everyone else and consisted of peasants, merchants, craftsmen and professionals. As such it was internally diverse with little internal coherence. Whatever coherence it had was drawn largely from its opposition to the other two estates and to the nobles in particular. Its opposition to the abuses of the First Estate, which is to say, to the Church, was far from uniform, and indeed, divisions in favour of and in opposition to the Church would eventually bring France to the brink of civil war before the Revolution would eventually be consolidated.

The social structure of estates bore within it social tensions that would be the seeds of its own destruction. In earlier centuries representatives of the three estates would meet in an assembly known as the Estates General in which each estate had a single vote. The privileged positions of the nobility and the clergy made them natural allies, and reform movements in favour of the Third Estate were readily vetoed. The ample range of privileges which were the exclusive domain of the nobles and the Church would be an irritant in any situation, but resentment was amplified by the spread of Enlightenment thought. Parisians in particular enjoyed a high level of literacy, and concepts of natural rights were debated in salons, coffee houses and philosophical societies, and in pamphlets that were produced in the thousands and that reached all levels of society. While it would take many years to decide who should have access to natural rights (for example, slaves, Jews, and especially women were denied civil rights for several years more), in an environment of privilege that was so patently abusive and contrary to the egalitarian principle, the concept of natural rights held great intellectual appeal.

At the centre of the debate around the abuse of privilege was the Queen of France, Marie Antoinette. She was an Austrian princess by birth, and typified what was wrong with the nobility. She enjoyed a well-deserved reputation for conspicuous consumption and luxurious living, and with her lavish lifestyle she was an easy mark for the frustrations of a people disillusioned with an entire social system. Pamphlets often portrayed her as sexually depraved and maintaining extra-marital relations with multiple lovers – an accusation that was at least exaggerated and never confirmed – but symptomatic of the disrespect into which the royalty had fallen. Yet a more immediate cause of social unrest is immortalized in an anecdote (probably a myth) whereby a servant reported to Marie Antoinette that 'the peasants have no bread to eat', to which she callously replied, 'Let them eat cake.' It is unlikely that she ever said anything of the kind, but the anecdote does highlight the shortage of bread in the fateful year of 1789. Grain harvests in the 1780s had often been poor, and the harvest of 1788 had been especially bad. Flour was scarce and of poor quality, prices were increasing rapidly, and hunger threatened to become famine. Bread was the basic staple of the diet and scarcity translated into severe hardship, especially for those who already lived on the edge under the burden of excessive taxation. The contrast between the hungry masses and the opulence of the royal court engendered passionate resentment. At one point tension around the shortage of bread grew so intense that market women massed together and marched on the palace of Versailles to demand relief from the king.

Thus a perfect storm was gathering, and the stage was set for violent upheavals. Paradoxically, when revolution came, it began quite calmly, and in circumstances initiated by King Louis XVI himself. The French State was at the point of bankruptcy after several disastrous wars with Great Britain in recent decades. Indeed, the support of France to the American Revolution in recent years would be the straw that broke the camel's back and carried the public debt to unmanageable proportions. It is ironic that Louis's government would eventually be driven to insolvency to support a republican form of government which he despised, but the desire for revenge on the British would outweigh his better judgement. When the direness of France's financial situation became public knowledge, creditors would give France no more loans, and the king was forced to find other means to raise funds. He had no choice in May 1789 but to call to session for the first time in nearly two centuries the Estates General, that assembly of representatives of the three segments of French society, to seek tax reform and financial support from within. However, convening the Estates General opened a Pandora's box of debate and confrontation with the crown which gradually grew more and more contentious. It would afford an opportunity for the Third Estate to voice its grievances toward both the nobles and the Church. Withdrawing from the Estates General, the members of the Third Estate declared themselves to be the National Assembly, establishing a model that in essence functioned like a constitutional monarchy (but without a formal document at this point until the constitution of 1791) and proposing reforms which the king would begrudgingly approve. It was in this period that the political designations 'left' and 'right' were coined, as the liberal factions sat on the left side of the National Assembly chamber and the conservative factions on the right.

With the convening of the Estates General events would snowball. In July the Parisian mob stormed the Bastille, and in the countryside peasants revolted against their feudal overlords, rattling the aristocracy and driving reforms in the National Assembly. While appearing to accede to the reforms, in fact Louis plotted to undermine them, even to the point of encouraging foreign intervention. At one point he fled from Paris with his family, hoping to seek refuge in the Austrian Netherlands (modern Belgium) from which he hoped to organize resistance, but he was stopped at the border and escorted back to Paris. As the radical elements pushed for a fully republican form of government instead of a constitutional monarchy, Louis's own position weakened and his popularity flagged. A republic was declared in September 1792. One of its first acts was to put Louis on trial in light of incontrovertible evidence of his duplicity and betrayal of the revolution.

An iconic image of the French Revolution is the guillotine. Louis would be executed in January 1793 in a public act celebrated by the audience with savage revenge. The guillotine would consume some sixteen thousand more as radicals sought to defend the Revolution from its perceived enemies. The reign of terror would be orchestrated, systematically and ruthlessly, by Maximilian Robespierre and the party of the Jacobins until he and many of his companions were themselves consumed by its flames. The terror evolved throughout the years of 1793 and 1794, in response to threats, perceived and real, to the very survival of the Revolution and the Republic. Royalist elements who had emigrated plotted against the regime in the exterior, and wars with Austria, Prussia, Great Britain and Spain drained energy on the borders on the north, northeast, south and southwest. Riots occurred in many cities, and armed insurrection in the conservative Vendée in the northwest – fiercely loyal to the Church – resisted the Revolution and the national guard for months. There were indeed many acts of counter-revolution, and the defence of the Revolution seemed to demand a decisive reaction. The terror was the response, implemented consciously and coldly as a 'necessary' step to save the Republic. Action and reaction led France into a downward spiral of polarization.

The terror was not limited to Paris, and in fact more died in the violence dispersed throughout the country than in Paris per se, polarizing society for generations to come. And if in the early days of the Revolution the Third Estate was united against the other two estates, once the aristocracy was overthrown the differences among social classes of the Third Estate would emerge and gradually become more violent. The successors of the Jacobins, referred to as Thermidorians, sought to control these inherent tensions through repressive measures and through a middle way that was no longer tenable. The contrasts of left and right, rich and poor, were accentuated. Under the Thermodorians the egalitarianism of the Revolution was called into question and the forces of reaction, now manifest in the bourgeoisie and the *nouveaux riches*, would set the tone for social tensions in the 19th century.

Enter the foremost iconic figure of the period, Napoleon Bonaparte. Napoleon is often portrayed as a megalomaniac bent on world conquest, but that is a gross oversimplification. He was also a shrewd diplomat and an able, albeit dictatorial, statesman who established a stable and progressive social order, including a code of law and an effective educational system, still largely intact to the present! Born in Italian-speaking Corsica, he was educated in France in the military tradition, and while he was an early proponent of the Revolution it was his military success which would always be the backbone of his political career. His action as a commander of artillery in 1793 served to lift the British siege of Toulon and gained him recognition within the army and the government. But it was his military success in Italy against the Austrians, and later in an invasion of Egypt, whereby his fame with the public grew and his star rose on the horizon of French politics.

From Egypt he marched north along the Mediterranean coast as far as Akka (St Jean d'Acre). Bahá'í pilgrims to the Holy Land can still see a hill on which he mounted his artillery, and the pockmarks of his cannon balls in the walls of the city – visible signs of the agitation that Western civilization wrought upon the world and upon which Bahá'u'lláh would comment. Returning to France, Napoleon dove into politics and engineered a coup in 1799 that overthrew the legislature and led to his own coronation as emperor in 1802. His ascension to the throne could only augment the fears of France's neighbours. Austria, Russia, Sweden, Britain and eventually Prussia leagued against France. Napoleon's military genius led him as far as the walls of Moscow, but he had overstretched his possibilities and of the 600,000 strong Grand Army that left France, only some 40,000 would return. Defeated and deported to Elba in the Mediterranean, he would steal back into France and make one last attempt before his final downfall at Waterloo.

Since the inception of the Revolution, France had attracted like-minded liberals from across Europe who dreamt of replicating it in their own countries. Some French revolutionaries suggested that France had the duty to extend liberty to all peoples. Still, no effort to promote a transformation of old-order Europe was so effective in shaping the rest of the 19th century as the Napoleonic wars of conquest. Although Napoleon had lost his zeal for egalitarianism years before, some remnants of idealism remained in the ranks. Napoleon's march across Europe rattled the old order and served to spread revolutionary ideals. Napoleon deposed kings, restructured governments, and flung the door open on radical change. He took steps to reduce the number of independent States and principalities in Italy and Germany, actions that foreshadowed their eventual unification as modern States. Although Napoleon was no friend of liberty and equality – a tyrant in the words of 'Abdu'l-Bahá – he was a consummate pragmatist, and some of the practical applications of the Revolution survived the defeat of Napoleon. His code of law and the establishment of meritocracy in state function set the tone for the modern era.

In particular, three long-term effects of the French Revolution deserve special attention in light of the progress of the 19th century.

Throughout the French Revolution, from its initiation in 1789 until the ascension of Napoleon to the throne and his self-declaration as emperor, the press of popular power played a key role in decisive moments and in setting the direction of events. When scarcity of bread threatened Paris with famine, the march of women to the palace at Versailles brought the king to Paris to attend to the emergency. A mass of artisans stormed the Bastille and destroyed that symbol of autocratic and despotic rule. Interest groups from the Third Estate regularly interrupted the National Assembly with their demands for reform. When the king sought to flee the country, it was an army of the masses that escorted him back to Paris, and it was a mob that accompanied Louis to his execution and celebrated savagely. Even normally conservative rural peasants participated in revolt in July of 1789 – an event that drove the abolition of the feudal system. Most dramatically, it was in the name of the people that the Great Terror carried out its grisly agenda. With the French Revolution, popular power burst upon the world with vengeful fury. The Great Terror was the grotesque prostitution of popular power, carried to the lowest levels of base animal instincts, and fulfilling the worst fears of the nobles who opposed the Revolution. Conservative monarchists had held up the spectre of mob rule as the ultimate outcome of the Revolution. Perhaps their opposition made this a self-fulfilling prophecy. Or perhaps the seeds of resentment were sown so deep that revenge would occur no matter what the proponents of the old order did. In any case, the cat of popular power was out of the bag.

Parallel to the expression of popular anger in the streets was the growing ascendancy of the middle class, the bourgeoisie represented by the lawyers, clerks and businessmen who manned the National Assembly and who were the leaders of the Revolution. As much as they detested the nobility, they likewise feared the mob and the Jacobins whom they viewed as instigators of violence. The First and Second Estates of the clerics and nobles had scarcely been dispensed with when tensions emerged between the more radical elements of the Revolution and the middle class. The latter flocked around the Thermidorians, but their greatest hero and defender was Napoleon Bonaparte. Yet the class tensions that emerged in revolutionary France would be only a taste of what was to shape many of the power struggles of the 19th century and the early 20th century. Still firmly rooted in the resentments of the previous era, this early expression of popular power in the French Revolution could not reflect the age of maturity that was dawning but rather the turbulent rebelliousness of adolescence. Its memory would stoke the fires of conservatism as European ministers sat at the table in Vienna in 1815 to draft the new 'old' Europe. While the forces of conservative Europe would have resisted change in any case, their resistance was made all the more stubborn by the memory of the Terror. The French Revolution would set in motion a pernicious dynamic of action and reaction that would inhibit social progress and make violence all the more likely. Yet the evolution of popular power could not be detained and would resurge inevitably in the course of the 19th century.

The second tendency of the Revolution that would continue in the next century was that of a decline in the prestige and position of the Church. Long before 1789 the Church had come under severe scrutiny in Germany and Switzerland with the Reformation in the early 16th century. Protestantism had made great inroads into France, remnants of which remained in the form of the Huguenot minority, but in the 18th century the primacy of Catholicism was undisputed. The position of the Catholic Church was sanctified as one of the three Estates of society, and in its position as the exclusive state religion, Catholicism was virtually synonymous with religion. As it was increasingly criticized for gross abuses of privilege, it was inevitable that rejection of the Church would lead to scepticism about religion per se. In 18th-century France resistance to the Church came not so much from Protestantism but from the Enlightenment, and among the intellectual leaders of the Enlightenment, it was Voltaire who attacked the Church most violently, earning the disapproval of 'Abdu'l-Bahá in later years.[1] Voltaire held pride of place among French Enlightenment thinkers, and his attitudes would have a baleful influence on the position of the Church. Once such a negative view was widely accepted, others would carry his ideas further and would openly declare themselves to be atheists. Perhaps this was the bitter fruit born of the Deist perspective, having replaced the vision of a loving God who is involved in history with One who is indifferent to human suffering, or at least does nothing about it, having all power to do so. As such, the Revolution maintained an antagonistic view toward the Church and to a large extent toward religion. At one point the revolutionaries went so far as to create their own religion to root out the influence of Christianity, including a new calendar that initiated with the declaration of the Republic, and that displaced Christian holy days.

Still, Catholicism held powerful sway over the masses, and when the National Assembly demanded that clergy swear allegiance to the Revolution, this split the Church and the country in two. Perhaps half of the clergy accepted this demand while others resisted. Imposition of the Revolution on the Church led to widespread discontent and violence in the population, with clergy being identified as for or against the Revolution with no neutral middle ground. Catholicism could not be dispensed with so readily, but it was severely divided.

Napoleon restored some privileges of the Church but neither

was he committed to Catholicism as a believer, by any means. In his Italian campaign he invaded the Papal States, exclusive domain of the Pope and the Church. At one point he had taken the Pope prisoner and carried him to France. Although the Pope's territories were restored by the Congress of Vienna in 1815, the tone was set for the 19th century. The Church would see its fortunes decline ever more dramatically over the next decades, culminating in the complete loss of its temporal authority in the days of Pius IX.

A third long-term effect that was stimulated by the French Revolution but that took on a life of its own over the course of the century was the growing force of nationalism. Many of the old order monarchies before and after the Napoleonic wars ruled over populations of diverse, distinct and restive ethnicities and were unrelated to their subjects except by brute force of repression. The Poles had been divided up and were ruled by Russia, Prussia and Austria in the mid-18th century, and the Austro-Hungarian Empire dominated Czechs, Slovenians, Croatians and Italians, among others. The Ottoman Empire likewise ruled over multiple nationalities on the frontiers with Austria and Russia and far beyond. In these lands peoples with a common language and culture longed to have governments that were coherent with their national identity. Germany was a very different situation, whereby a people with a common history and language was splintered into a plethora of small independent States of little consequence – a situation that created a longing for a viable united German State. Although France had been a strong State before the Revolution, even here a sense of national pride and 'French-ness' emerged more forcefully as revolutionaries saw themselves at the cutting edge of social progress with a mission to transform Europe.

Napoleon would give some practical stimulation to this incipient process of nation building when he reduced the number of German principalities to seventeen, and when he invaded Italy and subjected it to a common – albeit foreign – occupying power, and took the title of King of Italy. He even carved out a Duchy of Warsaw from the territory of ancient Poland occupied by foreign powers, suggesting the possibility of a Polish State. However, it was the inspiration of the principle of liberty disseminated from Paris that fuelled the hopes of nationhood beyond the defeat of Napoleon, as these peoples dreamt of having their own countries reflecting their national identities of language, culture and history. A growing sense of national identity would result in the modern States as we know them only after World War I, but would be a force to be reckoned with throughout the 19th century as old order empires sought to maintain their integrity in opposition to nationalistic currents. Furthermore, as States consolidated their power in centralized governments in the latter half of the 19th century, leaders would employ nationalism to rally support to their programmes. By the time war broke out in 1914, whole populations fell out to back the war effort of their respective governments, including socialists who had previously preached a gospel of an international brotherhood of workers.

In summary, from its very initiation the proponents of the French Revolution understood it as a social revolution and not merely a political revolution. Compared to the American Revolution, the French Revolution was much more ambitious in its goals for the transformation of society at the grassroots. In spite of its tragic direction and ultimate demise, the French Revolution will remain a hallmark in human history in the search for human improvement and social justice. It generated and encouraged public discussion about moral and social issues that would continue to plague society for decades, and in some cases into the present era: slavery; racism; colonialism; women's rights; the rights of religious minorities, especially Jews; unjust taxation systems; education; public administration. The Revolution produced the Declaration of the Rights of Man – the charter of revolutionary egalitarianism – that would inspire reformers around the world for years to come, for example, among the founding fathers of the Latin American republics. Arguably it was the forerunner of the Universal Declaration of Human Rights, promulgated by the United Nations in 1948. The French Revolution was a milestone in opening the modern age and in setting the tone of the 19th century.

4

The Industrial Revolution

Parallel to the French Revolution and its long-term effects, a second revolution transformed Europe in the late 18th and all of the 19th centuries. Compared to the French Revolution, this one began gradually and less violently, yet was to grow in tension and violence as time advanced, and would have comparable or even greater consequences on social relations. This was the Industrial Revolution. Much more than an economic revolution, this was a social transformation. Europe was recast into the mold of the capitalist system of production with its attendant tensions of socio-economic class that were incompatible with the egalitarian ideals of the French Revolution.

In 1776 Adam Smith published his seminal work that we know by its abbreviated name, *The Wealth of Nations*, in which he laid the foundations for modern economics. Living in Scotland, he could observe the Industrial Revolution in its infancy. He articulated the law of supply and demand, and if that was common sense for businessmen in any age, he was also the first to describe the power of division of labour in an assembly line approach, using a rather benign example of the steps required to produce a pin, from stretching the wire to placing the head on the pin. A modest group of workers, each one specialized in a single step, could produce many, many more pins per worker in a day by such specialization than could each one working separately.

While *The Wealth of Nations* described the broader fundamentals of modern economic theory, in this mundane example Smith illustrates the principle that made industrial production so much more efficient and a source of vastly greater wealth in society. The principle of specialization of labour would multiply labour productivity many fold, how much more when combined with the power of technology. But if increased labour productivity gave a spectacular boost to industry, there were, nonetheless, other more subtle effects as well. The fact of limiting the actions of any given worker to one step in a series of actions made the labour of that worker intolerably monotonous for someone who had been a master of all tasks. Furthermore, even this focus of work benefited factory owners, for in the former system the generalist worker was difficult to replace and was able by the nature of his multiple skills to demand higher wages, while a worker specialized in one task could be replaced by another with much less training, and thus could be paid less. Or in cases where industrial espionage was a threat, no one worker had knowledge of the entire productive process that he could share with others, nor could he strike out on his own to start his own business.

The first signs of a revolution in productive methods and capacities appeared in Great Britain, and especially in England. At the fore of the Industrial Revolution was the textile industry. Britain had for years been a producer of textiles but as a cottage industry wherein both women and men were engaged in different steps of the process carried out in their own home, and coordinated by some enterprising merchant who supplied raw material and purchased their production of cloth, especially woollens, although increasingly in the 18th century cotton imported from India and later from the United States came to dominate the industry. Under the Industrial Revolution these tasks were consolidated into a factory, with entirely different social relations and with loss of independence on the part of workers. Production was facilitated by water and steam power, and by inventions that assumed much of the time-consuming laborious hand work. In the United States the invention by Eli Whitney in 1794 of the cotton gin to separate fibre from seeds positioned cotton producers on the front line and made cotton the foundation of the southern economy, hand in hand with the institution of slavery. Machines for carding, for making thread, and for weaving vastly increased productivity.

The reasons for Britain taking the lead in industry have long been debated and are numerous: the availability of labour as rural workers lost their rights to communal land under the Enclosure Acts and migrated to cities; an abundance of water power and later coal; the ingenuity of its tinkerers who developed the simple but necessary machinery; an ample market for mass-produced products, both the internal market centred on London and that afforded by Britain's colonial possessions; the development of efficient internal transport systems, first as canals and then in the 1830s some of the first railroads. Indeed, there were several decades until the end of the Napoleonic wars when Britain was literally the only industrialized nation, and was able to experiment with mass production and marketing virtually without competition.

However, with the onset of peace on the continent, the Industrial Revolution moved from west to east, with Belgium being the first to follow Britain's example. Germany joined the ranks at mid-century, industrializing faster than any other country, and in the latter half of the century would rival Britain in industrial output. German scientists specialized in chemistry with companies such as Bayer being formed in this period and continuing until today. The Balkans and Russia on the eastern extreme of Europe were very slow, and even on the eve of World War I were scarcely in the early phases. Likewise, southern Europe engaged slowly. Although Portugal and Spain had taken the lead in imperial expansion in the colonial period, their entry into the industrial age was more gradual. Differences among countries in rates of economic growth across this period were also large. In 1830 per capita income between countries varied by a factor of 2 to 1. But by the end of the century its range was 4 to 1! Some countries clearly took far greater advantage of industrialization and/or improved agricultural technology that was needed to support it than others.

The Industrial Revolution could also be called the urban revolution, since it changed the distribution of population from rural to urban centres radically over the length of the century (Table 1). For centuries before, the proportion of urban and rural population was relatively stable, and Europe presented around 10% of its population in urban centres, using the arbitrary criterion for urban centres as places of 5,000 or more inhabitants – still only a very modest size of city. By 1830 this had grown only slightly to 12%, although differences among countries were already evident. Britain and the Netherlands were considerably higher, with Britain having fully a third of its population in cities while the Netherlands' urban tradition dated more to its commercial history as a world class trading nation than to early industrialization. Urban growth tracks the spread of industrialization, as rural populations migrated to cities in search of opportunities, and the relative contribution of several countries to world manufacturing closely follows the degree of urbanization. Again, Britain took the lead and at the end of the century nearly 70% of its population lived in cities. Germany and the United States started slowly but caught up very quickly by 1880. Germany was still urbanizing rapidly in the decade before the World War, while the process in other countries had slowed by this time. Russia at the other extreme lagged with 14% in urban centres. By any criterion, among the major players in 19th-century European history, Russia was at the bottom of the scale, with some of the Scandinavian and Balkan states similarly at the low end. By the end of the 'long 19th century' in 1914, Europe as a whole found itself with 33% urban population, or excluding Russia, at an estimated 43%. Furthermore, many cities were no longer large villages but centres of several hundred thousand inhabitants, the most numerous being London with more than six million city dwellers, the largest in the world!

Table 1. Level of urbanization for individual countries: Percentage of total population living in cities of 5,000 or more inhabitants[1]

	1800	1830	1850	1880	1900	1910
EUROPE	10.9	12.6	16.4	23.5	30.4	32.8
Austria-Hungary	6.5	7.1	9.7	16.0	25.6	28.5
Belgium	20.5	25.0	33.5	43.1	52.3	56.6
France	12.2	15.7	19.5	27.6	35.4	38.5
Germany	8.9	9.1	15.0	29.1	42.0	48.8
Italy	18.0	19.0	23.0	28.0	35.5	40.0
Netherlands	37.4	35.8	35.6	44.5	47.8	50.5
Russia	5.9	6.0	7.2	10.6	13.2	14.3
United Kingdom*	19.2	27.5	39.6	56.2	67.4	69.2
United States	5.3	7.8	5.3	25.0	35.9	41.6

* During the years cited here, the United Kingdom included the whole of the island of Ireland, which was largely rural.

Clearly great demographic changes had occurred, with attendant social changes. For 'ordinary' people, a change from independent rural dweller to urban slum resident represented an even greater change in daily routine and family environment than the change in their work environment. This demographic change of the 19th century set the direction for the 20th and 21st centuries, with the diminishing role of rural populations in society, and the eventual loss of the rural way of life in many countries. This is not to romanticize about a bucolic lifestyle set in an English country garden, since rural life was also very hard, but slum living was much, much worse. Although the middle class was increasing, the growth of urban centres largely reflects the expansion of the population in the lower economic strata. Translated into absolute figures, the percentages cited in Table 1 represent many millions of souls living in unhealthy and degrading circumstances, in the most appalling conditions of air and water pollution, inadequate sewage, industrial waste, in bleak quarters in close proximity to factories. The crowded living conditions were conducive to the spread of disease, as exemplified by the studies of John Snow, the English doctor who pioneered the science of epidemiology and mapped the spread of cholera around a public water supply in the 1848–49 epidemic in the Soho district of London. Tuberculosis and typhoid were also common. It is an astounding and bone-chilling fact that the death rate exceeded the birth rate in all major cities at mid-century, and that the spectacular growth of cities was due almost exclusively to rural migration.

In the 1840s Manchester was the epitome of everything that could go wrong with industrial urbanization. Accounts of its foul smell, its putrid water and streams, its open latrines, its smoke-filled and toxic air, its disease, its spiritless and depressed inhabitants, its young girls with vocabularies of street brawling drunkards . . . all that one can imagine as foul and repulsive is mentioned in the narratives of its visitors. In its early years Manchester did not even have the legal basis of a formal city whereby it could receive aid from the government and address these ills.

And while capitalism pre-dated the Industrial Revolution, and exploitation is as ancient as the Old Testament, the advantage of vastly improved productivity made industrial production a growth area for both capitalism and industrial slavery. The early period saw the vilest and most cynical expressions of industrial exploitation. If a century later when the worst abuses had been corrected, 'Abdu'l-Bahá would still charge the Americans with ending industrial slavery, we can scarcely visualize how debasing and tragic were the abuses at the dawn of this revolution. A dramatic example of these abuses was the use of child labour in factories, a reality experienced by the great-grandfather of this writer. While not invented in the Industrial Revolution, child labour then reached even lower depths of abuse. Children were favoured for industrial labour because unlike mature men who might revolt or purposefully damage machinery, children could be dominated readily, their small hands could work nimbly in and out of machinery, and they could fit neatly into the cramped spaces of factories jammed with machines and with low ceilings. They also were paid a fraction of what a grown man earned. Women were likewise preferred for the ease of domination. Men avoided factory work because they found it degrading, and early in industrialization only 23% of textile workers were grown men.[2] Even the freeing of the serfs in Prussia and Russia – a logical act in the light of modern egalitarian thought – was not entirely altruistic, as this served the ends of industrialization by freeing labour for factory work. In the feudal system serfs were tied to the land and were not available for industry, even if they were underemployed in the countryside. Breaking their bond to the soil was part of a strategy to facilitate the growth of industry.

Workers were not always silent, and as everywhere when machines replace hand labour and unemployment looms, worker revolts resisted the introduction of mechanization, occasionally damaging machines or even burning factories. In England in 1811 a movement known as the Luddites emerged, harassing factory owners and carrying on a virtual guerrilla war against the industrial process, with the vain hope of returning to the days of cottage industry. At one point as many British troops were employed in battling the Luddites as were fighting Napoleon's soldiers in Spain in the Peninsular War. The Luddites were only quelled when their leaders were captured and executed in a public display of punitive power, but to this day the term is used in a derogatory sense to refer to those who blindly resist progress. In another incident in 1819 several thousand workers gathered in a mass rally in Manchester were attacked and a number were killed in the so-called Peterloo massacre. In the same period a plot was uncovered to assassinate the prime minister and his cabinet – all events that contributed to the perverse dynamic of action and reaction that we saw in the French Revolution. Records show that working conditions were not the only concern of workers, and that the loss of independence also struck a bitter note and offended their human dignity. Workers were not alone in their concerns about the Industrial Revolution. The poet William Blake attempted to show the dichotomy between a spiritual and loving world, and the bleak and heartless life to which thousands, especially young children and women, were subjected.

Although often cited to justify a free market, which he did of course advocate, Adam Smith was first and foremost a moral philosopher, and made his living as such lecturing in the University of Glasgow. He thus was also sensitive to the abuses of the Industrial Revolution. In *The Wealth of Nations* he commented on the lop-sided relations between management and labour.

> The masters being fewer in number can combine much more easily and the law, besides, authorizes or at least does not prohibit their combination, while it prohibits those of the workmen. We have no acts of Parliament against combining to lower the price of work but many against combining to raise it . . . We rarely hear, it has been said, of the combinations of masters though frequently of those of workmen. But

whoever imagines upon this account that masters rarely com-
bine is as ignorant of the world as of the subject. Masters are
always and everywhere in a sort of tacit but constant and uniform combination not to raise the wages of labour above their
actual rate. To violate this combination is everywhere a most
unpopular action and a sort of reproach to a master among
his neighbours and equals. We seldom, indeed, hear of this
combination because it is the usual, and one may say, the
natural state of things which nobody ever hears of. Masters,
too, sometimes enter into particular combinations to sink the
wages of labour even below this rate. These are always con-
ducted with the utmost silence and secrecy til the moment
of execution and when workmen yield, as they sometimes
do, without resistance, though severely felt by them, they are
never heard of by other people.[3]

What is striking about this passage, apart from the fact that it
was penned by the recognized father of the free-market economy,
is that it was written in 1776, when the Industrial Revolution
was still only gathering momentum. For if man's exploitation of
man is not a modern phenomenon, Smith could already detect
a new and pernicious form of it in English industry fully half a
century before the Industrial Revolution reached full expression
in England, and nearly a century before it came into full swing
in Germany.

The analysis of David Ricardo, economist at the end of the
18th century, complemented that of Adam Smith in justifying
the free market. Ricardo saw labour as an input into production
that obeyed the same rules of supply and demand as any other
input or raw material – the more workers available, the lower
the cost of wages. Rising wages would reduce competitiveness
of industry, driving factories into bankruptcy and worsening the
fate of workers who would be reduced to even more desperate

conditions. Increasing wages would likewise improve diets and health of the masses, with increasing fertility rates, creating even more poor and driving them back into poverty. His thesis of *laissez faire* was based on the premise that these were immutable laws of economics and that any government intervention could only do harm – a thesis that was readily adopted by freewheeling industrialists, either because it was accepted as fact, or because it was to their advantage.

Similarly, the ruling elites had no desire to see the masses gain advantage and power. Old prejudices toward the lower classes were reinforced, both by worker revolts and by the French Revolution. Mob rule as evidenced in the French Terror was a doomsday spectre and was to be repressed at all cost. The ragged and hopeless masses, reduced to prostitution and thievery, were to be distrusted since indeed, they had 'nothing to lose but [their] chains' and could become a rabid dog if given too long a leash. Their sad state was the result of their own laziness and slovenly character, and so they had to be submitted to the most severe discipline. Such callous attitudes were formalized and institutionalized in England in the so-called Poor Laws that subjected the unemployed to rigorous physical exercise on the 'tread mill' – not a colloquial expression communicating a difficult day at the office but a real machine like that of hamsters in a cage! – and at sub-minimal wages, below the lowest rate on the street, to train them in the virtues of hard labour.

Social prejudices and economic exploitation acquired a sophisticated justification and a whole new philosophical basis at mid-century when in 1859 Charles Darwin published his landmark treatise, *On the Origin of Species*. An acrid debate was spawned immediately with traditional religion on one side and 'science' on the other, with no middle ground. Darwin himself was a mild-mannered country gentleman and was aware of the explosive potential of his work, which he shyly tried to avoid but which he eventually found inevitable in the interests of scientific truth. Dealing with the biology of organisms and their evolution, Darwin's ideas were quickly misappropriated and bastardized when placed into the context of social communities. In an age in which science was producing great wonders and industrial progress, science was the last word in any argument. 'Social Darwinism' argued that just as the laws of nature commanded that the strong should survive and the weak should perish, and thus lead to the improvement of the gene pool of plant and animal species, so too should the human gene pool be subject to the laws of natural selection. The strong and powerful, it was argued, had attained their position through their natural traits of superior fitness, and the weak of society likewise were manifesting their innate inferiority, and should be allowed to perish, or at very least their reproductive capacity should be held in check through malnutrition. Efforts to sustain the poor would only lead to degeneration of the gene pool in the long run by maintaining their inferior genes and permitting them to continue to breed and produce inferior offspring. Just as *laissez faire* ruled in the economic realm, so were government programmes to aid the poor viewed as interference in the laws of nature and as contrary to the best interests of society.

What was emerging from the early 19th century and the economic growth stimulated by the Industrial Revolution were stark differences of economic and social position that would solidify into two new and broad social classes. If the old order (at least on the European continent) had been based on the three estates, the new order saw the emergence of the industrial middle class and the industrial workers, with the aristocracy on the wane and relegated to the sidelines. The middle class would see themselves as being at the forefront of progress, driving economic growth, and would claim the right to confront the old order for political power. The middle class would promote the cause of the 'liberal' experiment, viewing economic freedom and *laissez faire* as the natural state of things. Throughout much of the 19th century the 'liberal' cause and 'liberal' democracy would be the cause of the industrial middle class – quite different from the way that we understand the term liberal today, yet in contrast to the old aristocratic order, the industrialists interpreted the Enlightenment's call to liberty in the context of freedom to function in a free market. The liberal movement would wrest power from the aristocratic powers, reinforced temporarily by the Congress of Vienna, and yet would oppose the expanding demands from the industrial workers.

At mid-century and in the midst of the debate around social Darwinism, Bahá'u'lláh would chide the kings in the *Súriy-i-Mulúk* for their neglect of the poor in a powerful indictment:

> Know ye that the poor are the trust of God in your midst. Watch that ye betray not His trust, that ye deal not unjustly with them and that ye walk not in the ways of the treacherous. Ye will most certainly be called upon to answer for His trust on the day when the Balance of Justice shall be set, the day when unto everyone shall be rendered his due, when the doings of all men, be they rich or poor, shall be weighed.[4]

He would subsequently return to this theme in His Tablets to individual monarchs, and Napoleon III in particular:

> Know of a truth that your subjects are God's trust amongst you. Watch ye, therefore, over them as ye watch over your own selves. Beware that ye allow not wolves to become the shepherds of the fold, or pride and conceit to deter you from turning unto the poor and the desolate.[5]

> Deal not treacherously with the substance of your neighbour.

Be ye trustworthy on earth, and withhold not from the poor the things given unto you by God through His grace.[6]

Bahá'u'lláh is explicit in His defence of the poor, and in other Tablets He encourages His followers to empathize with them, to seek their company and to acquaint themselves with their trials: 'If ye encounter one who is poor, treat him not disdainfully.'[7] 'They who are possessed of riches, however, must have the utmost regard for the poor, for great is the honour destined by God for those poor who are steadfast in patience.'[8] 'Flee not from the face of the poor that lieth in the dust, nay rather befriend him and suffer him to recount the tale of the woes with which God's inscrutable Decree hath caused him to be afflicted.'[9]

One might think that, in the words of Christ, 'the poor always ye have with you'[10] and therefore Bahá'u'lláh's words are a general call for charity and justice as might have been uttered at any time in history, but indeed, the poverty that existed in the early to mid-19th century was perhaps the most degrading and intense that the world had witnessed, short of the state and repression reserved for slaves and prisoners. The Age of Enlightenment that had stimulated scientific investigation, that had rebelled against the aristocratic order and opened the door on a progressive middle class, that had facilitated economic freedom and personal initiative, and thereby had fuelled the Industrial Revolution . . . the modernity so engendered by the Enlightenment had created a hell into which millions eventually sank. Indeed, against the backdrop of social Darwinism with its complete disdain for the poor, or even its calls for aggressive repression of their right to exist and procreate, the words of Bahá'u'lláh are in even starker contrast. Social Darwinism was the ultimate betrayal of the trust of God, a virtual religion of repression and social injustice, and a perverse complement to the industrial slavery that the Industrial Revolution had wrought – all in the name of science.

The Industrial Revolution, like the French Revolution, took a potential source of great good and prostituted it to particular ends and with sadly negative consequences. Eventually in England in the 1830s and 1840s laws were enacted to alleviate the abuses, although implementation would be slow and would drag out for another two generations. And though the increase in material wealth would eventually benefit the working classes as well, nigh well a century of the Industrial Revolution would pass before the masses of Europe saw benefits trickle down at the end of the 19th and the beginning of the 20th centuries. In part this was due to rising wages, in part due to much lower food prices in the 1880s thanks to greatly improved international shipping and cheap imports. Still, a survey in the 1870s revealed that twelve-year-old English boys in upper-class schools averaged a full five inches taller than boys in working-class schools, and as late as 1917, in mobilization for war, scarcely a third of Englishmen were fully fit for military service, with others in varying degrees of disability.[11] The previous century of social abuse and poverty had created an undernourished race now accustomed to its 'place' in the system. One can only imagine the state of the working class in the 1840s for which statistics are lacking but before conditions had improved.

Meanwhile, the industrial slavery that accompanied the Industrial Revolution flew in the face of the liberty, equality and fraternity promulgated by the French Revolution. The contrast between the revolutionary ideal and the crude reality would fuel discontent, and would give a new direction to the sentiments of 1789. The contrast was clearer to no one than to Karl Marx, who in 1848 would publish *The Communist Manifesto*, generating a movement that would proceed

systematically and with ruthless clarity of purpose towards the goal of world revolution. The Communist Party, deriving both its intellectual thrust and an unshakeable confidence in its ultimate triumph from the writings of the nineteenth century ideologue Karl Marx, had succeeded in establishing groups of committed supporters throughout Europe and various other countries. Convinced that the genius of its master had demonstrated beyond question the essentially material nature of the forces that had given rise to both human consciousness and social organization, the Communist movement dismissed the validity of both religion and 'bourgeois' moral standards.[12]

Years would pass before Marxism would have significant impact, but it was symptomatic that at a relatively early date in continental Europe's Industrial Revolution, social tensions were emerging so vigorously as to create such violent resentment, evolving into a viable political movement in the second half of the century, and opening another chapter in the evolution of the social role of the masses, however misguided and misdirected. In the end, the abuses of the Industrial Revolution and the neglect of the masses of industrial workers would arguably be the one of the most significant causes of the disasters of the next 150 years, as Communism overtook vast numbers of the world's population, first in Russia and later in Eastern Europe and beyond, and inspiring guerilla wars in a dozen countries.

Such were the forces that would increasingly dominate the 19th and 20th centuries. Still, what of the rural poor? If Europe as a whole was still less than 50% urbanized, what of the other half of society that still lived in rural areas? In France they maintained a voice in national politics as a largely conservative and Catholic force. In Italy they were widely limited by regionalism and language, as most inhabitants of the peninsula did *not* speak Italian but rather mutually incomprehensible dialects – a phenomenon that was not entirely unique to Italy – but toward the end of the century these rural masses too were being mobilized by the Church and by socialists. But as in most of history, almost until the end of the century the rural populations were a silent and neglected mass, passive observers of the forces of the times, farm labourers on their own small plots or on those of large landowners, and scarcely noticed except as a source of cannon fodder in times of war.

We close these reflections with a judgement drawn from *The Dawn-Breakers*, the narrative of Nabíl-i-Aẓam who shared the trials of Bahá'u'lláh from the earliest days, and whose account Shoghi Effendi adapted in English to a Western audience. We can only speculate as to the motivation of the author in noting these comments, but they are in any case a complement to Bahá'u'lláh's own observations on the contradictions of Western civilization and its misuse of intellectual and economic power.

> The peoples of the West, among whom the first evidences of this great Industrial Revolution have appeared, are, alas, as yet wholly unaware of the Source whence this mighty stream, this great motive power, proceeds – a force that has revolutionised every aspect of their material life. Their own history testifies to the fact that in the year which witnessed the dawn of this glorious Revelation, there suddenly appeared evidences of an industrial and economic revolution that the people themselves declare to have been unprecedented in the history of mankind. In their concern for the details of the working and adjustments of this newly conceived machinery, they have gradually lost sight of the Source and object of this tremendous power which the Almighty has committed to their charge. They seem to have sorely misused this power and misunderstood its function. Designed to confer upon the people of the West the blessings of peace and of happiness, it has been utilised by them to promote the interests of destruction and war.[13]

5

Basic Principles and Processes

These two revolutions, the French and the Industrial, would contribute heavily to the creation of the modern world in the storm centre of the European continent and among the nations that had assumed for themselves the role of world leadership. As such, the internal changes that Europe would experience, and the Enlightenment values and standards of human rights, would also have impact around the world through the channels of colonialism that European powers had created to establish their empires, inspiring Latin American revolutionaries like Bolívar and San Martín. Much later the United States would assume the leadership of this new world in the 20th century, and eventually the African colonies of the European powers would demand those same rights for themselves. But in the 19th century these forces were still taking form, were creating internal contradictions with forces of the old order, and were shaping the direction of Europe under the leadership of kings and politicians who left their personal stamp on events. These events and the personages who participated in them as national leaders would be the object of Bahá'u'lláh's commentaries, observing them from afar in Baghdad, Constantinople (Istanbul), Adrianople (Adirnih) and Akka, and visualizing their future consequences. However, the immediate events within France surrounding the French Revolution and the age of Napoleon, dramatic as they appeared, were secondary compared to the long-term effects of the Revolution on European thought and the course of the 19th century. Thus its underlying principles and their results merit special attention and analysis in light of the Bahá'í Writings. These principles are summarized in that emblematic slogan of the Revolution, 'Liberty, equality, fraternity'.

Liberty

The French Revolution gave practical expression to the Enlightenment concept of liberty in virtually all aspects of life, much more widely than the American Revolution in which liberty was largely a political concept. The French Revolution sought to transform society in all its aspects and at all levels, and this transformation initiated with an infusion of liberty, which was viewed as the key to a successful society. If mankind had not yet attained to its birthright of supreme happiness and virtue, it was due to the oppressive nature of social structures of the past that limited the possibilities of man, for '. . . everywhere he is in chains', according to Rousseau. Liberty was the magic ingredient that would create virtue in man and would transform society. This 'naive conviction' was a forerunner of that shared by later generations of revolutionaries, that 'if the particular part of the prevailing order that had become their target could somehow be brought down, the inherent nobility of the segment of humankind that supported their aims – or the assumed nobility of humankind in general – would by itself ensure a new era of freedom and justice.'[1] Liberty in the French Revolution was much more than a set of political rights, but extended to human relations and within the home. For example, greater liberty was to be permitted in choosing a spouse, reducing parental control and arranged marriages. Divorce was legalized and made permissible under very liberal justification, at least until the time of Napoleon, flying in the face of Catholic doctrine.

'Abdu'l-Bahá states that 'the conscience of man is sacred and to be respected; and that liberty thereof produces widening of ideas, amendment of morals, improvement of conduct, disclosure of the secrets of creation, and manifestation of the hidden verities of the contingent world'.[2] In His travels through the West, he expounded the benefits of liberty and yet when people expressed their joy that He was at last free, He emphasized that freedom was a state of the soul and not of the body. Indeed, rather than being contrary to the fundamental principles of the Faith, '[t]he spirit of liberty which in recent decades has swept over the planet with such tempestuous force is a manifestation of the vibrancy of the Revelation brought by Bahá'u'lláh.'[3] Yet liberty has its bounds. In its landmark statement *Individual Rights and Freedoms in the World Order of Bahá'u'lláh* the Universal House of Justice quotes Shoghi Effendi in describing relevant teachings of Bahá'u'lláh on this topic.

In his summary of significant Bahá'í teachings, Shoghi Effendi wrote that Bahá'u'lláh 'inculcates the principle of "moderation in all things"; declares that whatsoever, be it "liberty, civilization and the like", "passeth beyond the limits of moderation" must "exercise a pernicious influence upon men"; observes that western civilization has gravely perturbed and alarmed the peoples of the world; and predicts that the day is approaching when the "flame" of a civilization "carried to excess" "will devour the cities".'

Expounding the theme of liberty, Bahá'u'lláh asserted that 'the embodiment of liberty and its symbol is the animal'; that 'liberty causeth man to overstep the bounds of propriety, and to infringe on the dignity of his station'; that 'true liberty consisteth in man's submission unto My commandments'.

'We approve of liberty in certain circumstances,' He declared, 'and refuse to sanction it in others.' But He gave the assurance that, 'Were men to observe that which We have sent down unto them from the Heaven of Revelation, they would, of a certainty, attain unto perfect liberty.' And again, He said, 'Mankind in its entirety must firmly adhere to whatsoever hath been revealed and vouchsafed unto it. Then and only then will it attain unto true liberty.'[4]

Liberty among many Enlightenment thinkers was posed in the context of freedom from oppression, and this is totally comprehensible. The period of the 18th and 19th centuries was one of transition from arbitrary and sometimes capricious rule of the elite to a more rational state, and Bahá'u'lláh repeatedly admonished kings and leaders in His own time for such abuses as were the object of protests. Leaders of thought rightly saw intellectual liberty and freedom of expression as a necessary component of this historical change. That said, the healthy exercise of liberty requires limits both in the life of the individual and in the social context. In the extreme, the Terror was carried out in the name of the defence of liberty, and there is scarcely a starker example of the words of Bahá'u'lláh that:

> Whatsoever passeth beyond the limits of moderation will cease to exert a beneficial influence. Consider for instance such things as liberty, civilization and the like. However much men of understanding may favourably regard them, they will, if carried to excess, exercise a pernicious influence upon men.[5]

Equality

Equality was paramount among the foundational principles of the Enlightenment, and can be witnessed in the American

Declaration of Independence as set down by Thomas Jefferson: 'We hold these truths to be self-evident, that all men are created equal . . .' Indeed, if this truth was self-evident, it was not quite so clear how to apply this principle and who was to benefit from this standard, for in practice equality in creation did not translate into equal rights for the great majority of society and would be denied to slaves, women, and persons without property, among others, for years to come. However, equality was the central principle and substance of much of the French Revolution, and the French were ahead of their time in carrying this principle to many of its logical conclusions. The abuse of privilege by the nobles and the Church made this principle all the more attractive and the revolutionaries attempted to implement equality in every conceivable way. Universal suffrage for males would be implemented in 1792, albeit temporarily, and slavery was abolished in the overseas colonies in 1794. Equality pervaded the most basic of social relations and was even expressed in language. The terms *monsieur* (my lord) and *madame* (my lady) were replaced by 'citizen' and 'citizeness' to eliminate the implied subservience. Equality in an electoral system was incorporated in many walks of life, as equals would choose their leaders among themselves, even in some military units.

'Abdu'l-Bahá lauds equality as a necessary principle of a just society, within the context of equal rights and opportunities: 'Equality and Brotherhood must be established among all members of mankind. This is according to Justice. The general rights of mankind must be guarded and preserved. All men must be treated equally. This is inherent in the very nature of humanity.'[6] His reference to 'the nature of humanity' is reminiscent of the concept of natural rights of the Enlightenment thinkers, implying that the very existence of man, at a fundamental spiritual level, contains certain imperatives. Just as physical existence implies the right to breathe, the spiritual reality of man implies the right to equal treatment in the realm of application of the law. This was the first dimension of equality that the revolutionaries sought to establish as a principle *sine qua non*.

On the other hand, Bahá'u'lláh refers to the innate differences in capacity when He says of the grace of God that '[t]he portion of some might lie in the palm of a man's hand, the portion of others might fill a cup, and of others even a gallon-measure'.[7] 'Difference of capacity in human individuals is fundamental. It is impossible for all to be alike, all to be equal, all to be wise,' states 'Abdu'l-Bahá. He extends these natural differences in human capacity to social functions, and states that 'the community needs financier, farmer, merchant and labourer just as an army must be composed of commander, officers and privates. All cannot be commanders; all cannot be officers or privates. Each in his station in the social fabric must be competent – each in his function according to ability but justness of opportunity for all.'[8] But if such innate differences might lead to advantage and social tensions in a competitive world, then

> Bahá'u'lláh has revealed principles and laws which will accomplish the adjustment of varying human capacities. He has said that whatsoever is possible of accomplishment in human government will be effected through these principles. When the laws he has instituted are carried out, there will be no millionaires possible in the community and likewise no extremely poor. This will be effected and regulated by adjusting the different degrees of human capacity.[9]

In these paragraphs 'Abdu'l-Bahá both refers to the inherent and necessary distinctions between human beings, and states that in spite of these differences, all are equal before the law, and the law protects the weaker from any tendency for the stronger to dominate unjustly. 'The Law must reign, and not the individual;

thus will the world become a place of beauty and true brother-hood will be realized. Having attained solidarity, men will have found truth.'[10]

Furthermore, natural distinctions must never create a sense of superiority. 'Of all men the most negligent is he that dis-puteth idly and seeketh to advance himself over his brother.'[11] Equality should flow from the law but individuals, rather than clamouring for equality, 'must consider all those who are present as better and greater than himself, and each one must consider himself less than the rest'.[12] Much less should distinctions spawn envy, for 'the heart wherein the least remnant of envy yet lingers, shall never attain [God's] everlasting dominion'.[13]

Thus, equality applies not to the qualities and capacities of human beings, nor even to their functions of service in society that derive from their capacities, but to their essential rights. As clear as this is, humanity is still far from realizing such a 'self-evident' truth. The privilege of certain individuals and classes that the revolutionaries found to be so unjust continues to plague society, as economic and political power confer honour, opportunity and social benefit on their holders. The extension of political rights as universal suffrage is practically complete in most of the world but not all benefit equally from the fruits of the political process. As the Universal House of Justice writes:

> In many nations the electoral process has become discredited because of endemic corruption. Contributing to the widening distrust of so vital a process are the influence on the outcome from vested interests having access to lavish funds, the restric-tions on freedom of choice inherent in the party system, and the distortion in public perception of the candidates by the bias expressed in the media.[14]

How and why this self-evident principle was deflected from its course and bastardized is part of the story of the 19th century and of the modern world. However, 'Abdu'l-Bahá took equality a step beyond equal protection of the law. Speaking in Paris, the very storm centre of the French Revolution, He declared that 'Every human being has the right to live; they have a right to rest, and to a certain amount of well-being . . . one man should not live in excess while another has no possible means of existence.'[15] This dimension of equality is far more progressive and extends the essential rights inherent in man's existence to some basic level of physical, psychological and spiritual well-being. Just as Shoghi Effendi said that the principle of the oneness of mankind is 'no mere outburst of ignorant emotionalism or an expression of vague and pious hope'[16] but has practical implications for the organization of society, so too does the principle of equality have serious implications of social justice and economic well-being. 'Abdu'l-Bahá puts equality in the context of what each citizen can expect from society of the basic necessities of life, and implies significant refinement of social relations and social responsibility. These rights to physical and social well-being were recognized in the Universal Declaration of Human Rights, adopted and promulgated by the United Nations in 1948 as one of its first formal acts. But in the days of the French Revolution this was one of the most radical propositions of the Jacobins. Other less 'radical' revolutionaries claimed that equality was limited to equality before the law – which indeed was a great advance and benefit for the masses – but society was still not ready to assume the responsibility of providing a degree of social security as a basic human right. While modern society is more receptive to this principle, governments struggle to meet this standard for the masses of humanity.

Fraternity

Fraternity bears on the issue of essential human relationships and is a positive outcome of equality. While fraternity was a central value of the Revolution, it could not withstand the social tensions within the Third Estate among the several social classes once the aristocracy was overthrown. Factionalism soon emerged and created bitter rivalries, of which the Terror was but the tip of the iceberg. 'Abdu'l-Bahá's comments on fraternity are highly pertinent to the French Revolution and beyond.

> Brotherhood, or fraternity, is of different kinds. It may be family association, the intimate relationship of the household. This is limited and subject to change and disruption. How often it happens that in a family, love and agreement are changed into enmity and antagonism. Another form of fraternity is manifest in patriotism. Man loves his fellow-men because they belong to the same native land. This is also limited and subject to change and disintegration as, for instance, when sons of the same fatherland are opposed to each other in war, bloodshed and battle. Still another brotherhood, or fraternity, is that which arises from racial unity, the oneness of racial origin, producing ties of affinity and association. This, likewise, has its limitation and liability to change, for often war and deadly strife have been witnessed between people and nations of the same racial lineage. There is a fourth kind of brotherhood, the attitude of man toward humanity itself, the altruistic love of humankind and recognition of the fundamental human bond. Although this is unlimited, it is, nevertheless, susceptible to change and destruction. Even from this universal fraternal bond the looked-for result does not appear. What is the looked-for result? Loving-kindness among all human creatures and a firm, indestructible

brotherhood which includes all the divine possibilities and significances in humanity.[17]

The French Revolution and subsequent experiments in European nation building sought to employ the several foundations of unity that 'Abdu'l-Bahá refers to in this passage. In the earliest days of the Revolution the French based their efforts on the philosophical altruism of the Enlightenment but this faltered in the harsh realities and the 'change and destruction' of revolutionary political life. Patriotism was summoned but to generate hatred of foreign enemies, and in the 19th century nationalism would be cultivated as a tool to muster support for authoritarian regimes. The fantasy of racial superiority would unite one country but with disastrous consequences for others, especially in the phase of the colonization of Africa. If unity and fraternity served one camp, it became a weapon against others.

'Abdu'l-Bahá argues that the only firm basis of fraternity is that which flows from the Teachings of the Manifestations of God and from the Holy Spirit that is expressed therein.

The spiritual brotherhood which is enkindled and established through the breaths of the Holy Spirit unites nations and removes the cause of warfare and strife. It transforms mankind into one great family and establishes the foundations of the oneness of humanity. It promulgates the spirit of international agreement and ensures universal peace. Therefore, we must investigate the foundation of this heavenly fraternity. We must forsake all imitations and promote the reality of the divine teachings. In accordance with these principles and actions and by the assistance of the Holy Spirit, both material and spiritual happiness shall become realized. Until all nations and peoples become united by the bonds of the Holy Spirit in this real fraternity, until national and international prejudices are effaced in the reality of this spiritual brother-hood, true progress, prosperity and lasting happiness will not be attained by man. This is the century of new and universal nationhood.[18]

Even with regard to the internal workings of the Bahá'í Faith, where the members of an institution should support each other with pure intention and should manifest fraternity, their essential commitment is not to each other. The first loyalty of a Bahá'í administrator, and of any believer, is to God and to His laws through the bonds of the Holy Spirit. In the Bahá'í Writings, human relations emerge from obedience to the com-mands of God. Even Bahá'u'lláh's 'first counsel' that advises love and tenderness among God's children is posed in the impera-tive: 'possess a pure, kindly, and radiant heart'.[19] The Writings abound in counsels that merge into imperatives . . . to be for-bearing, tolerant, forgiving . . . until such time that obedience to these commands flowers into sincere love for each other, born of the love that God holds for us.

Institutional relationships and forms of government

The values of liberty, equality and fraternity raise the practical issue of how values can be carried to application in society, and what sort of social structure can be coherent with and foster such values. The French Revolution saw experiments with social organization evolve in rapid succession, with five distinct forms of government within a period of two decades, seeking to balance these fundamental principles with effective govern-ance, before Napoleon assumed power. With the fall of kings in Europe and the creation of a vacuum of power, this issue came to the forefront and was the cause of social unrest for much of the 19th century. Under the impetus of the French

Revolution, two broad and contrasting forms of government came into conflict on the European continent: monarchy and republicanism, with the latter divided in factions with different degrees of democratic tendency. Pure monarchy or aristocracy would soon become out of the question as the 19th century advanced and ended with World War I but would take a new form in the neo-absolutist regimes, the heads of which would be the object of Bahá'u'lláh's Tablets. The more complex issue was, has been, and even still is, the degree of popular participation in a republican form of government. To what extent should the masses be allowed to participate in government? To what extent should the power of the masses find expression in public power structures? How much democracy is enough? And what are the effective mechanisms for popular participation? Yet long before the Congress of Vienna sought to limit the spread of popular power, the proponents of popular participation in the French Revolution had done their own cause sufficient damage to put its future in doubt. It was severely divided between moderates and radicals, between regional interests and the leadership of Paris. The resort to violence in the Terror polarized society irreparably and spelled the end of any hopes of compromise. The very dynamic of the Revolution carried within it the seeds of its own destruction.

The Universal House of Justice refers to the pernicious inheritance of these 'models of the old world' in our own times, and hints at the root causes of their failure in the 19th century.

> The models of the old world order blur vision of that which must be perceived; for these models were, in many instances, conceived in rebellion and retain the characteristics of the revolutions peculiar to an adolescent, albeit necessary, period in the evolution of human society. The very philosophies which have provided the intellectual content of such

revolutions – Hobbes, Locke, Jefferson, Mill, come readily to mind – were inspired by protest against the oppressive conditions which revolutions were intended to remedy.[20]

The spirit of rebellion in the French Revolution, symptomatic of that age of adolescence and lacking the necessary maturity, generated a downward spiral of action and reaction, first in rebellion of the progressive elements against the excesses of the old regime; then in reaction of conservative elements against the emerging power of the Third Estate; and then further reaction against the King and all that he represented. This degenerative process eventually led to the ascension of Napoleon, the very antithesis of popular power that had initiated the process.

It is useful to refer to the Bahá'í Writings and reflect upon the response that Bahá'u'lláh, 'Abdu'l-Bahá and Shoghi Effendi gave to the question of a viable exercise of popular power under a legitimate authority, embodied in the Bahá'í Administrative Order. The Guardian notes that 'It would be utterly misleading to attempt a comparison between this unique, divinely-conceived Order and any of the diverse systems which the minds of men, at various periods of their history, have contrived for the government of human institutions.' The House of Justice states that the Bahá'í Administrative Order is 'a departure both in origin and in concept' from previous systems. Bahá'u'lláh's 'mission signals the advent of "an organic change in the structure of present-day society, a change such as the world has not yet experienced". It is a fresh manifestation of the direct involvement of God in history . . .'[21]

In recent years the House of Justice has defined three actors in this embryonic structure who participate in the unfoldment of the dynamic processes of the Faith: the individual, the institutions, and the community formed as an inclusive integral unit by its component parts. This means of defining the actors engenders a mature mentality by conceiving of these as an essential dynamic unit as opposed to being distinct, separate and even antagonistic parts. This mental structure is in itself a victory in overcoming the antagonism that has plagued relations within societies.

> Under the influence of Bahá'u'lláh's Revelation, the relationships among these three are being endowed with new warmth, new life; in aggregate, they constitute a matrix within which a world spiritual civilization, bearing the imprint of divine inspiration, gradually matures . . . By contrast, relations among the three corresponding actors in the world at large – the citizen, the body politic, and the institutions of society – reflect the discord that characterizes humanity's turbulent stage of transition. Unwilling to act as interdependent parts of an organic whole, they are locked in a struggle for power which ultimately proves futile.[22]

Having cited the rights and responsibilities of both individuals and institutions, and the implications of these for the relationship between these two components of the community, the Universal House of Justice notes that in contrast to the age of adolescence:

> The equilibrium of responsibilities [of individuals and institutions] . . . presupposes maturity on the part of all concerned. This maturity has an apt analogy in adulthood in human beings. How significant is the difference between infancy and childhood, adolescence and adulthood! In a period of history dominated by the surging energy, the rebellious spirit and frenetic activity of adolescence, it is difficult to grasp the distinguishing elements of the mature society to which Bahá'u'lláh beckons all humanity.[23]

Individuals can attain maturity in many ways and settings . . . through obedience, through acquiescence in tests, and above all, in the realm of service. The House of Justice cites one indicator of maturity that is emerging in the Bahá'í community, that of taking joy in the accomplishments of others. In the dawning of the age of the maturity of humanity, the requirement for maturity of the component parts of humanity is evidenced in many passages of the Bahá'í Writings. It implies an 'organic relationship between the internal and external realities of man'[24] whereby man's internal spiritual life is mirrored in a dignified and respectful demeanour. It demands moderation and courtesy in the exercise of self-expression or in constructive criticism of administrative decisions.

Within the context of liberty as Bahá'u'lláh has posed it and as the Universal House of Justice explains, 'the Administrative Order He has conceived embodies the operating principles which are necessary to the maintenance of that moderation which will ensure the "true liberty" of humankind. All things considered, does the Administrative Order not appear to be the structure of freedom for our Age?'[25] Although every State defines the extent and boundaries of freedom within the society that its government administers, it is rather different to say that an administrative structure is the 'structure of freedom'. This suggests that the Bahá'í Administrative Order – entity that binds the believers in a harmonious whole – more than fixing *limits* on freedom, is an opportunity to *exercise* freedom. Such a concept was shared in the document *The Prosperity of Humankind*:

> In a letter addressed to Queen Victoria over a century ago, and employing an analogy that points to the one model holding convincing promise for the organization of a planetary society, Bahá'u'lláh compared the world to the human body . . . the modes of operation that characterize man's biological

nature illustrate fundamental principles of existence. Chief among these is that of unity in diversity. Paradoxically, it is precisely the wholeness and complexity of the order constituting the human body – and the perfect integration into it of the body's cells – that permit the full realization of the distinctive capacities inherent in each of these component elements.[26]

This is in direct contrast to the thesis of Rousseau who saw man necessarily surrendering freedom under the social contract to be able to share life in society. Rather, the social context should offer new opportunities of freedom that require their own 'operating principles'. 'Abdu'l-Bahá said that 'the moderate freedom which guarantees the welfare of the world of mankind and maintains and preserves the universal relationships is found in its fullest power and extension in the teachings of Bahá'u'lláh'.[27]

If the Administrative Order is the structure of freedom, then the Nineteen Day Feast has a central role in the exercise of freedom.

The Nineteen Day Feast represents the new stage in this enlightened age to which the basic expression of community life has evolved. Shoghi Effendi has described it as the foundation of the new World Order . . . considered in its local sphere alone there is much to thrill and amaze the heart. Here it links the individual to the collective processes by which a society is built or restored. Here, for instance, the Feast is an arena of democracy at the very root of society, where the Local Spiritual Assembly and the members of the community meet on common ground, where individuals are free to offer their gifts of thought, whether as new ideas or constructive criticism, to the building processes of an advancing civilization. Thus it can be seen that aside from its spiritual significance, this common institution of the people combines an array of elemental social disciplines which educate its participants in the essentials of responsible citizenship.[28]

Considered in light of that emblematic slogan of the Revolution, 'liberty, equality, fraternity', the Nineteen Day Feast is where liberty can best be exercised freely within the boundaries of courtesy, moderation and respect for the institutions and for one's fellow believers. It is in every sense the perfect expression of equality, where the friends meet without distinction in a devotional attitude before God. It is where fraternity is the reigning principle. The Feast among all Bahá'í institutions is a divinely ordained association where spirituality and community administration unite in an event in which all participate, the 'common institution of the people' that 'combines an array of elemental social disciplines which educate its participants in the essentials of responsible citizenship'. While in Bahá'í administrative elections the right to vote is limited essentially by age, it is noteworthy that in the Administrative Order that He established, the Nineteen Day Feast is the 'arena of democracy' where all participate in constructive consultation, without even limits of age. Children, youth and adults express themselves, in what is likely the most democratic institution of its kind in the world.

Such is an outline of the values and principles that motivated the French Revolution and the popular movements that followed it, and the response of the Bahá'í Writings to these. In subsequent chapters we will see how these values and principles played out in the 19th century, and in particular in the domains of those kings to whom Bahá'u'lláh directed His Tablets.

6

Voting Rights, Education and Civil Society

The French Revolution and its egalitarianism unleashed the power of the masses as a motif of the modern age, but the expression of popular power brought destruction to France in the Great Terror. Destruction spread to all of Europe as Napoleon's wars propagated revolutionary principles including popular power, even as he himself had little enthusiasm for them. The immaturity of humanity did not permit the flowering of popular power into the greater good of humankind, but rather it was directed into revenge. The healthy development of this power would be a long and painful process extending well beyond the 19th century.

The French Revolution was not the first time that popular power found extensive expression. For example, ancient Rome had seen a massive slave revolt led by Spartacus that nearly threatened the existence of the existing order. However, in the French Revolution under the Jacobins and in lesser degree in the American Revolution, popular power was legitimized as the basis of the State. Thus, as the 19th century dawned, the power of the masses was a force to be reckoned with, and the leaders of society would have to decide how to deal with it. They could seek to stifle it, or they could channel it to their own ends, or they could cultivate it. It would, however, advance against all efforts to resist it. Within the scope of this study, what became of popular empowerment after the French Revolution? This review is a brief accounting of major influences on the development of the capacity of the masses to forge their own destiny and to contribute to an ever-advancing civilization. It is of necessity superficial but seeks to give the reader a sense of the changes that were spreading across the European continent as democratization gained momentum. The dimensions of popular empowerment considered here are: voter suffrage or enfranchisement; education; and freedom and willingness to form associations. While falling far short of the standard of Bahá'u'lláh for spiritual empowerment, these criteria nonetheless reflect the emergence of the masses from the restrictive and oppressive environment of previous centuries.

Voter suffrage

One common criterion of mass empowerment and an expression of liberty and equality is enfranchisement in political processes and the right to vote in public elections. As different versions of republican government were adopted across Europe in the wake of the Napoleonic wars, the issue of participation in elections came to the forefront. In a new world in which liberal democracy was becoming the norm, who should have the right to participate? While initially the middle classes retained this right, inevitably the popular classes would seek representation in the choice of their governing officials. While the percentage of adults with voting rights is a significant datum, it reflects more the willingness of those in decision-making positions to extend the franchise, than voter empowerment per se. A second indicator of empowerment is the actual participation in elections of those with the right to vote. Neither criterion necessarily reflects the capacity of the voter to make rational decisions about the best interests of a nation, nor the voters' inclination to elect on the basis of common good or of personal gain. Recognizing that enfranchisement is an imperfect measure of empowerment, and that it often implies no more than the opportunity to engage the powers that be on their own terms, it does still offer a relatively objective measure of the relaxing of those barriers that held the masses captive in the old regime, and a general sense of participation in public life that was widely denied to the masses in the 18th century.

Enfranchisement expanded slowly over the 19th century, as barriers to voting were eliminated gradually. Limitations on enfranchisement were often based on property ownership under the pretext that those who owned property had a stake in society and therefore were the most responsible in exercising their vote. Enfranchisement based on property ownership was first extended from rural to urban property owners, before this requirement was abolished altogether. Wealth, taxes rendered to the State, and educational level were other criteria used to limit the voting public, justified as either reflecting the required capacity to vote rationally, or as evidence of commitment to the State by investment through taxes.

Adapting data presented by Bartolini[1] in a detailed analysis of voter suffrage over the course of the 19th and 20th centuries, it is evident that enfranchisement was a process that advanced unevenly over the continent. Taking 25% of the adult population as an arbitrary measure of wider voter enfranchisement (and noting that this watermark is in fact 50% of males, since women were uniformly excluded), only France, Switzerland and Denmark had obtained this level before the mid-19th century. Some 36% of adults could vote in France, 30% in Switzerland, and 25% in Denmark by 1849. From the very start French voters turned out in large numbers (about 75%), reflecting perhaps her long electoral tradition that was applied in many dimensions of society during the Revolution. Voter participation was lower (about 50%) in Switzerland. The next country to reach this watermark level of voter suffrage was Germany with 35% of enfranchised population in 1867 – quite a substantial achievement considering that it only recently had been formed as a nation. However, German voters assumed the exercise of this right gradually, rising from 55% to 80% by the end of the century.

A major step in voter enfranchisement occurred in Britain in 1832 with the Reform Act which doubled the number of eligible voters, but even in this landmark legislation only 14% of males were permitted to vote. Nonetheless, it opened the door on the participation of an emerging middle class and eventually to the gradual incorporation of nearly all men as voting public, although a much wider extension of voting rights would delay for another half century! In the decade of the 1880s the United Kingdom enfranchised 29% (1885) and Ireland 27% (1886). Although the United Kingdom had the longest tradition of representative democracy among the Great Powers, its tradition of class structure and its suspicion of the working classes reinforced by the French Terror slowed enfranchisement. Voter participation in the United Kingdom fluctuated from 50 to 80%.

In the 1890s Belgium (37% in 1892) and Austria (34% in 1896) reached this watermark level, while the Netherlands (25% in 1909) only broadened the franchise in the 20th century, in spite of a long republican history. The Scandinavian countries tended to be slow in this regard: Norway (34% in 1900, although it had had a quite liberal policy at the start of the 19th century), Finland (76% in 1906), and Sweden (32% in 1911). Voter turnout was lackadaisical (50% or less) when voting was limited to a small elite, but gradually increased as the franchise was amplified.

In contrast, in the United States universal male suffrage came relatively early, though unevenly since voting requirements were set by individual states. Popular participation in the political process received a great boost with the election of Andrew Jackson in 1828. A proponent of popular power, his philosophy has come down to us as 'Jacksonian democracy'. We shall return to this theme in the history of the United States in Chapter 14.

Women in Europe were denied enfranchisement across the board until the 20th century. However, when Finland expanded its franchise rapidly from 9% in 1904 to 76% in 1906, women were included in this move and Norway followed in 1907, these being the only European countries to grant the franchise to women before the war, although in Australia women were given the right to vote in federal elections in 1902, following the lead of South Australia (1894) and Western Australia (1899). It was only after the war that enfranchisement was extended to women more generally, although in France women were only given this right in 1945, and in Switzerland in 1971. This is a paradox given France's egalitarian tradition, and the fact that both countries had led the move to wider enfranchisement in the 1840s. In the United States women were assured of the franchise by the nineteenth amendment in 1920. Voter participation was maintained at 80% or higher in most countries after the First World War.

Education

The spread of education among the masses was a major contribution to empowerment, and its progress paralleled in general terms the advances in voter enfranchisement on the timeline of the 19th century. Education had long been the domain of religion, and as education was extended to the masses by civil authorities, control of the educational process would be a bone of contention between the State and the Church on many fronts. Scattered experiences in education in the mid-late 18th century displayed surprising creativity on the part of some vision-ary individuals who saw great innate potential in the human being, but these models were isolated experiments and were not adopted by governments to be scaled up. Systematic education for the masses would take far longer to implement.

The United States, or rather, certain of the original thirteen colonies and especially those in New England, were pioneers in public education. The fact of individual colonial administration that grew into semi-autonomy among states in the subsequent union permitted a more localized experimentation in public education. Schools were established as early as the 17th cen-tury and shortly after the founding of the Massachusetts colony, typically with the purpose of promoting religious education in a Puritan society. Curiously, reading and writing were considered separate skills. Reading was taught to both boys and girls, with the purpose of giving access to sacred scripture, while writing was reserved largely for boys. In 1690 the New England Primer was published as the first widely used text until Noah Webster created the 'blue-backed speller' in the 1780s, a landmark in public education in which learning was scaled by age group. Indeed, Webster admired the Prussian model (see below) and used elements of it in his system. He had little use for traditional religious content but employed secular education to fortify a budding American nationalism, rejecting conventional spell-ings and creating 'American English' as opposed to that of Great Britain. His text would be used until the McGuffey Reader was published in 1836, a text with which this writer's grandfather learned to read in the 1880s.

Surprisingly, in Europe it was authoritarian Prussia that took the lead in popular education in a process that preceded even the French Revolution. In 1763 Frederick the Great, authoritar-ian absolutist but rationalist par excellence, established publicly funded education for children between the ages of 5 and 13.

Frederick had no special love for the popular classes of society, and while he was an avowed atheist, he was the classic 'enlightened despot' and could see the advantages of an educated public for the progress of the nation. Teacher training was developed in parallel to support systematic education, and secondary education was also strengthened. Horace Mann, an influential pioneer of public education in the 1830s in Massachusetts, sought to emulate the Prussian example after personally visiting Prussia in 1843. In Austria the Emperor Joseph II, another enlightened despot, launched similar efforts in public education in the 18th century.

In France, education in the 18th century was largely in the hands of the Catholic Church, and by 1790 literacy was reported at 47% among men and 27% among women.[2] The French revolutionaries recognized the importance of education and enacted laws to extend its reach to all classes, although the Revolution in fact disrupted education for some time due to the persecution of the Church. Efforts to promote public education progressed, especially in the Thermidorian period, thereby seeking to limit the influence of Catholicism. However, education could not receive its just due until Napoleon's reign, when it became a high priority for the State. Like Frederick, Napoleon saw education as a requisite for a nation at the cutting edge of progress in a competitive world, although Napoleon had little interest in the masses and in primary education, much of which was devolved to the Catholic Church. Rather, Napoleon's priority was secondary education as embodied in the system of *lycées*. These schools would serve to create an elite cadre of civil servants and military personnel in service to the State. This system of secondary education is still largely operational today. Indeed, education was a cornerstone of nation building of France, since all instruction was carried out in French and thus served to combat dialects and the regionalism that they reinforced. France was not alone in this regard, as we shall see in the case of Italy in its efforts at nation building, or even in 21st century Spain. A common language is a prerequisite of a sense of nationhood, and modern European nations had to struggle with the challenge of dialects and functional illiteracy that many African countries still face today.

Great Britain, with its traditional system of social classes and its distrust of revolutionary ideas that had disrupted the continent so tragically, was cautious about extending education widely among the masses. Indeed, educational opportunities were heavily marked by social class, especially in England.[3] Much early work in education of the lower classes was carried out by individual initiatives such as the Sunday Schools of Robert Raikes, initiated in 1780, which met on Sunday as the only time that young boys were not working, and which focused on the Bible as their primary text. Even so, Raikes's schools were the subject of ridicule and some were closed under the pretext that this represented working on the Sabbath. Only in 1833 did Parliament approve funds for the building of public schools for the poor – its first involvement in public education (although in Scotland universal education had existed since 1561!).

School attendance was slowed, nonetheless, by economic realities, as many working-class families preferred to send their children to work in the mills and so gain modest income for the home. But as labour laws gradually limited child labour in factories, this freed children to attend school. The extension of public education in Great Britain was also slowed by religious infighting and competition among sects over which doctrine would be taught in schools. Anglicans in England, Presbyterians in Scotland, Nonconformists such as Quakers in Wales, and Catholics in Ireland – all saw in education a rightful area of religious instruction and resisted ceding this domain or submitting their children to the precepts of another denomination. However, by 1861 a government report could state that 2,535,462 out of 2,655,767 children in England and Wales were registered in schools and were receiving some education, albeit at times very little. A diverse and gradual movement toward universal public education was consolidated and reached a landmark in the Forster Elementary Education Act of 1870. This was a decisive move toward making education compulsory, a tendency that was strengthened in subsequent acts of Parliament. It was motivated in part by the sense that Britain was falling behind in its economic development compared to its competitors on the continent, especially Germany, and that an educated work force would help correct this.

In Italy education was a particular challenge and only received systematic attention after 1870 and the consolidation of the Italian State. Emerging from the union of a multitude of small princedoms, an effective educational system was a crying need to solidify the nationhood of a multicultural, multilingual population. Furthermore, educational levels were among the lowest in Europe. At the start of the 19th century perhaps 90% of the population was illiterate, and as late as 1921, one-fourth of men and one-third of women still suffered from illiteracy.[4]

Thus, for many parts of Europe, free and *effective* public primary education was not a reality until the second half of the century. However, two aspects can be highlighted about education in the 19th century. First, education was a long-term battleground between religion and the State as the latter sought to impose a secular order under Enlightenment principles. In the several examples cited above, religious organizations figured prominently in the field of education and viewed the entry of the State as an encroachment in their traditional domain. Both the Church and the State understood education as the key to winning the hearts and minds of future generations. The struggle between Church and State over education was especially intense in countries with a Catholic majority, and Pope Pius IX himself participated in this debate. Early in the French Revolution the National Assembly sought to dislodge the Church from its monopoly, and though Napoleon struck a balance between roles of the Church and State, this would be a point of contention even late in the 19th century. Belgium was a particularly stark and bitter example of this battle after its constitution of 1831 which culminated in its final separation from the Netherlands.[5] The Catholic Church held a virtual monopoly on education for the first half of the century, and was only challenged at mid-century as the liberal political movement gathered strength. From then to the end of the century and up to the First World War, educational policy bounced back and forth between Church-dominated tendencies and those of Enlightenment-inspired liberals as power alternated between liberal and Catholic parties.

Secondly, and closely related to the issue of state-sponsored versus religious education, was that of the education of girls and women which was often severely restricted and lagged behind that of boys. Unlike progressive thought in other areas of human endeavour, the Enlightenment generally did not place women on a par with men, and Rousseau went so far as to say: 'Thus the whole education of women ought to be relative to men. To please them, to be useful to them, to make themselves loved and honoured by them, to educate them when young.'[6] Some French revolutionaries had more progressive views on education, but most thinkers and leaders of society viewed the biological difference between the sexes as having implications for social roles and intellectual capacities. The view that the place of the woman was in the home was predicated upon 'scientific' premises, that in their role as childbearers and caregivers, women were naturally more compassionate but also less rational and less capable of logical decision-making.

This perceived distinctive nature of woman influenced the education of each of the sexes. Public schools were considered to be conducive to developing manliness in boys, while girls might often be educated at home. As private schools for girls developed, curricula included basic subjects of reading, writing, literature, history, arithmetic, geography, and often Latin, and also included moral education that was supplemented by activities of dance and needlework, or those relevant to domestic chores. The tendency toward distinct curricula was reinforced by resistance to co-education, which was viewed as potentially dangerous to morality. One curious distinction that was rooted in perceived biological differences was reflected in teaching methods. Boys were assumed to benefit from discipline and concentrated effort on a single subject, while girls were thought incapable of such concentration and thus were offered a varied but sometimes superficial curriculum. A finding of a government commission in Britain in 1868 is revealing about attitudes. The report stated that girls scored every bit as well as boys on exams, but condescendingly noted that women could be over-eager to learn and needed to be protected from their own enthusiasm that could lead to excessive workload and negative health consequences.[7] Indeed, even as the State expanded its role in education, resources were often directed first to schools serving boys. This was especially true in Italy where Catholic schools continued to be the primary supplier of female education until late in the century, although normal schools for teacher training were a frequent path of self-improvement for women.

At the end of that long 19th century 'Abdu'l-Bahá would set forth an unambiguous position regarding education:

The education and training of children is among the most meritorious acts of humankind and draweth down the grace and favour of the All-Merciful, for education is the indispensable foundation of all human excellence and alloweth man to work his way to the heights of abiding glory.[8]

Furthermore, the education of women is of greater importance than the education of men, for they are the mothers
of the race, and mothers rear the children. The first teachers
of children are the mothers. Therefore, they must be capably
trained in order to educate both sons and daughters.[9]

'Abdu'l-Bahá's view on the social role of women as educators of
children and therefore of society is consistent with the thinking
of both liberal and religious participants in the century-long
debate around education (each seeking to promote their own
vision of society). Furthermore, like the philosophers in the
18th century and later years, 'Abdu'l-Bahá noted unique poten-
tials that distinguish women from men: 'In some respects
woman is superior to man. She is more tender-hearted, more
receptive, her intuition is more intense.'[10] However, those earlier
thinkers created a false dichotomy, seeing sensitivity as incompatible with rational thought. They concluded that as a result
of women's sensitivity, women should therefore receive a more
'domestic' education and should be limited to the home. To the
contrary, 'Abdu'l-Bahá declared that 'Women shall receive an
equal privilege of education. This will enable them to qualify
and progress in all degrees of occupation and accomplishment.'[11]
The compassion and intuition of women are added value and
not limitations on their scope of service and attainment.

Associationism of civil society

One of the most noteworthy changes of the 19th century,
the significance of which is still hotly debated, is the formation of voluntary associations in support of what we today call
'civil society'. As early as 1780 but much more when Europe
had returned to some degree of stability after the Napoleonic
wars, an outburst of associations and clubs occurred across the

continent in a nascent movement that one could view as an expression of fraternity, and that would come to involve a significant proportion of society. While 'clubs' had existed before, these were largely male-dominated and not infrequently for sociable purposes involving significant consumption of spirits. In contrast, the flowering of associative activity in the 19th century was a phenomenon on a scale not seen previously, and is still the subject of study as to its nature and significance. The upsurge of social organizations in the 19th century is an established fact, and seems coherent with the counsels of Bahá'u'lláh voiced in the mid-late century:

> It is permitted that the peoples and kindreds of the world associate with one another with joy and radiance. O people! Consort with the followers of all religions in a spirit of friendliness and fellowship. Thus hath the day-star of His sanction and authority shone forth above the horizon of the decree of God, the Lord of the worlds.[12]

> With the utmost friendliness and in a spirit of perfect fellowship take ye counsel together, and dedicate the precious days of your lives to the betterment of the world and the promotion of the Cause of Him Who is the Ancient and Sovereign Lord of all. He, verily, enjoineth upon all men what is right, and forbiddeth whatsoever degradeth their station.[13]

> O contending peoples and kindreds of the earth! Set your faces towards unity, and let the radiance of its light shine upon you. Gather ye together, and for the sake of God resolve to root out whatever is the source of contention amongst you.[14]

Many of the formal associations in the 1820s and 1830s were constituted by men of aristocratic or middle classes, and like the salons of the 18th century, they served as platforms for discussion of specific issues of scientific or literary nature. Of more significant importance is the role of associations as mechanisms for social action. A particular type of association emerged in Great Britain, referred to as 'subscriber democracy' – voluntary associations that carried out their internal business in a formal manner, with a chairperson and secretary, keeping formal records, and reflecting Britain's parliamentary tradition. Some associations would even publish their proceedings in local newspapers. These associations were generally open to the public, participants would 'subscribe' with a member's fee, and meetings were directed as if they were a session of Parliament.[15]

In Europe in the first half of the century associations seldom had political ends. A major exception to this was the Chartist Movement in Britain which gained widespread support among workers, receiving the allegiance of millions, and making unsuccessful appeals to Parliament on behalf of the working classes. Originally a scattered mix of local organizations with varying objectives, it coalesced in 1838 with the creation of the People's Charter, calling for political reforms including male suffrage. The Chartist Movement surged anew with the enthusiasm surrounding the revolts of 1848 that swept over Europe, but declined in the 1850s.

Conservative elements viewed this broad tendency of associations with suspicion as promoting unbridled democracy. In repressive environments in which associations were suspected of hiding political or revolutionary motives, salons permitted informal private discussions that otherwise would have been impossible. For example, in pre-unification Italy where the Austrian presence was still evident and associations were carefully scrutinized, most formal associations had some benign purpose such as scientific exchange, while aspirations for political unity could be expressed only privately. In Russia and

Austria-Hungary, state police viewed civil society with suspicion, but in Hapsburg Austria restrictions were relaxed in 1867 and associations grew in numbers in various parts of the empire in a long-term tendency. The Catholic Church likewise was highly sceptical about associations and especially Freemasonry which flourished widely, much to the chagrin of the Church.

Ironically, in France in the very cradle of liberty, equality and fraternity, associations were tightly controlled for most of the 19th century, and complete freedom of association was only granted in 1901.[16] This is in contrast to the application of near universal suffrage to adult men in the 1840s. After the Revolution, France remained highly politicized and divided, and whichever group that was in power at a given moment – republicans, monarchists, Bonapartists, liberals – all feared that freedom of association could be used to organize groups of opposition against the government. The franchise was counted as sufficient for the masses, beyond which further participation was suspect and deemed unwise. As such, the opportunities to associate freely would expand gradually and then contract again after violent events such as the Revolution of 1848 and the coup of 1851 when controls were reinforced.

The working classes also participated in this new tendency in these early decades, but their associations were typically of a more applied nature that dealt with the demands of day-to-day living through mutual help organizations on the level of neighbourhoods or localities. Significantly, associationism was also a channel for the wider participation of women in society. Referring to charitable associations of the period, Prochaska notes: 'In a typical charity in the 1790s only about 5 percent of subscribers were female. By 1830, the figure had risen to about 30 percent; by the 1870s it had risen to about 60 percent.'[17] The century saw a radical shift in the participation of women in charity, for example, Florence Nightingale among the English and Clara Barton, founder of the American Red Cross.

However, in the 60s and 70s the formation of associations accelerated dramatically in both the middle and working classes, and with more associations taking on political goals. This spectacular growth is termed 'association mania' by social historians, and occurred on both sides of the Atlantic. A tendency that had been gestating for wellnigh two generations suddenly burst into full flower, and thousands of associations were formed within the next few decades, including in areas where they had been repressed systematically by state police power. For example, in Prague the number of associations doubled within a decade between 1890 and 1901.

Labour unions were a special class of association, but unlike other associations that enjoyed ample freedom to form and carry out their chosen field of activity, labour unions were illegal or closely monitored with highly restricted activity. We note the comment of Adam Smith in 1776 about the imbalance between industrialists and workers in the right to form associations, the latter being forbidden to establish 'combinations'. This total ban in Great Britain was repealed in 1825 but unions were severely limited in the scope of their activity until well into the second half of the century: until 1871 in Britain, until 1884 in France, and until 1897 in Germany with the repeal of anti-socialist laws. In spite of repression, workers formed organizations over the length of the 19th century, sometimes under the cloak of other purposes. As the 19th century was drawing to a close and restrictions on associations were relaxed, the movement of the working classes was increasingly associated with socialism, which claimed centre stage as the spokesperson of the masses with the right to take the lead in workers' associations. From a common point of departure of indignation at social injustice, socialism resulted in a diverse array of responses about how to craft a more just society. Socialism was destined to be a movement with stark differences of opinion that could grow into bitter rivalries.

During most of the 19th century the associative movement had been an active urban phenomenon, but its role in rural areas is subject to question. Rather, the traditional structure of rural life lent itself to 'associative behaviour' with or without a formal structure, certainly based on family relations and probably shared culture. In Italy such relations were a potent force in attracting the allegiance of the masses. Urbanization and massive relocation of populations weakened but did not destroy such traditional links and allegiances. However, toward the end of the century, even in rural areas associations are better documented. For example, two opposing movements competed for the allegiance of the rural population in Italy, the Church and the socialists. Here and elsewhere even the Catholic Church joined the movement toward associations and sought to recover from its reverses at mid-century, while socialists found a receptive audience among the disenfranchised farm labourers who had no share in the progress of liberal economy.

What motivated this drive toward public participation and involvement? While societies were formed for any conceivable theme or special interest, a common thread in these early associations was the cultivation of virtue – a noble ideal that crossed social strata and specific objectives. This was a conscious effort that viewed social action as originating in values that required nurturing. De Toqueville, a French aristocrat who observed American democracy at work in 1831, attributed much of the relative success of democracy in the United States to the unfettered and widespread functioning of free associations, with the view that these cultivated human virtue which was the foundation of the individual's input into social processes and the cornerstone of democracy. He viewed the impact of associations not in a cold organizational context but in very human terms, and at the level of the human spirit: 'Sentiments and ideas renew themselves, the heart is enlarged, and the human mind is developed only by the reciprocal action of men upon each other.'[18] We will return to Tocqueville in a later chapter.

While causes and effects of the associational movement are hotly debated, what is striking about the movement is – very simply – that *it happened!* Recognizing the importance of voting rights as a component of public participation, and the role of education as essential to empowerment, the associational wave that swept across Europe and America could someday be considered to be the most significant component of the empowerment of the masses in the 19th century. Temporally and spatially, these dimensions of popular power and popular participation followed patterns similar to industrialization and urbanization as component dimensions of modernity – from West to East, with concentration in urban areas, and in much the same period. In a Europe that was emerging from a millennial history of a vertical medieval power structure, and frequently from societies with very explicit restrictions on freedom of association, in which 'clubs' were the near exclusive domain of 'gentlemen' . . . in such societies and in distant and varied cultures, and within a scant two generations, people of every social class were frantically developing every sort of association imaginable, from temperance unions, to sports clubs, to literary groups, to charities, to religious organizations, and eventually, to groups with political ends. This represented a vast change in the sense of possibility that filtered through society, and though frequently opposed by conservative forces and governments, voluntary associations surged forward in even some of the most repressive of circumstances. Just as some modern companies of the 21st century emerged from the Industrial Revolution in the 19th century, so did some well-known associations such as the American Red Cross and Germany's Social Democratic Party appear in this period.

What is important is that voluntary associations were a potent force in democratizing the 19th century – 'democratizing' not in the narrow sense of a system of government and in which they are sometimes studied – but democratizing in the sense of the internet in the 20th century. The internet put the power of knowledge (of all types – both good and evil!) at the fingertips of everyone with access to a computer, and opened the potential of new intellectual vistas. In the 19th century voluntary associations broadened the perspectives of the 'man in the street' about his or her potential to act for his or her own good and for the betterment of society, and were a major force of empowerment of the masses. As significant a development as this was, the association movement should not be a surprise. 'Abdu'l-Bahá comments on the essential need for man to live in association with others:

> It seems as though all creatures can exist singly and alone. For example, a tree can exist solitary and alone on a given prairie or on the mountainside. An animal upon a mountainside or a bird soaring in the air might live a solitary life . . . On the contrary, man cannot live singly and alone. He is in need of continuous cooperation and mutual help. For example, a man living alone in the wilderness will eventually starve. He can never, singly and alone, provide himself with all the necessities of existence. Therefore, he is in need of cooperation and reciprocity.[19]

The formation of associations is a natural impulse that is inherent in man's being. However, as important as associations or 'collective centres' are, and as productive as they are of progress in many fields of human endeavour, they did not prevent the tragic war that was soon to rage over Europe and around the Holy Land as 'Abdu'l-Bahá penned those reflections. Only the collective centre of the Holy Spirit could do this. In the *Tablets of the Divine Plan*, written during those years of agonizing conflict in Europe, He observes the following:

In the contingent world there are many collective centers which are conducive to association and unity between the children of men. For example, patriotism is a collective center; nationalism is a collective center; identity of interests is a collective center; political alliance is a collective center; the union of ideals is a collective center, and the prosperity of the world of humanity is dependent upon the organization and promotion of the collective centers. Nevertheless, all the above institutions are, in reality, the matter and not the substance, accidental and not eternal – temporary and not everlasting. With the appearance of great revolutions and upheavals, all these collective centers are swept away. But the Collective Center of the Kingdom, embodying the institutions and divine teachings, is the eternal Collective Center. It establishes relationship between the East and the West, organizes the oneness of the world of humanity, and destroys the foundation of differences. It overcomes and includes all the other collective centers. Like unto the ray of the sun, it dispels entirely the darkness encompassing all the regions, bestows ideal life, and causes the effulgence of divine illumination. Through the breaths of the Holy Spirit it performs miracles; the Orient and the Occident embrace each other, the North and South become intimates and associates, conflicting and contending opinions disappear, antagonistic aims are brushed aside, the law of the struggle for existence is abrogated, and the canopy of the oneness of the world of humanity is raised on the apex of the globe, casting its shade over all the races of men. Consequently, the real Collective Center is the body of the divine teachings, which include all the degrees and embrace all the universal relations and necessary laws of humanity.[20]

It is significant that these passages about the power of the Kingdom to resist conflict and to unite East, West, North and South were written precisely as the Great War – whereby 'all these collective centers are swept away' – was shaking the very foundations of Europe and tearing down its civilization. Moreover, those limited collective centres or associations that 'Abdu'l-Bahá cites were by and large products of the 19th century that had just ended and to which the peoples of Europe had subscribed enthusiastically. Participation in a collective centre is motivated by a sense of belonging to that centre, by a sense of shared identity. Some such centres represented emerging identities that had caught the imagination of Europeans, especially 'nationalism' that prospered in the hundred years before the War and contributed to the ongoing conflagration. Similarly, 'political alliances' flourished under liberal democracy. 'Identity of interests' can describe the multitude of associations with narrow focus covering topics as diverse as sports and temperance. Even the 'union of ideals' that should have raised the moral consciousness of humanity as expressed in the French Revolution and adopted by the socialists could not assure the peace and tranquillity of humanity. As critical as collective centres or associations are to 'the prosperity of the world of humanity', they had not prevented the conflict that was engulfing mankind. These collective centres were emblematic of the 19th century, but they failed due to the lack of the one essential collective centre, that one that was offered to humanity by Bahá'u'lláh and neglected by potentates and paupers alike. And at the heart of that essential collective centre was the spiritual identity as the essence of the human being – a universal identity that 'Abdu'l-Bahá sought to propagate in all His travels through the West.

The history and significance of associations – broadly equated with civil society – in the 19th century and up to the present is the subject of intense study and heated debate. Within this debate the topic of associations has been approached from at least two different perspectives that are of interest to this treatise, that of an outward-looking approach examining the role of associations in the broader sweep of society and often in relation to systems of government; and a second inward-looking perspective, that of the impact of associations on the individual. De Toqueville and others of his age saw these two perspectives as one, insomuch as association among citizens was seen to breed civic virtue in the individual that was the basis of good social organization. This remains an area of learning within the scope of the Bahá'í Faith, as relations develop among the three actors in an evolving dynamic: the individual, the institutions, and the community – under the collective centre of the Kingdom. Indeed, the structures of the Bahá'í Faith through which it functions – its Local Spiritual Assemblies, its committees and dependencies – offer the opportunity to revive that spirit of participation that flourished in the 19th century, with the conscious purpose of promoting virtue and the betterment of society. In this context, the Nineteen Day Feast can play a particular role, as that scenario where every Bahá'í, young and old, can contribute actively in an institution that 'combines an array of elemental social disciplines which educate its participants in the essentials of responsible citizenship'.[21]

7

Dawn of a New Day

As the Industrial Revolution gathered momentum in England, and while Napoleon was arming his campaigns that would disrupt the old order of Europe, a spiritual awakening was stirring in the East. In the first years of the 13th century of the Muslim calendar (ca. 1792 AD), as the French revolutionaries declared the French Republic and instituted a new calendar as symbolic of a new era that they thought was dawning, Shaykh Aḥmad-i-Aḥsá'í (1753–1826/27 AD; 1166–1242 AH) arose to revive the fortunes of Islam. Born on an island of the kingdom of Bahrain, at the age of forty years he set forth to stir the world of Islam from the lethargy into which it had fallen, establishing himself first in Najaf and Karbila in Mesopotamia where he came to be recognized as a *mujtahid* (a doctor of the law). As Europe was sucked into a maelstrom of war and Napoleon marched across Europe, Shaykh Aḥmad set his sights on Persia, traveling first to Shiraz, and then to Yazd where he established his residence. In 1815, while Metternich entertained the ambassadors and crowned heads of Europe at the Congress of Vienna, Shaykh Aḥmad received a youthful seeker of twenty-two years of age, Siyyid Káẓim, who would be his successor. Setting out from Yazd, Shaykh Aḥmad travelled throughout Persia, first to Mazindaran and then to Tehran. In 1817 as the old order of Europe celebrated the death of revolution and settled into its 'renewed' role of dominance, Shaykh Aḥmad found himself a guest of Fatḥ-'Alí Sháh in Tehran. In those days was born One Who was destined to transform the world, not through radical revolution and violence, but through the invisible hand of the Spirit and the power of His Pen. Two years later His forerunner would be born in Shiraz.

The next three decades saw Bahá'u'lláh and the Báb grow into manhood, while Siyyid Káẓim struggled in the face of Muslim orthodoxy that opposed his inspired and insightful interpretations of the Islamic traditions. Nabíl paraphrases the attitudes of those who first resisted Shaykh Aḥmad, and who intensified their resistance when the mantle of leadership fell upon the shoulders of his youthful disciple:

> 'For forty years,' they clamoured, 'we have suffered the pre-tentious teachings of Shaykh Aḥmad to be spread with no opposition whatever on our part. We no longer can tolerate similar pretensions on the part of his successor, who rejects the belief in the resurrection of the body, who repudiates the literal interpretation of the "Mi'ráj", who regards the signs of the coming Day as allegorical, and who preaches a doc-trine heretical in character and subversive of the best tenets of orthodox Islám.'[1]

> How grievously Siyyid Kázim suffered at the hands of the people of wickedness! What harm that villainous generation inflicted upon him! For years he suffered silently, and endured with heroic patience all the indignities, the calumnies, the denunciations that were heaped upon him.[2]

Only the choicest of the spiritually insightful would carry his message forward into the new day when it finally dawned upon the stygian darkness of Persia.

In Europe these three decades would be marked by a deceptive calm, at least on the international scene, while the forces of change gathered momentum under the surface. For if messianic fervour simmered among the Persians, in Europe the period between 1815 and 1848 was a period of social and intellectual ferment known to some as the Age of Revolution. Fully conscious of these undercurrents, the traditional powers of the Congress of Vienna were vigilant to oppose and snuff out any hint of revolutionary fervour, as secret police in Austria and Russia monitored suspicious activity, and the English Parliament supported military action against worker organizations. This was a period of soul-searching among students and intellectuals in countries as distant as Italy, Germany and Russia, where earnest young men met in clandestine societies, avoiding the vigilance of government authorities, to dream of the fruits of liberty within the context of new national identities. The Carbonari in Italy, the Intelligentsia in Russia . . . across Europe a vital force was stirring that was born of the lofty principles of the Enlightenment and propagated through the French conquest. Internal social pressures waxed and waned, bursting occasionally into riots and revolts. In France in particular a major revolt broke out in 1830, forcing the abdication of King Charles X and the ascension of Louis-Philippe to the throne.

In spite of the social tensions of the period, wars of the sort that had decimated its population in the days of Napoleon were avoided. The international peace of this period in Europe reflected an act of volition on the part of the crowned heads when they met in Vienna in 1814–15 under the guidance of the Austrian Count Clemens von Metternich. Austria was relatively weak militarily compared to other powers, but Metternich assumed the role of host and prime negotiator to bring about the accords that sought to conserve the consensus among the Great Powers. On that occasion they set about to restore the old order of aristocracy and monarchy. All the major powers – Britain, Austria, Prussia, Russia – and several minor ones were at the table to restore monarchies where these had been upset by the Napoleonic wars; to take decisions on borders, for example in the case of Germany where Napoleon had reduced the number of principalities drastically; and to decide on the fate of France that was represented by Count Talleyrand. Rather than a punitive peace, France was welcomed back into the circle of nations by reestablishing the monarchy, and Louis XVIII was designated king of France, later to be succeeded by Charles X.

The powers set themselves the goal of avoiding more disastrous conflicts as had brought such ruin upon their countries. For this purpose they created the Concert of Europe, a consultative body meant to serve as a sounding board, and a means for peaceful settlement of their international frictions and to maintain the status quo among the Great Powers. The same major powers who attended the Congress also sat at the Concert where they would meet to maintain the balance of power that they had established. In this regard they were substantially successful in maintaining the peace, and for three decades there were no major conflicts among European nations. The Concert of Europe was comparable to the Security Council of the United Nations in preserving the peace. Indeed, this similarity is more than skin deep, and it is not a coincidence that three important actors in 19th-century Europe – England, Russia and France – are among the five permanent members of the Security Council. These permanent members were derived from the victorious allies of the Second World War, which in essence was an extension of the First World War where the major actors of the 19th century clashed.

In the mid-19th century as wars again overtook Europe, in the *Súriy-i-Mulúk* Bahá'u'lláh would call upon the kings of the earth to:

Compose your differences, and reduce your armaments, that the burden of your expenditures may be lightened, and that your minds and hearts may be tranquillized. Heal the dissensions that divide you, and ye will no longer be in need of any armaments except what the protection of your cities and territories demandeth.[3]

And again in the Tablet to Queen Victoria He directs His attention to the kings and presidents of the world.

O rulers of the earth! Be reconciled among yourselves, that ye may need no more armaments save in a measure to safeguard your territories and dominions . . . Be united, O kings of the earth, for thereby will the tempest of discord be stilled amongst you, and your peoples find rest, if ye be of them that comprehend.[4]

Later in the 20th century Shoghi Effendi would clarify that Bahá'u'lláh's call to unity was an imperative for a fundamental transformation in society:

The principle of the Oneness of Mankind – the pivot round which all the teachings of Bahá'u'lláh revolve – is no mere outburst of ignorant emotionalism or an expression of vague and pious hope . . . Its message is applicable not only to the individual, but concerns itself primarily with the nature of those essential relationships that must bind all the states and nations as members of one human family.[5]

If the unity of nations was still a distant vision in the 19th century, it was not a remote possibility that the European powers might have resolved their differences peacefully, since prior to the time that Bahá'u'lláh penned these words, they had had such a mechanism for this purpose in the Concert of Europe. It would have been perfectly feasible to heed the counsel of Bahá'u'lláh, but this the powers failed to do, and with fatal results. Rather, the forces of disintegration had fractured the consensus and corroded the common will to maintain the status quo, and nations were on the move to seek advantage over each other. This would have tragic consequences that eventually would lead to two world wars.

However, in the 1840s the dangers of war were only just looming, while the façade of the stability of tradition would soon be shattered by the forces that had been gestating for a generation. Forces of change would come to the forefront, the veneer of calm would break, and events would accelerate in both the East and the West. In Persia the Báb declared His Mission in 1844, opening a new era in the history of the world as anticipated by Shaykh Aḥmad and Siyyid Káẓim, and releasing a wave of religious fervour that would shake the foundations of Persian society. Thousands would respond to His call, thousands would render up their lives as the powers of orthodoxy mustered their all to quell the groundswell of God's Cause.

Meanwhile, across Europe a wave of revolutions broke out spontaneously in 1848, startling the noble classes and revealing the depth and the geographical scope of underlying discontent and the intensity of aspirations. Historians see no effort at coordination among these rebellions, rather they appear to have been similar responses to frustrated expectations of freedom. In Italy and France, later in Austria, Prussia and the lesser German states, students arose to demand constitutions and representative government. While these were internal conflicts recalling the aspirations engendered by the French Revolution, they would presage a period of international conflict that would shatter the peace of the Congress of Vienna.

While Europe slipped back into widespread violence, the

Báb languished as a prisoner in the mountain of Chihríq. In that same year of 1848 the Báb was called to Tabriz to an interrogation by the mullas of the city, and soon after Mullá Husayn mustered the faithful to their meeting with destiny and to the first violent encounter in the history of the young Faith in the fort of Shaykh Tabarsí. Both the popular uprisings of 1848 and the upheaval of Shaykh Tabarsí were put down decisively and violently by the respective governments, passing to history as tragic but heroic events symbolizing the hopes and aspirations placed on a new era. On both continents armies assured the existence of the old order. European monarchs reneged on constitutions granted in the face of revolution. By 1850, when the Báb was martyred in midsummer, in both the East and the West the forces of the old order appeared to have conquered once again, although the foundations of that order had suffered a severe challenge from which they would never recover.

In most cases the revolutions in Europe did not involve multiple countries, though in one exceptional case Austria called upon Russia to help quell rebellion. Nonetheless, the revolutions would bring important changes that would eventually impinge on relations among countries. The most immediate of these was the rise of Napoleon III to whom we will refer in Chapter 8. In Austria also, revolution precipitated a change in leadership when Francis Joseph ascended the throne, to be in that position until his death in 1916. In the spiritual realm Pope Pius IX, installed on the throne of Peter only two years before, would recede into reactionary conservatism in response to the events of 1848.

Coincidentally the year of 1848 was also the year that Karl Marx published the *Communist Manifesto*. Destined to shape much of the intellectual content of mass movements in the latter years of the 19th century and much of the 20th century, Marxism understood itself as the inheritor of the legacy of the

French Revolution, as interpreter, articulator and promoter of the principles of Jacobinism in a more radical and philosophically coherent form based on scientific materialism, amplifying its scepticism about religion, and expounding the need for violent change. The *Communist Manifesto* played no role whatsoever in the revolutions of 1848, but rather, what is of interest for current purposes is its analysis as a reflection of the social tensions that were coming to a head, and its symbolic role as symptomatic of the unrest of the age. Marx was accompanied in his quasi-messianic mission by his long-term colleague Frederick Engels, who was, ironically, an industrialist with investments in England. Engels could witness first-hand the abuses of the Industrial Revolution, and authored an account of the miserable conditions surrounding factories in Manchester, then the heart of industrial England – thousands of workers huddled together in shanty towns, without sanitary conditions and receiving starvation wages.

While the misery of the masses moved many to sympathy, Marx went far beyond an emotional outburst and gave a conceptual framework to the exploitation of workers by industrialists, posing it in terms of a historical imperative of class struggle. Marx was not the first to expound revolutionary socialist ideals, but he was the most effective in presenting them in what to many would seem a coherent structure. He articulated a social reality that was most obvious in the context of factory production where owners and workers found themselves in frequent opposition, but that Marx extended to the generality of the owners of the means of production, and to those whose labour contributed to production. Putting this reality in the context of political power, Marx saw three social classes competing for power in the long term. First, with the rise of a middle class, the bourgeoisie opposed and wrested power from the aristocracy. This had occurred in the French Revolution, in particular when the Thermidorians and later Napoleon promoted the interests of the bourgeoisie, overriding the actions of the Jacobins. The next logical step, according to Marx, would be the rise of the proletariat to take their rightful command of the means of production, by violence if necessary through a revolutionary government representative of the proletariat – a dictatorship of the proletariat. The socialist State, derived from the necessary conflict between haves and have-nots, would be the happy result of class warfare. Independent of the interpretation that Marx gave to the social context and his conclusions about conflict as the motor of social progress, what is important is that he was describing a social reality of human misery – a reality that had been evolving over previous decades, especially under pressures of the Industrial Revolution, and that contributed to the revolutions of 1848. While the participation of the working classes in 1848 was still not organized in opposition to the industrial class, they expressed their own aspirations for social justice as propounded by the French revolutionaries a generation earlier.

The Marxist historian Eric Hobsbawm saw the revolutions of 1848 to be a watershed in defining the future political landscape of Europe, as the revolutionaries would gradually diverge into different tendencies: the liberal democracy of the upper middle classes, the radical republicanism of the lower middle classes, and eventually socialism of the working classes.[6] The term 'liberal' in this context is quite different from its use today, and refers to representative government much as we currently know it. Originally liberal democracy was a creation of the middle classes as a mechanism for the expression of political rights born of natural rights. The basic components of modern democracy such as national constitutions, representative legislatures, and political parties emerged in this period. Liberalism was often allied to industry and *laissez-faire* policies of governmental non-intervention in business, with the voting franchise limited by income or property. Governments representing the middle class and remnants of the aristocracy adopted these policies and suppressed worker organizations in favour of factory owners. Subsequent to 1848, working-class frustrations would take on a life of their own. An urban working class, now vastly expanded as industrialism grew, was ever more restive. Thus, the emerging dichotomy of the middle class and proletariat became increasingly explicit, mimicking the course of the French Revolution – a dichotomy of social classes that would grow more conflictive with the advance of the century, and in which socialism and eventually Marxism would present a carefully crafted ideology, and would claim to speak for the masses. This would ultimately bear its bitter fruit in the Bolshevik revolution that would mark the course of most of the 20th century.

The revolutions of 1848 would end a period of relative calm and would initiate an eventful period of turmoil of some twenty-odd years that would see the transformational processes of East and West come together as one. Germany and Italy would be formed as nations, France would rise and fall again, and the balance of power in Europe would be altered dramatically. Neo-absolutism, or the renewed concentration of power in monarchs, would dilute tendencies toward democracy. It was also the period that would see the dawn of the Revelation of Bahá'u'lláh and His Declaration in the garden of Riḍván. Especially significant for our current purposes, it was the period of His exile and establishment on European soil, and His proclamation to the kings of East and West. It was the climactic period during which Bahá'u'lláh would turn His face to Europe and condemn those who held the reins of power, and who had contributed to the agitation of the world. Inevitably, these two currents of change would merge into one and East and West would meet, unsuspected by the crowned heads of Europe.

8

Napoleon III and France

For what thou hast done, thy kingdom shall be thrown into confusion, and thine empire shall pass from thine hands, as a punishment for that which thou hast wrought. Then wilt thou know how thou hast plainly erred.[1]

The story of Charles-Louis Napoleon, better known as Napoleon III, starts with the termination of the revolts of 1848 when he is elected president in that same year, and comes to the forefront on the continental scene with one of the most significant events of mid-century Europe, the Crimean War. Napoleon III was the son of Louis Napoleon, one of the Bonaparte brothers, and had been raised on the model of his uncle, Napoleon Bonaparte. He envisioned himself from his very youth as chosen by Providence to bring both glory and prosperity to a France humiliated by the Congress of Vienna.

> Possessed of a fixed and indestructible ambition, he aspired to emulate the example, and finish the interrupted work, of his imperial uncle. A dreamer, a conspirator, of a shifting nature, hypocritical and reckless, he, the heir to the Napoleonic throne, taking advantage of the policy which sought to foster the reviving interest in the career of his great prototype, had sought to overthrow the monarchy.[2]

Practically all of the high points of his career, before and after becoming President and then Emperor, can be viewed in the light of his emulation of the life of Napoleon Bonaparte. Yet if the original Napoleon was possessed of an iron will and a crystal clear vision of his objectives and the path to obtain them, Napoleon III was given to meddling and scheming in his games of self-aggrandizement, of poor judgement and occasional vacillation in execution of his plots. Napoleon Bonaparte had dethroned the crowned heads of Europe and established new republican governments, albeit subservient to Paris, while the Congress of Vienna turned the clock back and reestablished the old regimes. Napoleon III longed to open the door once again on more liberal regimes (ironically, since he had himself overthrown the Second Republic and named himself Emperor), and visualized a messianic role for himself at the head of a new Europe. Yet time and again he would fail to 'screw his courage to the sticking point', and would falter in carrying out his grandiose schemes. Even in his youth he was given to ill-conceived political adventures. He had made more than one attempt to enter into politics by force, participating naively in a war of liberation in Italy as a mere youth. He engineered two unsuccessful coups against the monarchy, in 1836 and 1840, to reclaim the throne of France which he considered rightfully his. He was imprisoned, filling himself with a sense of noble martyrdom, but escaped to England in 1846.

The revolutions of 1848 created the environment for him to attain to his aspirations. Although little known in France at the time, in the turmoil surrounding the revolutions his name served him to be elected as President in December of that same year by a wide margin. Not content to serve the single term due him in the constitution, he organized a coup in 1852, whereby literally from the evening to the next morning, he declared himself President for life – reminiscent of the actions of his uncle in deposing the National Assembly – and arbitrarily converted a fledgling democracy into a centralized dictatorship. Napoleon was especially resentful of the Treaty of Vienna, which, if it did not extract heavy reparations from France, was symbolic of the humiliation of France and of the Napoleonic line.

The Concert of Europe had served to maintain the peace among nations for three decades – no small feat in a continent given to settling the most trifling of issues through arms – but the Crimean War (1853–56) broke with that thirty-year tradition of peace, and opened up a new period of international conflict. While little remembered today, the Crimean War was indeed a costly conflict in terms of life. Yet its long-term effects were to pit Great Power against Great Power, and so upset that delicate balance that the Treaty of Vienna had established. The Crimean War reflected in part the existing residual tensions from the social conflicts of 1848 that left resentments between the more liberal nations – i.e. Britain and France – and the more conservative elements, Russia, Austria and Prussia, who had employed heavy-handed repression to deal with the revolts. But in essence, the Crimean War centred on spheres of influence, and suspicions of the British and French toward aspirations of the Russian Czar Nicholas I to exercise leadership over Slavs, and specifically Orthodox Christian Slavs in the Balkan States controlled by the Ottoman Turks. The Ottoman Empire, the so-called 'sick man of Europe', had been in decline for nigh well two centuries, and the Czar was eyeing Turkish lands with intentions of expanding his own frontiers. This aspiration of the Czar had military and commercial implications, as he sought exclusive control of the Black Sea and the Bosphorus that gives access to the Mediterranean. As such, Napoleon did not start the war, but schemer that he was, he did not lose the opportunity to forward his interests and to raise his own profile on the continental scene.

Curiously, the tensions between Russia and France had a religious dimension as well. The Orthodox Church had traditionally cared for the Christian holy sites in Jerusalem, then within the Ottoman Empire. Napoleon, perhaps to ingratiate himself with French Catholics, or perhaps to irritate the Czar, had finagled a treaty with the Ottoman Sultan to assume responsibility for the holy sites, much to the offence of the indignant Czar who dispatched a diplomatic mission to Istanbul to berate the Sultan in no uncertain terms. With the pretext of protecting Orthodox Christians in the Balkans, the Czar's troops occupied the Ottoman territories of Moldavia and Wallachia (Romania) in June 1853, and the Ottoman Sultan declared war on Russia, which in short order sank the Turkish fleet in the Black Sea in November 1853. The British Prime Minister Benjamin Disraeli had insistently backed the Ottomans, and Napoleon – ever the adventurer as demonstrated in subsequent events – signed up to the conflict.

In brief, the war was an unfortunate and unsatisfying event for all. Russia lost, but there were no real winners. Loss of life was great on all sides, perhaps half a million, due as much to unsanitary conditions as to battlefield deaths. Austria dithered on the sidelines for most of the war, neither aligning with Russia as its traditional partner in conservatism, nor taking a stand against Russian expansionism into its backyard of the Balkans. Austria finally entered on the side of the allies – too late to gain the affection of the British and French, but soon enough to gain the long-term distrust of Russia. Camillo de Cavour, Prime Minister of the Italian state of Piedmont, and whom we shall meet shortly, also entered late but as a minor power on the winning side; the presence of Piedmont at the peace table gained prestige for the Italian cause in its opposition to the Austrian presence in the peninsula. For its part, Britain was chastened for launching into a no-win situation. Among the Great Powers, France did not gain great glory but it suffered less than others and so won by default, as Britain, Russia and Austria all lost prestige and Prussia wisely sat on the sidelines, biding its time.

The most significant result of the war was not the allied victory per se, but a shift in the balance of power in central Europe. Britain withdrew from continental affairs after a bitter experience. Russia's influence as a moderating force on Prussia and Austria was severely diminished. Austria lost much of its prestige and most of its friends, and the Concert of Europe, brainchild of Metternich, was left severely debilitated, much to the glee of Napoleon who detested everything associated with the Treaty of Vienna. France and Prussia were left as the big players on the stage, and Napoleon was set to take advantage of the situation. Ironically, the disgrace of Austria and the realignment of the Great Powers, which Napoleon celebrated, also served the Prussian chancellor Bismarck in his ambition to extend the influence of Prussia among the German states, uniting them under Prussian leadership and eventually contributing to the fall of Napoleon.

The ascension of Napoleon to the presidency in 1848 occurred as the Báb suffered imprisonment in the mountain of C̲h̲ihríq. Napoleon declared himself Emperor in that period after the martyrdom of the Báb when His followers awaited 'Him Whom God shall make manifest'. The Crimean War began shortly thereafter in October 1853, when Bahá'u'lláh had established His residence in exile in Baghdad, and conflict raged while He had removed to Sulaymáníyyih. Yet more than ten years would pass before Bahá'u'lláh directed these retrospective words to Napoleon, alluding to the destruction of the Turkish fleet by the Russian navy:

O King! We heard the words thou didst utter in answer to the Czar of Russia, concerning the decision made regarding the war. Thy Lord, verily, knoweth, is informed of all. Thou didst say: 'I lay asleep upon my couch, when the cry of the oppressed, who were drowned in the Black Sea, wakened me.' This is what We heard thee say, and, verily, thy Lord is witness unto what I say. We testify that that which wakened thee was not their cry but the promptings of thine own passions, for We tested thee, and found thee wanting . . .³

In the interim Bahá'u'lláh had directed another epistle to Napoleon, to which Bahá'u'lláh refers in this same Tablet, highlighting Napoleon's characteristic arrogance and duplicity:

Hadst thou been sincere in thy words, thou wouldst have not cast behind thy back the Book of God, when it was sent unto thee by Him Who is the Almighty, the All-Wise. We have proved thee through it, and found thee other than that which thou didst profess. Arise, and make amends for that which escaped thee. Erelong the world and all that thou possessest will perish, and the kingdom will remain unto God, thy Lord and the Lord of thy fathers of old. It behoveth thee not to conduct thine affairs according to the dictates of thy desires. Fear the sighs of this Wronged One, and shield Him from the darts of such as act unjustly.⁴

Bahá'u'lláh concluded this passage with a severe judgement, unique in its directness among the epistles that He directed to the European kings:

For what thou hast done, thy kingdom shall be thrown into confusion, and thine empire shall pass from thine hands, as a punishment for that which thou hast wrought. Then wilt thou know how thou hast plainly erred. Commotions shall seize all the people in that land, unless thou arisest to help this

Cause, and followest Him Who is the Spirit of God in this,
the Straight Path. Hath thy pomp made thee proud? By My
Life! It shall not endure; nay, it shall soon pass away, unless
thou holdest fast to this firm Cord. We see abasement hasten-
ing after thee, whilst thou art of the heedless. It behoveth thee
when thou hearest His Voice calling from the seat of glory to
cast away all that thou possessest, and cry out: 'Here am I, O
Lord of all that is in heaven and all that is on earth!'[5]

As is widely known, the prophetic words of Bahá'u'lláh came
to pass when France declared war on Prussia on 19 July 1870
and the armies of William I of Prussia overran the French at
the battle of Sedan on 1 September of that year. Sedan lies in
the north of France near Luxembourg and in the watershed of
the Rhine river. In a Tablet that He wrote before World War I,[6]
'Abdu'l-Bahá explained that Bahá'u'lláh referred to the battle of
Sedan in the following verse of the *Kitáb-i-Aqdas*: 'O banks of
the Rhine! We have seen you covered with gore, inasmuch as
the swords of retribution were drawn against you; and you shall
have another turn.'[7] Indeed, this region lying on the frontier
between these two rivals would know no peace for many years.
The trenches of World War I traversed this land from northwest
to southeast, and a second battle of Sedan took place in 1940.
When Bahá'u'lláh prophesied 'and you shall have another turn',
might He not have foreseen these bloody struggles?

Still seeking to emulate the example of his uncle but lacking
his military genius, Napoleon led his own troops into battle. He
was made a prisoner and went into exile in Britain in humiliation, suffering the same fate of banishment as the Prisoner
whom he ignored so arrogantly. Curiously, as Napoleon faced
complete defeat at the end of 1870 and initiated his exile in
March of 1871, the Lord of the Age was leaving His prison in
Akka, initiating a gradual process of house arrest that would

eventually permit Him to live in relative freedom outside the walls of the city. For at mid-year, as cataclysmic events that would alter the course of Europe for the rest of the century were unfolding in the heart of the European continent, in the Holy Land occurred what must be regarded as one of the most significant events of the new era. On 23 June 1870 after His youngest son Mírzá Mihdí had suffered a fatal accident that would claim his life, Bahá'u'lláh 'offered up His martyred son as a ransom for the redemption and unification of all mankind',[8] acceding to his request to be a sacrifice that the gates of the prison be opened. Thus were the fall of Napoleon and the accelerated disintegration of Europe counterbalanced by the supreme act of sacrifice for the integration of the world.

The fall of the empire brought another tragic period for the French, opening old wounds of class tensions. Leftist workers in Paris established the Paris Commune and declared it to be the legitimate government of France, while similar communes were formed in other cities. Conservative powers smothered the popular revolt with forces that included peasants – largely Catholics – who had no sympathy with revived Jacobin ideology. The suppression of the Paris Commune would see some of the bloodiest internal warfare since the days of the Great Terror, and would leave a scar on the memory of liberal thinkers who witnessed it, creating for many doubts about the viability of the liberal experiment.

As a national leader, Napoleon could have gone down in history as a better than average progressive liberal who brought a period of considerable prosperity to France. His government developed not only the country's industrial capacity but also promoted social programmes in favour of the poor. Nonetheless, his leadership was autocratic and authoritarian, eliciting from Bahá'u'lláh the statement, 'It behoveth thee not to conduct thine affairs according to the dictates of thy desires.'[9] In his dealing with the French public, he was the master of manipulation, employing plebiscites at key moments to fortify his position as emperor, much as Napoleon Bonaparte had done. Reducing complex issues to simple statements with foregone conclusions, carefully executed plebiscites both justified authoritarian rule and raised the sense of public participation. Napoleon's plebiscites were eminently successful in this regard, and bolstered his public support.

One of his greatest downfalls in his official capacity was his meddling in foreign affairs such as in the Crimean War, for which Bahá'u'lláh found him wanting and self-serving. He also meddled extensively in the politics of Italy (not unlike Napoleon Bonaparte), actually plotting a war with Camillo di Cavour against Austria in 1858, through which Cavour sought to drive Austria out of Italy. 'Though able to initiate far-reaching movements, he possessed neither the sagacity nor the courage required to control them,' writes Shoghi Effendi.[10] Still, the chaos, rioting and street fighting that broke out in France upon his demise and that claimed thousands of lives testify to an even greater failure, his inability to deal over a twenty-two year reign with the forces of change working at mid-century and to create a united and coherent nation. France was still – and would be for many years to come – divided between radicals and conservatives, rural areas and Paris, Catholics and sceptics, left and right, with incompatible undercurrents that would emerge in times of crisis all the way up to end of the century: 'thy kingdom shall be thrown into confusion . . . Commotions shall seize all the people in that land.'

In closing, we cite 'Abdu'l-Bahá's summary account of the impact of Bahá'u'lláh's Revelation on the crowned heads, and on Napoleon in particular.

When Bahá'u'lláh arrived at 'Akká, through the power of God He was able to hoist His banner. His light at first had been a star; now it became a mighty sun, and the illumination of His Cause expanded from the East to the West. Inside prison walls He wrote Epistles to all the kings and rulers of nations, summoning them to arbitration and universal peace. Some of the kings received His words with disdain and contempt. One of these was the Sultan of the Ottoman kingdom. Napoleon III of France did not reply. A second Epistle was addressed to him. It stated, 'I have written you an Epistle before this, summoning you to the Cause of God, but you are of the heedless. You have proclaimed that you were the defender of the oppressed; now it hath become evident that you are not. Nor are you kind to your own suffering and oppressed people. Your actions are contrary to your own interests, and your kingly pride must fall. Because of your arrogance God shortly will destroy your sovereignty. France will flee away from you, and you will be overwhelmed by a great conquest. There will be lamentation and mourning, women bemoaning the loss of their sons.' This arraignment of Napoleon III was published and spread.

Read it and consider: one prisoner, single and solitary, without assistant or defender, a foreigner and stranger imprisoned in the fortress of 'Akká, writing such letters to the Emperor of France and Sultan of Turkey. Reflect upon this: how Bahá'u'lláh upraised the standard of His Cause in prison. Refer to history. It is without parallel. No such thing has happened before that time nor since – a prisoner and an exile advancing His Cause and spreading His teachings broadcast so that eventually He became powerful enough to conquer the very king who banished Him.[11]

9

Kaiser William I and Germany

O King of Berlin! Give ear unto the Voice calling from this
manifest Temple: 'Verily, there is none other God but Me, the
Everlasting, the Peerless, the Ancient of Days.' Take heed lest
pride debar thee from recognizing the Dayspring of Divine
Revelation, lest earthly desires shut thee out, as by a veil, from
the Lord of the Throne above and of the earth below. Thus
counselleth thee the Pen of the Most High. He, verily, is the
Most Gracious, the All-Bountiful. Do thou remember the
one whose power transcended thy power, and whose station
excelled thy station. Where is he? Whither are gone the things
he possessed? Take warning, and be not of them that are fast
asleep. He it was who cast the Tablet of God behind him
when We made known unto him what the hosts of tyranny
had caused Us to suffer. Wherefore, disgrace assailed him
from all sides, and he went down to dust in great loss. Think
deeply, O King, concerning him, and concerning them who,
like unto thee, have conquered cities and ruled over men. The
All-Merciful brought them down from their palaces to their
graves. Be warned, be of them who reflect.[1]

It is fitting, having considered the adventures, misdoings, arrogance and downfall of Napoleon III, to next turn our attention
to that realm and its leaders who dealt him that God-determined

blow. We described briefly the results of the Crimean War, that pivotal event that restructured the relations of power in central Europe, releasing both France and Prussia from the influence of Russia and Britain. We also referred to the disastrous defeat of the French forces at the hands of the German/Prussian army in the battle of Sedan. Let us now review those major events and persons that led to the establishment of a modern German State that inflicted a humiliating defeat on Napoleon III, and that set the stage for the upsurge of what would become the major power in Europe in the second half of the 19th century.

Reference to 'Germany' prior to 1860 is in fact a misnomer, for such a State did not exist in the first half of the 19th century nor before. Since the decay of the Holy Roman Empire of Charlemagne, the region that we know as Germany had been divided into a plethora of mini-states under minor princelings, in some cases as dominions of the Church, and with a few mid-sized states. Division was accentuated by the Reformation in the 16th century, leaving the north largely Protestant, and the south traditionally Catholic. The Thirty Years' War (1618–48), born of religious strife, devastated much of the region, exhausting its resources, slaughtering an estimated one-third of its population, and leaving little more result than the further decline in the prestige of the Holy Roman Emperor, and the conclusion that the German states would be both Protestant and Catholic, much as they had been at the outset of the war. By the 18th century, while still boasting a Hapsburg ruler at its head, the Holy Roman Empire was a symbolic anachronism and a dead letter. Germany in this period was still an unlikely candidate to become a super-power, with more than 300 mini-states – the sad remnants of an empire. Still, a few larger states were emerging, of which Prussia, under the Hohenzollerns, would take precedence.

The House of Hohenzollern, like the Hapsburgs, was one of the ancient dynasties of Europe, though for its early years it was limited to minor principalities of little importance, ruling Brandenburg since 1415. Its first leader of note, Frederick William the Great Elector, was born in the midst of the Thirty Years' War, and ascended to the throne of Brandenburg-Prussia in 1640 while the war still raged. As a Protestant kingdom in the storm centre of the war, Brandenburg-Prussia had suffered intensely and Frederick William's task was to rebuild a shattered country, a task that he achieved admirably. The Treaty of Westphalia in 1648 ended the bloodshed but did not guarantee a lasting peace, and Frederick William's first priority was to assure an adequate defence. In the course of his efforts, his most lasting contribution and one that would have tragic consequences in the long run of history, would be the firm establishment of a standing army – a policy that would be greatly extended by subsequent monarchs and would shape the character of the nation.

Prussia (as the kingdom would be called, though ironically the historic territory of Prussia no longer is part of Germany but of Poland) would gain international prestige and respect, in particular under the reign of Frederick II the Great (ruled 1740–86), one of the most brilliant monarchs of all history and a military genius. He would continue to expand Prussia's boundaries, personally leading his armies on the battlefield, and would establish Prussia's military prowess as a force to be reckoned with. Frederick was the classic 'enlightened despot', inspired in the Enlightenment, one-time patron of Voltaire and Rousseau, who promoted not only military development but a creative and progressive educational system, one of the first and best in the world that would eventually fuel industrialization. These two strengths, military might and effective mass education, would put Prussia and eventually Germany on the front lines of Europe in the 19th century.

The German states would again come under sustained attack in the Napoleonic wars, and with the advent of the

Napoleonic invasion and conquest, revolutionary structures were implanted and modernizing principles promoted among the German principalities. In particular, Napoleon had reduced the hundreds of German states and units to nineteen, which the Congress of Vienna left as thirty-nine states in a loose German confederation and with a Diet (a weak consultative body with its seat in Frankfurt). Germany was on the road to unification. But in a century marked by a careful balance of power, in the very heart of Europe among the German principalities a power vacuum existed, and the surrounding larger countries vied for dominance. In the German confederation, Austria held the presidency and was the beacon of tradition, boasting the Hapsburg throne, while Prussia sat in the vice-presidency and was the up-and-coming dynamic young state, far more open to experimenting with the benefits of the Industrial Revolution. The uneasy marriage of Austria and Prussia within the Confederation combined two incompatible competitors that were set on a course of conflict. Yet Prussia was not yet ready to challenge the primacy of Austria. Frederick William III, though overseeing the restoration imposed by the Congress of Vienna, would be weak and vacillating, and as we approach the opening of the new era, in 1840 Frederick William IV took the throne – a romantic conservative in the medieval tradition of the divine right of kings with little or no use for liberal ideas. Indeed, Frederick William IV had participated in the war against Napoleon, and so had firsthand experience on the battlefield in the custom of the warrior kings of old. His tenure would witness the uprisings of 1848, in response to which a constitution was created. Even after the revolution was suppressed, the constitution survived although Frederick William did all that he could to subvert it. Falling victim to a stroke in 1857, his brother William (soon to be William I) would assume power, first as regent and then as king in 1861. Of Kaiser William I, Shoghi Effendi notes that

'William I, first German Emperor and seventh king of Prussia, whose entire lifetime had, up to the date of his accession, been spent in the army, was a militaristic, autocratic ruler, imbued with antiquated ideas . . .'[2]

We have noted that in the *Súriy-i-Mulúk*, His first joint address to the kings of the world, and again in His Tablet to Queen Victoria, Bahá'u'lláh admonished the monarchs for their growing militarism. In light of the military history of the Hohenzollerns, and the subsequent address of Bahá'u'lláh to William in the *Kitáb-i-Aqdas*, these words bear repeating:

> Compose your differences and reduce your armaments, that the burden of your expenditures may be lightened, and that your minds and hearts may be tranquillized.[3]

> O rulers of the earth! Be reconciled among yourselves, that ye may need no more armaments save in a measure to safeguard your territories and dominions. Beware lest ye disregard the counsel of the All-Knowing, the Faithful.[4]

In the *Kitáb-i-Aqdas* Bahá'u'lláh refers to that military tradition that characterized the Prussian throne, and reminds William of the example of Napoleon III, again singling out the issue of militarism and conquest. 'Think deeply, O King, concerning him, and concerning them who, like unto thee, have conquered cities and ruled over men.'[5] It was this military tradition, in the hands of an unwise, ambitious and capricious leader, that would spell the downfall of Germany a generation later.

As the new relations of power in Europe took shape after the Crimean War, entered upon the stage Otto von Bismarck, appointed chancellor in 1862 by William I – Bismarck, the arch-conservative who more than anyone else would shape the face and destiny of Europe in the second half of the 19th century.

Bismarck's reputation has come down through history heavily coloured by his own very pragmatic and blunt statement at the outset of his chancellorship, that the course of events would be determined not by speeches or majority votes but by 'blood and iron'. Nonetheless, it was he 'to whose sagacity Bahá'u'lláh had paid tribute', 'a statesman rightly regarded as "one of the geniuses of his century"',[6] who instituted some of the most progressive social policies of the age, well ahead of Great Britain or France, and whose astuteness created the modern German State on the foundation of the Prussian monarchy. Setting out to extend Prussian influence, Bismarck defied Austria and joined the smaller German states to Prussia through encouragement, coercion, or outright war, employing the early fruits of industrialization including railroads for the mobilization of troops and supplies.

> This policy was pursued with characteristic thoroughness and perfected through the repressive measures that were taken to safeguard and uphold it, through the wars that were waged for its realization, and the political combinations that were subsequently formed to exalt and consolidate it, combinations that were fraught with such dreadful consequences to the European continent.[7]

By 1870 Bismarck was ready to confront France for the leadership of central Europe. Goading Napoleon into war, German forces won a quick victory in the battle of Sedan in September, and occupied Paris in January 1871, permitting William I to be proclaimed Emperor of Germany in the palace of Versailles. With this victory, Prussia – now Germany – had a free road open to exercise its undisputed hegemony in the heart of Europe. Ever the master of *realpolitik* or unprincipled political pragmatism, Bismarck's foremost goal was the preservation of aristocratic privilege and with this, the maintenance of the Kaiser's position. While Bismarck is rightly credited for engineering the unification and progress of Germany, mention is also due to the Junkers, those aristocratic and conservative landowners among whom Bismarck arose, and who were an important component of his power base and the core of his army's officer corps. Virtual remnants of the medieval period, the Junkers were scarcely two generations removed from the abolition of serfdom, and maintained their conservative attitudes in opposition to many of the reforms that even Bismarck promoted.

The experience of Germany with modernization was unequalled in the history of the 19th century in speed and quality, as well as in its social dimension. Its adoption of the Industrial Revolution was phenomenal under Bismarck, as reflected in its rapid urbanization after mid-century. Between 1850 and 1880 its urban population grew from a mere 15% to nearly 30%, and continued to grow up to the outbreak of war in 1914 to become the most urbanized country after the traditional leaders of the United Kingdom, Belgium and the Netherlands that initiated the 19th century with large urban populations. In the last quarter of the century, Germany converted its economy from a traditional agrarian focus to be a powerhouse of heavy industry, and overtaking every other industrial aspirant. Students were dispatched to England to learn engineering and the art of manufacturing, and soon Germany would surpass even Britain in total production. The Krupp family would contribute no small part to the industrial growth, and made German arms the most innovative and powerful in the world – a fact to which even 'Abdu'l-Bahá referred in 1875![8] German scientists found a niche in chemistry, evidenced even today in companies like Bayer.

The rapid growth of industry was paralleled by an expansion of socialist thought and action, perhaps as Marx might have expected. Socialism grew faster and more widely in Germany than anywhere else in spite of Bismarck's opposition, with branches ranging from hard-core Marxists dedicated to violent revolution, to pragmatists who sought to work within the electoral system. Indeed, even Marx was angered by the willingness of German socialists to seek election to the Reichstag, in contradiction to his own dogma that violent revolution would be the only possible route to social transformation. So powerful was the movement of the left that the Social Democratic Party soon became the largest in all of Germany, but confronted with Bismarck's obstinacy, it could never exercise power in proportion to its popular vote. Internally Bismarck manipulated politics to assure that no real opposition could function, playing both sides of the fence to relieve social pressures but also to limit the expression of popular power. Even as the franchise was extended to nearly all males, Bismarck did his best to circumvent its logical outcomes. The periodic and inevitable bone of contention between Bismarck and the socialist Reichstag was the military budget, which Bismarck defended tooth and nail, and which he assured by conjuring up crises of national security at key moments of parliamentary votes in the Reichstag. Furthermore, what Bismarck could not suppress he co-opted, promoting innovative social programmes to placate the masses and the left. Indeed, Germany in the late 19th century was in some ways one of the most socially progressive countries in the world, establishing programmes in health and old-age insurance.

Thus did Bismarck deal with the forces of democracy, which he was committed to repress at all costs, through administrative or legislative means if convenient, or by unconstitutional means if not. He jailed socialists under pretext of being conspirators in two assassination attempts against the Kaiser, and he passed anti-Catholic legislation in a so-called 'culture war'. Although Germany enjoyed remarkable progress materially and socially in the latter half of the century, in many ways it remained much as the Congress of Vienna would have wanted it. Thus, Bismarck's Germany was a contradiction. Bismarck certainly did not show much love toward the popular classes, yet his policies – implemented with the vigour of the iron fist – did more for the popular classes than did more liberal regimes in other countries.

On the international front, Bismarck understood better than anyone the delicate situation of Germany, sitting in the middle of Europe between the Great Powers of France and Russia. His nightmare was having to fight a war on two fronts, and his efforts in diplomacy were directed toward avoiding this possibility. Indeed, Bismarck struggled to maintain a balance of power through a complex web of treaties, whereby Germany could avoid facing off against an alliance of enemies. In this regard, he might be considered the heir to Metternich, maintaining the peace but always within the context of the hegemony of Germany in Central Europe. Thus, Bismarck gained the reputation of 'sagacity' attributed to him by Bahá'u'lláh, maintaining the domestic tranquillity in an ever more volatile social milieu, and balancing the powers in the external environment to assure peace in the region.

Yet someday the inevitable would come to pass. Kaiser William I died in 1888 followed soon by his son Frederick II who succumbed to cancer after a reign of scarcely three months, and in turn, William II ascended to the throne.

William II, temperamentally dictatorial, politically inexperienced, militarily aggressive, religiously insincere, posed as the apostle of European peace, yet actually insisted on 'the mailed fist' and 'the shining armor'. Irresponsible, indiscreet, inordinately ambitious, his first act was to dismiss that sagacious statesman, the true founder of his empire, to whose sagacity Bahá'u'lláh had paid tribute, and to the unwisdom of whose imperial and ungrateful master 'Abdu'l-Bahá had testified.[9]

Like many ambitious and egocentric personalities, William II could not tolerate one much more competent than himself, and Bismarck's demise came when William dismissed him, wishing to run Germany on his own terms. With vast industrial power at his disposal, employing the autocratic and efficient system constructed by Bismarck, and emboldened by the aggressive military tradition of the Hohenzollerns, the stage was set for Germany's entry into war, and for what we might well speculate would be the fulfilment of Bahá'u'lláh's remarkable prophesy set down in 1873, and to which we referred in the previous chapter: 'O banks of the Rhine! We have seen you covered with gore, inasmuch as the swords of retribution were drawn against you; and you shall have another turn. And We hear the lamentations of Berlin, though she be today in conspicuous glory.'[10]

William II pursued a policy of confrontation with neighbours, with France in Morocco and with Britain in a naval arms race on the high seas. His foolhardiness unsettled his neighbours and stimulated their suspicions and alliances to oppose him, but ironically it would not be William who would set off the conflagration. Rather, it would be Germany's cousin and long-term competitor, Austria, in reprisal for the assassination in Sarajevo of the Archduke Ferdinand, heir to the Hapsburg throne. Germany backed Austria's overreaction and declaration of war on Serbia, and the rest is history – bloody, tragic history that ripped Europe apart at the seams and sealed the fate of some of its oldest dynasties.

Held in check by repression and co-opted by Bismarck's progressive policies, the popular forces of the masses had been channelled into parliamentary democracy, yet resentment simmered under the surface. When Germany surrendered in 1918 and the Kaiser fled in disgrace, Communists revolted in several cities and the country was threatened with chaos and class warfare. Berlin itself was taken by Communists and the government was driven out, establishing its seat in the city of Weimar. The anaemic and unpopular Weimar Republic, burdened with debt and accused by its people of betraying Germany to the allies, was headed by its Social Democratic president Friedrich Ebert who was unable to contain the revolt except by brute force as right-wing thugs were loosed upon the Communists. 'And We hear the lamentations of Berlin, though she be today in conspicuous glory.'

The chaos that gripped Germany and Berlin in particular was reminiscent of the disorder that followed the fall of Napoleon and the suppression of the Paris Commune. Bahá'u'lláh had warned Napoleon, saying, 'thy kingdom shall be thrown into confusion, and thine empire shall pass from thine hands,' and later He admonished William I, 'Do thou remember the one whose power transcended thy power, and whose station excelled thy station. Where is he? Whither are gone the things he possessed? Take warning, and be not of them that are fast asleep.' The flight of Kaiser William II, grandson of William I, mirrored the exile of Napoleon III after his battlefield disaster, and like Napoleon, the Kaiser's realms also passed from his hands and fell into confusion as leftist revolt broke out and was brutally suppressed in his capital city.

No one man can change history alone, and Bismarck's achievements must also be taken as those of a German people disciplined by an iron fist for generations – producing qualities that under the guidance of religion could produce wonderful results. When 'Abdu'l-Bahá visited Germany briefly in 1913, He was extremely happy to find the Bahá'ís united and characterized by exceptional devotion and humility – marks of the highest qualities of a nation that Bismarck was able to channel toward material progress.

'The humility, love and devotion of the German believers', wrote an eyewitness, 'rejoiced the heart of 'Abdu'l-Bahá, and they received His blessings and His words of encouraging counsel in complete submissiveness . . . Friends came from far and near to see the Master. There was a constant flow of visitors at the Hotel Marquart. There 'Abdu'l-Bahá received them with such love and graciousness that they became radiant with joy and happiness.'[11]

It was apparently the Bahá'ís of Germany to whom Shoghi Effendi referred in 1938 as a persecuted community 'in the heart of the European continent . . . which, as predicted by 'Abdu'l-Bahá, is destined, by virtue of its spiritual potentialities and geographical situation, to radiate the splendour of the light of the Faith on the countries that surround it . . .'[12]

The fact that the country that Bismarck built with such single-mindedness could be undone by yet another ambitious, shortsighted and aggressive autocrat is still another sad chapter in the history of 19th-century kingship. Worse yet, the war that was spawned by the ambition of Kaiser William II would lead to the victory of the Bolshevik movement in Russia and the rise of the left foreseen by the Master, and within scarcely two decades would create the Second World War – the greatest holocaust to yet ravage mankind, and that would engulf that community of believers so loved by 'Abdu'l-Bahá.

10

The Papacy and Italy

O Supreme Pontiff! Incline thine ear unto that which the Fashioner of mouldering bones counselleth thee, as voiced by Him Who is His Most Great Name. Sell all the embellished ornaments thou dost possess, and expend them in the path of God, Who causeth the night to return upon the day, and the day to return upon the night. Abandon thy kingdom unto the kings, and emerge from thy habitation, with thy face set towards the Kingdom, and, detached from the world, then speak forth the praises of thy Lord betwixt earth and heaven. Thus hath bidden thee He Who is the Possessor of Names, on the part of thy Lord, the Almighty, the All-Knowing. Exhort thou the kings and say: 'Deal equitably with men. Beware lest ye transgress the bounds fixed in the Book.' This indeed becometh thee. Beware lest thou appropriate unto thyself the things of the world and the riches thereof. Leave them unto such as desire them, and cleave unto that which hath been enjoined upon thee by Him Who is the Lord of creation. Should anyone offer thee all the treasures of the earth, refuse to even glance upon them. Be as thy Lord hath been. Thus hath the Tongue of Revelation spoken that which God hath made the ornament of the book of creation.[1]

The history of the papacy in the modern era is intimately intertwined with the history of the French Revolution and the evolution of Italy as a modern State. We have seen how the French Revolution convulsed continental Europe and induced radical change in social and governmental structures. Italy was another case whereby its own particular history and social reality interacted with these forces of revolution, with the papacy caught in the middle. For hundreds of years before the 19th century, Italy consisted of small independent princedoms and republics, separated by language and culture, and with power in the hands of local social elites. Indeed, 'Italy' as we think of it today simply did not exist and at best was a mental construct of a geographical area stretching from the Alps in the north to the tip of the boot in the south, plus Sicily and Sardinia. Among these mini-nations of the peninsula, the Pope enjoyed a temporal authority as head of state of several of the political units surrounding Rome, the so-called Papal States. These extended east to the Adriatic Sea and up the coast, and westward to the coast of the Mediterranean, dividing the Italian peninsula in two with Sicily and Naples to the south, and the states of Venice, Lombardy, Piedmont and others to the north. The domain of the Pope would wax and wane as politics swirled around Rome and neighbouring regions, subject to the Great Powers and forces that were beyond the control of the Church.

Throughout the 16th and 17th centuries and before, the states of the Italian peninsula were often subject to domination by foreign powers, especially Spain and France. Charles V, Hapsburg king of Spain, held the greatest sway in the 16th century, although Spanish influence diminished and finally terminated at the end of the 17th century when Charles II, the last Hapsburg king, died without leaving a son. The War of Spanish Succession (1701–15) pitted a Bourbon against a Hapsburg candidate who was backed by England, Austria and Netherlands. When the

Bourbon finally retained the throne of Spain, other Hapsburg territories were divided up under a peace treaty, and the Austrian Hapsburgs 'inherited' the dominion of the Italian republics and kingdoms. This set the stage for a long-term Austrian presence in the peninsula, and Austria would continue to seek to impose its will throughout the first half of the 19th century.

With the French Revolution, thoughtful Italians of the intelligentsia admired from afar the social changes wrought in Paris and around the country, as if this would satisfy their own aspirations for a united country free from foreign domination, although there was little active agitation to create a local revolution. Napoleon invaded Italy in 1796, and while he had enjoyed other military victories, Italy was his first notable triumph on the battlefield that launched him into the public eye in France. He seemed to take a personal interest in the immediate future of Italy, which was also his first experiment in extending French influence into neighbouring lands through new structures of government. 'Sister republics' were set up as experiments in puppet States that would serve French ends. Revolutionary institutions and processes were put in place, following the model in Paris. Napoleon withdrew but returned in 1800, declaring himself King of Italy on 17 March 1805.

In the anticlerical tradition of the Revolution, Napoleon displayed little regard for the Church and the papacy suffered great indignities at his hands. When the French confronted a hostile attitude in the Vatican, Napoleon invaded the papal territories and Rome in 1798, declaring the Roman republic, while Pope Pius VI withdrew to Tuscany. Later, under Pius VII, a Concordat or treaty defining the respective domains of the Church and the State was signed with Napoleon in 1801. When Napoleon assumed the position of Emperor in 1804, he received the crown from the hands of the Pope but placed it upon his head with his own hands in a gesture that detracted from the prestige of the

Church. Subsequently, animosity between Napoleon and the Church continued. In 1805 the Pope declared neutrality when France went to war with Austria, and Napoleon was furious. He made the Pope a prisoner in 1808, and a year later abolished the temporal authority of the Pope, for which Pius VII excommunicated him and those who had violated the sanctity of the Church and its properties which were the 'patrimony of Jesus Christ'. Pius VII was removed to Savona on the Mediterranean coast near France and was a prisoner of Napoleon until 1814, surviving as Pope until 1823.

With the Congress of Vienna in 1815 many of the Italian 'mini-states' were reestablished, from Lombardy in the north to Sicily in the south, but with substantial disorder still. Austria attempted to exercise certain 'legal' rights over the Italian peninsula, especially in the north with Piedmont, Lombardy and Venice, while its puppet Bourbon kings ruled in the south. Following its mode of action in the rest of Europe, the Congress of Vienna also reestablished the position of the Church within the revived old order, and the sovereignty of the Pope in the Papal States was restored. And like the kingdoms of Europe, the Church slipped further into the trap of action and reaction that typified the surrounding political environment. The Church consolidated a reactionary mode under Gregory XVI, who is most remembered for his opposition to street lights and railroads which he viewed as corrupting the social order. Such reactionary policies hardly addressed the real crises of the Church and its dependencies. Shoghi Effendi writes:

Corruption, disorganization, impotence to ensure internal security, the restoration of the inquisition, had induced an historian to assert that 'no land of Italy, perhaps of Europe, except Turkey, is ruled as is this ecclesiastical state.' Rome was 'a city of ruins, both material and moral.'[2]

Parallel to the reactionary position of the papacy in the first decades of the 19th century, the idea of a united Italian peninsula free from Austrian intervention simmered, ebbed and flowed. The road ahead was not clear, but the seeds of a free Italian State had been sown. Although associations were generally repressed, and freedom of association was guaranteed only in the Kingdom of Piedmont in its constitution of 1848, lively discussions took place in secret or in private salons, attempting to create a vision that would galvanize a national identity. Intellectuals and revolutionaries were known as Carbonari, so-called because they supposedly met at night around a charcoal brazier for heat and light while they discussed the possibilities for a progressive Italian nation.

As Europe moved into the 1840s and unrest boiled to the surface, the stage was set for the appearance of Pius IX who ascended to the throne of Peter in 1846, serving in that capacity until 1878 – the pontiff of longest tenure in the history of the Church. It fell to him to confront those two eventful decades of the 50s and 60s that would change the face of Europe for the rest of the century, and it was he to whom Bahá'u'lláh directed His fateful epistle. Shoghi Effendi describes Pius IX in the following terms:

> Authoritarian by nature, a poor statesman, disinclined to conciliation, determined to preserve all his authority, he, while he succeeded through his assumption of an ultramontane attitude in defining further his position and in reinforcing his spiritual authority, failed, in the end, to maintain that temporal rule which, for so many centuries, had been exercised by the heads of the Catholic Church.[3]

Ironically, prior to his election as Pope, Pius IX had been a relatively liberal cleric, and he initiated his papacy by freeing political prisoners of the Papal States, but events rapidly drove him back into a reactionary mode from which he never relented. He would become one of the most stubbornly reactionary popes who would seal by his obstinacy the reduced prestige of the Church.

With the revolutions of 1848, events in Italy followed suit as in the rest of the continent. Revolt broke out in Naples in January, followed by Paris in February. As rebellion spread, the Pope escaped from Rome once again, but was restored as revolutions were quelled and foreign troops protected him from revolutionary, nationalistic forces that had driven the rebellions. Their visionary was Giuseppe Mazzini who dreamt of a united Italy with Rome as its capital, which he hoped would result from a spontaneous uprising of the masses. Mazzini together with Giuseppe Garibaldi would be the embodiment of popular aspirations, in contrast to those of the liberal middle classes represented by King Victor Emmanuel of Piedmont and his prime minister Camillo de Cavour in the north. As in France where the inherent social tensions of liberals and the popular classes had existed independent of the Industrial Revolution, so also in Italy where questions of the structure of a future Italian State were even less clear.

In pursuit of an Italian State, Cavour sought the support of Napoleon III, meeting secretly in 1858 and plotting a war against Austria that would serve to liberate the northern states and pave the way to unification. Napoleon viewed Austria as a stalwart of conservatism and a natural opponent that had engineered the Congress of Vienna and France's dishonour. Napoleon was all too ready to see Austria humiliated. Unknown even to Napoleon's foreign minister, Napoleon committed to give military backing in case of aggression from Austria, emboldening King Victor Emmanuel of Piedmont to declare war on Austria. A brief but vicious war ensued, engaging France and

Piedmont against Austria and leaving both sides bleeding, but soon Austria had to withdraw. In an inherently unstable situation, Cavour played his cards well and outmanoeuvered both France and Austria. In 1860 Cavour managed to join the northern Italian mini-states to Piedmont, and a proto-Italian entity emerged with Victor Emmanuel as king. Suddenly Napoleon III was faced with a nearly-united Italian State – another power on his southern flank and much more than he had bargained for! – and true to character, he wavered in his commitment and got cold feet. He withdrew from the war, made peace with Austria, and stationed his troops in Rome to protect the Pope against the advance of the Piedmontese army that was uniting the rest of Italy, lest he face the ire of French Catholics for permitting the papacy to be absorbed by the new State. The troops would stay there until 1870. Giuseppe Garibaldi led the war effort against the Bourbon puppet kings in the south with an invasion of Sicily and eventually brought the southern states under the sway of a united Italy.

Garibaldi was certainly one of the most colourful characters of this century. His fame had spread far and wide, and Abraham Lincoln even offered him a commission in the US army during the Civil War. Garibaldi is the personification of other more popular democratic tendencies and was also a master of what today we call guerilla warfare. With a modest band of compatriots called the 'Red Shirts' (for their standard dress that identified them), he was able to advance the nationalist cause in the south. He would reach the gates of Rome, where he was met by Victor Emmanuel and his army. In an act of statesmanship and to avoid a civil war, he recognized Victor Emmanuel as king, not of Piedmont but of a united Italy. Cavour, the architect of modern Italy, would die soon after, but his comment on the event of the unification reflected the social condition of the day: 'We have created Italy. Now we must create Italians.' For Italy at that point was still more of a mental construct than a social reality. Although political boundaries had been erased, cultural and linguistic boundaries would hamper nation building for years to come.

As the move toward unification advanced in the mid-19th century, the Papal States shared the fate of other mini-states. As these were absorbed into the new Italian nation in 1860, Papal authority continued in Lazio around Rome and was a thorn in the side of the democratic or modernizing forces. Did it make sense to have a State within a State, which did not adhere to the emergent Italian State? . . . especially when that State was Rome and the natural capital of a united republic! Yet the French army protected the Pope and stood in the way of integrating Rome into the new national entity. The 'Roman question' would simmer for another decade and its resolution would depend on external happenings far beyond the borders of Italy.

Throughout the 1860s, having lost most of his territory already, the Pope counterattacked against what he considered the robber State and all that it stood for. In the *Syllabus of Errors*,[4] a document that summarizes the conclusions of no less than twenty-five encyclical letters from 1846 when Pius assumed the pontificate until 1864, he defended some essential principles of religion such as the existence of God and the validity of divine revelation. However, most of the points reflect opposition, in several cases justified, to the then-current environment that grew out of the Enlightenment and the rise of the secular mindset. By 1864 the concepts of the Enlightenment that had been championed by the French Revolution and promoted by the proponents of liberal government were generally accepted as standards of social values. We saw how liberal thought was spread by Napoleon's conquests, often at the expense of the Church, for example in the field of education. While these concepts contravened the traditional basis of society in which the Church was supreme, they were made all the more abhorrent by the advance of the secular State in Italy – a State which was born of these liberal principles and which absorbed almost all of the Papal States. In the *Syllabus of Errors* the Pope paraphrases these far-ranging concepts of modernity, one after the other, as misguided standards of the social order.

He attacks the position of many Enlightenment thinkers that reason is the highest and sole basis for establishing truth, and that the 'faith of Christ is in opposition to human reason'. He rejects the idea that 'The decrees of the Apostolic See and of the Roman congregations impede the true progress of science', and that 'Philosophy is to be treated without taking any account of supernatural revelation'. He apparently alludes to the advance of industrialization when he criticizes the growing sense of materialism, that 'accumulation and increase of riches' has replaced the 'rectitude and excellence of morality . . .' He abhors the democratic idea that 'authority is nothing else but numbers and the sum total of material forces'.

However, the most prominent theme of the *Syllabus* is a defence of the prerogatives and primacy of the Church. He rejects the idea of religious freedom – a freedom that had emerged as a compromise at the end of the disastrous wars of religion two centuries earlier, and that declared that 'Every man is free to embrace and profess that religion which, guided by the light of reason, he shall consider true,' and that 'Man may, in the observance of any religion whatever, find the way of eternal salvation, and arrive at eternal salvation.' Indeed, these 'false doctrines' had led to the erroneous belief that 'Protestantism is nothing more than another form of the same true Christian religion . . .' Recognizing the dire state of affairs of the Church, he blames this situation on the 'frauds and machinations of these sects'. He denies that 'The Church is not a true and perfect society, entirely free' and that 'The Church has not the power of defining dogmatically that the religion of the Catholic Church is the only true religion.' He laments that 'it is no longer expedient that the Catholic religion should be held as the only religion of the State, to the exclusion of all other forms of worship' and objects to the idea that persons migrating to a Catholic country 'shall enjoy the public exercise of their own peculiar worship'.

Touching on one of the great bones of contention of the age, he objects to the marginalization of the Church in the education of youth, and 'that popular schools open to children of every class of the people, and, generally, all public institutes intended for instruction in letters and philosophical sciences and for carrying on the education of youth, should be freed from all ecclesiastical authority, control and interference . . .' and that 'Catholics may approve of the system of educating youth unconnected with Catholic faith and the power of the Church . . .'

Fully a quarter of the 80 points of the Syllabus are dedicated to attacking the civil authority of the State and its perceived incursions into the domain of the Church, reflecting the immediacy of the growth of the Italian State. He denies that 'Roman pontiffs and ecumenical councils have wandered outside the limits of their powers, have usurped the rights of princes . . .' Of immediate importance for the Pope and in the historical setting of the erosion of ecclesiastical dominion over the Papal States, he attacks the growth of secular power and its dominance over the Church, and rejects the idea that 'The sacred ministers of the Church and the Roman pontiff are to be absolutely excluded from every charge and dominion over temporal affairs.' Another section is dedicated to 'SOCIALISM, COMMUNISM, SECRET SOCIETIES, BIBLICAL SOCIETIES, CLERICO-LIBERAL SOCIETIES'. These errors would apparently be far too abundant to enumerate, for they are not detailed, but it is sufficient to say that 'Pests of this kind are frequently reprobated in the severest terms' in various other encyclicals. While resistance to socialism and Communism is understandable, the broader attack seems to reflect discomfort with associations that were flowering in civil society at that moment in history, especially the Freemasons and including those 'clerico-liberal societies' that could lead to reflection on religion in the context of the social milieu.

The gist of the *Syllabus* is summed up in the last error among the 80 errors cited, that 'The Roman Pontiff can, and ought to, reconcile himself, and come to terms with progress, liberalism and modern civilization.' With this the Pope declared war on the 19th century in all of its multiple aspects and historical tendencies. Rather than engaging with the spirit of the age and the social currents that were shaping the continent, and offering spiritual and moral guidance when it was most needed, the Supreme Pontiff took refuge in the past and condemned himself and the Church to increasing obscurity for much of what remained of the 19th century.

Against the historical backdrop of the advance of the Italian State, Bahá'u'lláh's counsel to 'Abandon thy kingdom unto the kings' and to 'Beware lest thou appropriate unto thyself the things of the world and the riches thereof. Leave them unto such as desire them,' are more than general calls to spiritual detachment. When He penned those words in 1867 or 1868, the all-consuming obsession of the Pope was to maintain his temporal authority over Rome and the Papal States. In 1860 the Pope had already lost his dominion over the Papal States except for Rome, and Rome was his last bastion of temporal authority, and also the last obstacle to completing the dominion of the secular State. When Bahá'u'lláh addressed the Pope, it was a decisive moment for Pius. It was his last opportunity to make a graceful peace with the forces of modernity and so to contribute positively to progress, and Bahá'u'lláh was addressing the central issue of the papacy in that period.

Heedless of the counsels of Bahá'u'lláh and of the forces of the times, throughout the decade of the 1860s the Pope struggled to muster his authority against the inevitable, and to regain his temporal power. Rather than concerning himself with temporal power, Bahá'u'lláh called upon the Pope to assume his pastoral role at the highest level and to admonish the kings to establish justice. 'Exhort thou the kings and say: "Deal equitably with men. Beware lest ye transgress the bounds fixed in the Book." This indeed becometh thee.' This role would be coherent with Bahá'u'lláh's own actions and the insistent message in His epistles, initiating with the *Súriy-i-Mulúk*, urging the kings to be concerned with the welfare of their subjects and to establish justice. Indeed, in all 80 points of the *Syllabus of Errors*, there is no mention of social justice, nor of the errors of the Industrial Revolution and its abuses over the poor, apart from an indirect reference to the evils of the 'accumulation and increase of riches'. Concern for the welfare of the masses is inexplicably absent.

Within scarcely three years of Bahá'u'lláh's epistle to Pius, the end would close in about him. After the war of 1861 the papacy had enjoyed the protection of French troops, but with Napoleon's own demise in 1870, the new government of the Third Republic withdrew French troops and Victor Emmanuel occupied Rome. Thus did the Papal States as such come to an end, victims of the crush of history, and the worldly realm of Pius IX disappeared. The Pope receded into self-imposed imprisonment inside the Vatican, stubbornly refusing to recognize the civil authority, a situation that endured beyond his papacy and into the 20th century. Embittered but unbending, Pius IX continued to resist the nascent Italian State. From his refuge deep within the Vatican he at first discouraged and then forbade all Catholics to have anything to do with the new State, even to the point of voting in elections.

The Italian public was one of the most illiterate in all of

Europe at that time, and its peoples were divided by regional languages, constituting a formidable barrier to the process of nation building. The only real bond that could link them together in those first years of the Italian State was their Catholic faith, and the Pope refused to lend his support to developing a sense of unity around the fledgling State. Quite the contrary – rather than exercising moral leadership to heal the social tensions, the Church organized its own associations among the masses in opposition to the liberal State and in competition with the socialists.

Pius IX seemed to be oblivious to any wrongdoing of the Church throughout history. He recognized no faults that had led to the Protestant Reformation. He turned a blind eye to the abuses that had fuelled the French Revolution. He even denied any responsibility in the schism with the Eastern Orthodox Church centuries before! Pius took a stand on the basis of 1,500 years of Church doctrine: the exclusive primacy of Peter; the exclusive inheritance of Peter's authority through the bishops of Rome; the doctrine of original sin and the futility of attaining salvation except through the sacraments administered by the Catholic Church; the supremacy of Church over State; the right of the Church to temporal authority over the 'patrimony of Jesus Christ'. He can be categorized as reactionary without a doubt, but he was also a prisoner of accumulated dogma and he drew the logical conclusions in the *Syllabus of Errors* from a much longer history of errors.

The epistle of Bahá'u'lláh to the Pope is unusual in its repeated insistence in warning against the dangers of 'human learning'. 'Beware lest human learning debar thee from Him Who is the Supreme Object of all knowledge . . . Tear asunder the veils of human learning lest they hinder thee from Him Who is My name, the Self-Subsisting . . . Rend asunder the veils of your idle fancies!'[5] It is striking that the Pontiff, who should have been the

exponent of divine learning, should be so endangered by human
learning, and Pius must have felt that he was indeed combatting
'human learning' in his opposition to the Enlightenment project. One wonders if Bahá'u'lláh might not have been referring
to those doctrines which blinded Pius IX, not only to His own
advent, but to the march of history that was enveloping him.
In this regard Pius IX was not unlike others of his age. Like the
revolutionaries who blindly and blithely proclaimed the universal benefits of liberty; like Marx who claimed to have discovered
the immutable and scientific laws of history; like the prophets of
economic growth who promulgated the laws of the free market
and *laissez faire*, Pius IX based his actions on the immutable
laws of the Church.

Indeed, the call of Bahá'u'lláh is still current, and is relevant for the Church as it struggles with its own tests of the 21st
century:

O concourse of monks! Seclude not yourselves in your
churches and cloisters. Come ye out of them by My leave, and
busy, then, yourselves with what will profit you and others.
Thus commandeth you He Who is the Lord of the Day of
Reckoning. Seclude yourselves in the stronghold of My love.
This, truly, is the seclusion that befitteth you, could ye but
know it. He that secludeth himself in his house is indeed as
one dead. It behoveth man to show forth that which will benefit mankind. He that bringeth forth no fruit is fit for the fire.
Thus admonisheth you your Lord; He, verily, is the Mighty,
the Bountiful. Enter ye into wedlock, that after you another
may arise in your stead. We, verily, have forbidden you lech-
ery, and not that which is conducive to fidelity. Have ye clung
unto the promptings of your nature, and cast behind your
backs the statutes of God? Fear ye God, and be not of the
foolish. But for man, who, on My earth, would remember

Me, and how could My attributes and My names be revealed? Reflect, and be not of them that have shut themselves out as by a veil from Him, and were of those that are fast asleep. He that married not could find no place wherein to abide, nor where to lay His head, by reason of what the hands of the treacherous had wrought. His holiness consisted not in the things ye have believed and imagined, but rather in the things which belong unto Us. Ask, that ye may be made aware of His station which hath been exalted above the vain imaginings of all the peoples of the earth. Blessed are they that understand.[6]

11

Francis Joseph and Austria

O Emperor of Austria! He Who is the Dayspring of God's Light dwelt in the prison of 'Akká at the time when thou didst set forth to visit the Aqṣá Mosque. Thou passed Him by, and inquired not about Him by Whom every house is exalted and every lofty gate unlocked. We, verily, made it a place whereunto the world should turn, that they might remember Me, and yet thou hast rejected Him Who is the Object of this remembrance, when He appeared with the Kingdom of God, thy Lord and the Lord of the worlds. We have been with thee at all times, and found thee clinging unto the Branch and heedless of the Root. Thy Lord, verily, is a witness unto what I say. We grieved to see thee circle round Our Name, whilst unaware of Us, though We were before thy face. Open thine eyes, that thou mayest behold this glorious Vision, and recognize Him Whom thou invokest in the daytime and in the night season, and gaze on the Light that shineth above this luminous Horizon.[1]

Of all the dynasties of Europe, none could compare with the Hapsburgs regarding their longevity and dominance over a vast geographical area, and their role in the history and wars of previous centuries. At various times over a period of four centuries, the Hapsburgs ruled not only Austria, but Hungary, Bohemia, part of Poland, much of the Balkans, the Netherlands, Belgium, Italy, Spain, the Philippines, and most of Latin America. Originating in the 11th century in what is today modern Switzerland, the Hapsburg dynasty showed little early indication of its future glory, and for four hundred years was a modest royal family participating in the horse trading of kingdoms and thrones in central Europe. For many years its internal family policy of dividing lands among all male heirs limited its potential for great political or military power. Its destinies took a turn for the better when a Hapsburg, Frederick V, occupied the position of Holy Roman Emperor in 1452, a position that would stay in the family for three and a half centuries. Dating to the acceptance of Christianity by Charlemagne and his designation as Holy Roman Emperor by Pope Leo III in the year 800, the Holy Roman Empire in its early years united a vast range of medieval feudal States under the powerful central figure of the Emperor. As local kings and warlords gained in power, the position of the Emperor became more symbolic. Frederick V of Austria, later to be known as Emperor Frederick III, was still not a powerful ruler, but his descendants would soon change that.

The Hapsburg domains grew vigorously, not by conquest of war, but by romantic conquest, for the Hapsburgs were experts at the strategic art of choosing a spouse, hence the refrain, 'Let others wage wars; you, fortunate Austria, marry.' Frederick's son Maximilian optimized this strategy in a marriage that won him the control of the Netherlands, and his son Philip, in turn, married Joan the Mad, heiress to the Castilian throne of Spain. Their son became Charles V of Spain, the youthful successor to Isabel and Ferdinand who came to Iberia from the Low Countries, and as a Hapsburg heir, extended the domain of the Hapsburgs over nearly half the lands of the western hemisphere. Thus, in four short generations, and in the space of some sixty years, strategic marriages had launched the Hapsburgs from the status of a run-of-the-mill royal family of central Europe, to being the masters of half of that continent and another half of the New World, and with a foothold in Asia in the Philippines.

The Holy Roman Emperor had originally been closely allied with the papacy, but in later years had entered into frequent competition with the Pope for leadership of Christendom. In any case, the position of Emperor held an aura of at least nominal leadership of Christians of Europe. Symbolic or not, several emperors took seriously their duty as protector of the Catholic Church. A fervent Catholic like Isabel and Ferdinand before him, Charles V assured the establishment of Catholicism in Latin America. No small part of the colonial effort was indeed driven by a sense of missionary zeal to evangelize the natives of the western hemisphere. This was also the age of the Reformation, and his son and successor as king of Spain (though not emperor), Philip II, launched widespread attacks on countries associated with the Protestant movement, famously represented in the disastrous plan to invade England with the Spanish Armada, and so frittering away the riches flowing from the New World and bankrupting the royal treasury. Likewise, the Protestant Netherlands were in rebellion in a war that would only be resolved in the mid-1600s. In the 17th century Ferdinand II of Austria, in his role as Holy Roman Emperor (1619–37), renewed the war on Protestantism, pursuing the Thirty Years War that devastated northern Europe and slaughtering an estimated third of the population in many regions. Napoleon Bonaparte abolished the position of Holy Roman Emperor in 1806, an act that was maintained by the Congress of Vienna, but the memory of the Austrian Hapsburgs as the natural heirs of this position sustained a firm commitment to traditional Catholicism. Indeed, Austria would remain a bastion of tradition of the old regime, even as modernism swirled around it.

Given the central position of Austria-Hungary in Europe, and its extension into new dominions, it was inevitably involved with conflicts on all sides. As the dominant force in the Low Countries in the early 17th century, Austria came into direct conflict with the French as they extended their own influence north, and later as the Napoleonic wars gathered momentum, Austria would be a consistent enemy of France. To the south we have seen that Austria held sway over Italy, including with 'legal rights' bestowed by the Congress of Vienna. Wars were fought, most recently with Piedmont with the backing of Napoleon III. On the east the Empire confronted the intrusions of the Ottoman Turks, and later extended its influence into those same Ottoman territories with their Slavic peoples. However, given that many Christians of the Balkans were Orthodox, this also implied entering into the sphere of influence claimed by the Russian Czar. On the north, Austria was in competition with Prussia for the leadership of the German states, but was no match for the manoeuvering of Bismarck. Furthermore, as a Great Power of the old order, Austria felt obliged to have a presence in virtually any significant conflict, such as the Crimean War which did not involve Austria directly but did involve almost all the other Great Powers. And if wars with neighbours were not enough, the multi-ethnic nature of the Empire lent itself to internal unrest, especially after an infusion of revolutionary ideas from the French Revolution.

Indeed, as for much of Europe, the French Revolution was the determining factor in the course of Austria in the 19th century. The radicalism of France created a backlash among the monarchs of Europe, with Austria taking a prominent role in opposition early in the Revolution, and when the Napoleonic wars finally ended it would be the Austrian Metternich who engineered the reestablishment of the old order. Ironically, the Austrian monarchy had not always been so conservative. Maria Theresa (Queen from 1740 to 1780) had been a modernizer, and her son, Joseph, was the proverbial enlightened despot and an aggressive proponent of Enlightenment principles who sought to use dictatorial powers to promote education and other benefits of modern society. But as the 19th century dawned and Austria took a dominant role in opposing the French Revolution, its policies became decidedly conservative and reactionary.

What is remarkable about the role of Austria (or Austria-Hungary after 1867), in the period that parallels the Heroic Age of the Bahá'í Faith, was that it was led by the same absolutist monarch for almost all of that period and into the Great War – Francis Joseph, Emperor from 1848 to 1916, a remarkable span of sixty-eight eventful years! Like his rival Napoleon III, Francis Joseph came to the throne as a result of the revolutions of 1848, but at the other end of the political spectrum. At one time mentored by Metternich, there was no question where his heart lay as the continent debated its destiny between the past and the future. Indeed, in his youth he had participated in the military action to put down the rebellious Italians in the spring of 1848, thus having first-hand experience in defending the old order with force. At the age of eighteen he ascended to the position of Emperor of Austria upon the abdication of his uncle in December of that same year. A proponent of 'neo-absolutism' and highly devoted to duty, he assumed many decisions personally and the State was inextricably linked to his own personality.

Bahá'u'lláh's address in the *Kitáb-i-Aqdas* to Francis Joseph does not refer to either specific or even general events surrounding his tenure as head of state. Rather He chides the Emperor for rejecting Him and cites the negligence of Francis Joseph in not seeking the presence of Bahá'u'lláh when on pilgrimage in the Holy Land. The pilgrimage of Francis Joseph took place in 1869, when Bahá'u'lláh had been transferred to Akka from Adrianople and while He still was held within the barracks of the prison, which is to say, during one of the most troubling and testing periods of His life. With the opportunity afforded by the opening of the Suez Canal in 1869, Francis Joseph, who bore the honorific title of King of Jerusalem, made his pilgrimage to the Holy Land on behalf of the Hapsburg monarchy.

Francis Joseph was not the only crowned head to make acts of religious devotion, or in favour of religious interests. We have mentioned that Czar Nicholas I claimed the right to defend Orthodox Christians in the Balkans, invading Turkish territory for that purpose and sparking the Crimean War. Napoleon III, often at loggerheads with the Church, obtained a concession from the Ottoman government to have France recognized as having sovereign authority over all Christian holy sites in Palestine, probably to curry favour with French Catholics but to the chagrin of the Czar. However, the pilgrimage of Francis Joseph held a special significance for Catholics, as he was the first Catholic monarch to visit Jerusalem since the Crusades – no small event! The significance of this visit was heightened by the fact that it was carried out by the natural heir of the now-defunct position of Holy Roman Emperor, an institution closely allied to Catholicism since its inception in 800 AD. Indeed, Shoghi Effendi notes that the Austro-Hungarian monarchy was 'the most powerful unit which owed its allegiance to, and supported through its resources the administration of, the Church of Rome'.[2]

Thus, Francis Joseph had a unique opportunity among the crowned heads of Europe in coming within closer proximity of the Lord of the Age than any other, short of the Sultan himself. The timing of his pilgrimage – and the end of the decade of the 1860s – was also significant in the context of surrounding events. Bahá'u'lláh had issued His proclamation to the kings a scant two years before. Circumstances were coming to a head that would lead to the downfall of Napoleon and the humiliation of the Pope a year later in 1870. Soon the entire course of events would change the direction of Europe for the rest of the century. Francis Joseph, unknown to himself, was at a decisive moment in European history, and among the crowned heads of Europe, he had a unique opportunity to seize the moment and to avoid impending disaster.

Francis Joseph failed to intervene on behalf of Bahá'u'lláh, in spite of his proximity to Akka and the prison where Bahá'u'lláh languished. This, despite the fact that Christian kings and governments of Europe had never been reticent to intervene in affairs of the Ottoman Empire, and their failure to do so on behalf of Bahá'u'lláh cannot be attributed to any respect for diplomatic protocol. In contrast, a review of the history of the Faith reveals that Christians had in fact played a role out of proportion to their small numbers in the Middle East, and had rendered great services to the Central Figures. Manúchir Khán, Christian governor of Isfahan, had sheltered the Báb with the unfulfilled intention to put his vast fortune at His disposal,[3] and the Armenian Christian Sám Khán had refused to execute the Báb. A physician, Dr Shishman, reputed to be a Christian,[4] sacrificed his own life for the life of Bahá'u'lláh when He lay agonizing from an attempt to poison Him. When the Holy Family was subject to indignities in Adrianople, Bahá'u'lláh Himself testifies that the lamentation of the Christians was greater than that of others.[5] Finally, a Christian merchant of Akka, Údí Khammár, permitted the exiles to be lodged in his property, and his son-in-law 'Abbúd amplified the living quarters so that 'Abdu'l-Bahá could marry. Subsequently Bahá'u'lláh would occupy Bahji, the mansion of Údí Khammár on the outskirts of Akka. Bahá'u'lláh praised Údí Khammár in a Tablet, and the tomb of Údí Khammár lies within the holy precincts near Bahá'u'lláh's own Sanctuary, the only other person whose grave is in proximity to that of Bahá'u'lláh, and whose tomb Shoghi Effendi left undisturbed.

But like the Pope and others to whom Bahá'u'lláh directed His epistles, Emperor Francis Joseph – heir to the title of Holy Roman Emperor and the tradition of defender of Catholicism

– failed to live up to the example of the Christian faithful in rendering service to the Lord of the Age. In failing to seize the opportunity, his expression of piety in fulfilling his pilgrimage came to naught, reminiscent of another passage in the very same *Kitáb-i-Aqdas* where Bahá'u'lláh left graven for all time His judgement on acts of piety:

> Were anyone to wash the feet of all mankind, and were he to worship God in the forests, valleys, and mountains, upon high hills and lofty peaks, to leave no rock or tree, no clod of earth, but was a witness to his worship – yet, should the fragrance of My good pleasure not be inhaled from him, his works would never be acceptable unto God.[6]

Austria was a victim of the times and its own sluggish response to the changing world around it. At every turn it seemed that Austria was 'born to lose'. Stubbornly committed to the 'old Europe' in the autocratic personality of Francis Joseph, slower than Prussia among the German states to incorporate the benefits of industrialization, the 19th century did not go well for Austria. Gaining no more from the victory of the Crimean War than Russia's animosity; being out manoeuvered in Italy by Cavour, and in Germany by Bismarck; facing restive nationalistic Slavs in the eastern provinces of the Empire; dealing with the demands of conservative Magyars (the ruling class of Hungary) – Francis Joseph had no significant victories to claim glory for the Empire. In the words of Shoghi Effendi:

> The House of Hapsburg, in which the Imperial Title had remained practically hereditary for almost five centuries, was, ever since those words [of Bahá'u'lláh] were uttered, being increasingly menaced by the forces of internal disintegration, and was sowing the seeds of an external conflict, to both of

which it ultimately succumbed. Francis Joseph, Emperor of Austria, King of Hungary, a reactionary ruler, re-established old abuses, ignored the rights of nationalities, and restored that bureaucratic centralization that proved in the end so injurious to his empire.[7]

Beyond disasters of state, Francis Joseph suffered many personal tragedies. The Empress was assassinated in Geneva. His brother Maximilian, at the manoeuvering of Napoleon III in a scheme to reassert European dominance in the New World, was imposed as Emperor of Mexico, only to be executed after three years in a revolution. Another brother died after drinking contaminated water while on pilgrimage in Jerusalem, an ironic result of another act of piety. Crown Prince Rudolph, his son and heir apparent, committed suicide at a young age over a love affair, while the next heir to the throne of Hapsburg, Archduke Francis Ferdinand, was assassinated in Sarajevo in the Balkans, at the hands of a Serbian nationalist. Serbia had been a hotbed of resistance against Austria, and many of the Austrian hierarchy thought that war with Serbia would be inevitable sooner or later. Not disposed to patience, Austria declared war in August of 1914, setting off a domino effect of intertwined treaties that dragged the rest of Europe into its disastrous maelstrom.

It fell to Francis Joseph to witness and administer the final demise of the once mighty House of Hapsburg, that dynasty whose rule had encircled the world in an earlier age. It was perhaps God's one last mercy to him that he died before seeing Austria's ultimate humiliation in the First World War, for he passed from this world in 1916 'closing a reign which is unsurpassed by any other reign in the disasters it brought to the nation,'[8] and as the Great War which his government initiated was tearing down both those remnants of the old order and the achievements of the previous century.

12

Alexander II and Russia

O Czar of Russia! Incline thine ear unto the voice of God, the King, the Holy, and turn thou unto Paradise, the Spot wherein abideth He Who, among the Concourse on high, beareth the most excellent titles, and Who, in the kingdom of creation, is called by the name of God, the Effulgent, the All-Glorious. Beware lest thy desire deter thee from turning towards the face of thy Lord, the Compassionate, the Most Merciful. We, verily, have heard the thing for which thou didst supplicate thy Lord, whilst secretly communing with Him. Wherefore, the breeze of My loving-kindness wafted forth, and the sea of My mercy surged, and We answered thee in truth. Thy Lord, verily, is the All-Knowing, the All-Wise. Whilst I lay chained and fettered in the prison, one of thy ministers extended Me his aid. Wherefore hath God ordained for thee a station which the knowledge of none can comprehend except His knowledge. Beware lest thou barter away this sublime station. Thy Lord, verily, doeth what He willeth. What He pleaseth will God abrogate or confirm, and with Him is the knowledge of all things in a Guarded Tablet.[1]

Russia was one of the Great Powers of the 19th century, yet unique due to its ultra-conservative nature, its cultural history as the foremost Orthodox Christian nation after the fall of Constantinople in 1453, and with a geographic position that accentuated its distinctive nature. Russia fell outside of the western Latin tradition of Roman law, and clearly outside of the domain and influence of the Roman Church. Even into the second millennium it was dominated by Mongol tribes who demanded tribute from the local population. Christianity arrived relatively late to Russia, around 1000 AD. Yet its history lacked a decisive turn toward modernity until the advent of Peter the Great who ruled from 1689 to 1725. A dynamic and imposing figure, measuring nearly seven feet tall, Peter gave Russia its most significant modernizing impulse, symbolized quite emblematically in the construction of St Petersburg, his new capital on the Baltic coast that looked to the West, and promoting western technology such as shipbuilding. Still, while Peter was an ardent and active admirer of the West, this did not in the least extend to any lessening of his own absolute autocratic power, and he deployed his power without hesitation. Although Russian explorers had reached the Pacific Ocean in the 1500s to the extent that the Czar had signed a treaty with China in 1585, after 1721 Peter initiated an expansion on the southern borders of Russian territories, coming into contact with other cultures and empires, and waging war with Persia. Thus initiated a permanent presence in this region that would eventually bring the Russian State into contact with the history of Bahá'u'lláh a century and a half later.

In the 18th century Catherine the Great dominated Russian history as Czarina from 1762 to 1796, a reign encompassing the years that saw the flowering of Enlightenment thought in the West. Catherine was in fact a German princess who adopted Russian culture and the Russian cause, extending Russia's engagement in Europe and under whose rule Russia participated in the partition of Poland with Prussia and Austria. And although elevated discussions about reform took place during her reign, no action was taken, least of all as the French Revolution unfolded in all its grisly details.

While Peter and Catherine had sought to copy the West and had influenced the nobility, Russia's wider engagement with the West was forcefully imposed when Napoleon invaded in 1812, in his disastrous and near-suicidal attempt to conquer the sleeping giant on the eastern borders of the continent. Indeed, Napoleon succeeded in what he set out to do – conquering the vast expanses and even the city of Moscow, but those vast expanses devoured his army with disease, hunger and cold, and in the final insult the Russians burned Moscow to the ground, causing his one trophy to slip through his fingers. Still, the Napoleonic wars of the 19th century drew Russia into the European circle of nations as no other event could have. Russian armies marched all the way to Paris and occupied the city, and Russia sat at the table in the Congress of Vienna as one of the Great Powers on which rested the stability of Europe. The Russian delegation was headed by no less a personage than Czar Alexander I, an unusual personality of mystical inclinations who proposed a Holy Alliance of Christian kings to which only the conservative leaders of Prussia and Austria subscribed. At home, Alexander I participated in the same sort of liberal discussions as had occurred in the days of Catherine, including the prospect of a constitution, but as with Catherine, these discussions bore no fruit and absolutism continued unabated.

Alexander I died in 1825, and was succeeded by his younger brother Nicholas I. This event was accompanied by an abortive but telling incident in December of that year, the so-called Decembrist Revolution. A half-baked scheme of a handful of liberal army officers, the revolt fell apart almost on the day of its initiation, but it reflected the disillusionment of a young generation who had been inspired with the vision of the Enlightenment, and who were disheartened by the lack of any prospect for substantial change. The revolt did however steel the resolve of Nicholas to stamp out any hint of liberal thought. Of more long-term significance than the Decembrist Revolution in this period was the birth of a movement of young intellectuals who came to be known as the *Intelligentsia*. While this term has been applied to comparable groups in other countries and ages, in fact its origin is Russian. Inspired by Enlightenment principles, its early proponents were largely educated aristocratic youth, and were characterized by passionate investigation of reality, by devotion to sacrificial service for the betterment of Russia, and by an ardent search for a Russian identity that transcended crass absolutism. Some viewed the future of Russia in closer association with the West, others sought identity in the traditions of Russian folklore and collectivist rural life. Nor were they disposed to seek the source of Russian identity in the Orthodox Church which they viewed as a bulwark of absolutism. Much as similar fervent discussions flourished in secret in Italy and in German universities among youth who sought a redefinition of nationhood during this so-called Age of Revolution, the intelligentsia would become the backbone of the drive toward reform, and eventually toward socialism.

In contrast to the passionate commitment of the intelligentsia, in the 18th and 19th centuries Russia suffered from ambivalence about its future, with successive czars and czarinas alternating flirtation with reform followed by subsequent reversion to unquestioned absolutism. Nicholas I represented the extreme of the latter tendency, as expressed in the explicit and official dogma set forth as a standard for the educational system. The three pillars of education – which reflected the pillars of society – were orthodoxy, autocracy and nationality. Orthodoxy implied unquestioned authority of the Russian Orthodox Church that extended to the Czar himself as God's chosen representative. Autocracy was the unhindered exercise of that authority by the Czar, and nationality was the union of the Russian people under the paternalistic and absolute power of the 'father' Czar. Indeed, these three pillars were knit together as one. One contemporary Russian commentator noted: 'Our law is interested in religion primarily as the basis of nationality, as the spiritual nerve of the various tribes and peoples, not as one or another form of a person's relation to God.'² Indeed, to be Russian was to be faithful to the Church, and therefore to the Czar. If this model had been implicit in the reigns of other monarchs and in other countries of the period, Nicholas believed in this simplistic model of society to a degree that few others could equal, and he acted decisively on this model.

In spite of its remoteness from the heart of Europe, Russia would be the watchdog of the East, keeping an eye on any resurgence of revolution; and beneath the arch-reactionary vigilance of Nicholas, Russia was a key player in maintaining the stability of Europe under Metternich's anti-revolutionary scheme. To the extent that revolutionary ideas had fuelled France's wars of conquest and would most certainly threaten the renewal of monarchical power, Russia was an uncompromising proponent of the status quo, maintaining the role and prerogatives of the aristocracy, and ready to act against any new signs of revolution. Indeed, when the revolutions of 1848 threatened the very existence of the Hapsburg dynasty in Austria, it was Russia who came to its aid and quashed the rebellious and liberal forces.

Together with Austria, Russia's geographic position made it an especially active player in relations with the Ottoman Empire, known as the 'sick man of Europe'. The Turks had advanced to the very gates of Vienna in the mid-1500s but by the 19th century the decline in Ottoman power made its future – the so-called 'eastern question' – a matter of concern for the stability of Europe. Who would inherit those lands of the Balkans under Ottoman domination, and what shape would the different ethnicities take? These questions implied a vacuum of power in the Balkans and potential changes in the status quo of international boundaries, and Russia – that very watchdog of the status quo – would be one of the first to seek to expand its influence. The Christian population of the Balkans was largely Orthodox, and the Russian czars felt a special responsibility to extend protection to them. Still, when Czar Nicholas invaded Turkish territories and the Crimean War broke out, its principal motivation would be geopolitical with Russia competing with Turkey for control of the strategic straits of the Bosphorus, and Britain acting on its long-term suspicions of Russian expansionism, with Napoleon III signing on for the ride and Austria entering at the last minute. The war was a disaster for Russia, and indeed, Nicholas I died before it formally ended, precipitated, it was said, by sadness at what was viewed as treachery on the part of Austria after Russia had saved the Hapsburg throne.

It fell to Czar Alexander II to deal with the consequences of the war and to seek to modernize the State and its army. Thus, in 1855 when Alexander II took the throne, he inherited an empire from his father that was smarting from defeat in a disastrous war, betrayed by its European partners, and with internal contradictions – longing for the change that other European countries were enjoying but shackled by custom and an explicit dogma of absolutism that had created a sullen and dispirited population overwhelmingly composed of serfs.

The Tablet of Bahá'u'lláh to Alexander II has a unique tone, for it is both cordial and foreboding. Bahá'u'lláh states that having heard the supplication of the Czar, God answered his prayers: 'We, verily, have heard the thing for which thou didst supplicate thy Lord, whilst secretly communing with Him. Wherefore, the breeze of My loving-kindness wafted forth, and the sea of My mercy surged, and We answered thee in truth. Thy Lord, verily, is the All-Knowing, the All-Wise.'[3]

The Hand of the Cause of God 'Alí-Akbar Furútan cites a story of one Áqá Muḥammad-Rahím who, in a conversation with a Russian consul, was inspired to suggest that the supplications of the Czar were for victory over the Ottoman Empire, after his recent defeat in the Crimean War – an interpretation that 'Abdu'l-Bahá reportedly validated. Áqá Muḥammad relates that he said to the consul:

> To me, the rulers of the various nations desire nothing from God except assistance in defeating the enemy and conquering new lands, and inasmuch as the army of Russia had been defeated in the war of Sebastopol, the Czar in his prayers had expressed the wish to overcome the Ottoman Empire.[4]

If these were the aspirations of the Czar, his hopes were fulfilled in the Russo-Turkish War of 1887–88, when Russia led a coalition of Orthodox Christian nations (Bulgaria, Romania, Serbia and Montenegro) against Turkey, defeating it soundly and resulting in the establishment of de facto independent States.

Bahá'u'lláh continued, saying 'Whilst I lay chained and fettered in the prison, one of thy ministers extended Me his aid.' Alexander was not yet Czar when Bahá'u'lláh lay in prison in the Síyáh-Chál, but rather, his father Nicholas I still held that position. Perhaps when Bahá'u'lláh refers to 'one of thy ministers', He addresses Alexander as representative of the Romanov dynasty in previous years. He then reminds the Czar of the New Testament story of the flight of Joseph, Mary and Jesus into Egypt to escape the perfidy of Herod,[5] implicitly comparing that instance of Divine Protection with His own preservation in migrating to Baghdad – a deliverance that was facilitated by the Russian minister. While God had destined a special reward for the Czar, apparently out of consideration for his support to the Manifestation of God, the Czar was still called upon to take the next step and to lend full support. In this sense Alexander was unique among the sovereigns addressed by Bahá'u'lláh. He benefited from being held in special favour by God, yet he was adjured not to sacrifice this special favour by neglecting the explicit and insistent Call to recognize his Lord in His new manifestation. Thus, the story of Alexander's demise has a particular poignancy of lost opportunity. Indeed, Shoghi Effendi notes that in the Tablet that Bahá'u'lláh had directed to him, Alexander II 'had been thrice warned: "beware lest thy desire deter thee from turning towards the face of thy Lord," "beware lest thou barter away this sublime station," "beware lest thy sovereignty withhold thee from Him Who is the Supreme Sovereign".'[6]

Among the czars of the 19th century, Alexander II would be the great reformer, breaking with the reactionary policies of Nicholas I and of Alexander's successors, Alexander III and then Nicholas II. Establishing reforms in the period of 1861–64, the latter half of the 19th century saw a seismic break with the past, marked by the liberation of the serfs in 1861 and accompanied by progress in education, industrialization and the extension of railroads. One of the most significant reforms in institutional terms was the establishment of an independent judiciary, with authority in all but crimes against the State (although the Czar maintained the right to intervene on any matter).[7] An unexpected consequence of this reform in an environment in which public criticism of the State was still severely limited by police action, was to give a public stage to those with revolutionary inclinations. In the 1870s a number of passionate revolutionaries, both men and women, who were found promoting revolution in the villages were put on trial, and disdainful of both the reforms and their own fate, they used their own trials to publicize their cause with drama and theatrics. Subsequently trials were not open to the public.

But in spite of reforms that were relatively transformative

for the most backward of the Great Powers, discontent boiled beneath the surface. Russia had gone too long without reform, and when it came, it satisfied neither the liberals who sought a representative legislature with real power to institute laws, nor the peasants who received land but were obliged to pay for it. The Czar could not change Russia fast enough to meet the expectations of either the peasants, the intelligentsia or the students. 'In the latter part of his reign', writes Shoghi Effendi, 'he initiated a reactionary policy which, causing widespread disillusionment, gave rise to Nihilism, which, as it spread, ushered in a period of terrorism of unexampled violence, leading in its turn to several attempts on his life, and culminating in his assassination.'[8]

Alexander II fell victim to an assassin's bomb in St Petersburg in 1881. His son Alexander III came under the influence of reactionary advisers and reverted to the traditional conservatism, only to be exceeded in opposition to liberal tendencies by Nicholas II. Only in the latter years of the century was a long overdue commission convened to revise the code of law. When in 1905 revolution broke out further changes were promised, including a representative parliament or Duma, but Nicholas refused to yield any significant degree of power, to the extent of arbitrarily dismissing the Duma. Russia's history in the modern era was one of alternating between reform and reactionary conservatism, imitating that wider dynamic of action and reaction that typified so much of Europe. In spite of the efforts of Peter, Catherine and Alexander II to modernize, and in spite of wide engagement with Europe since the Napoleonic wars, at the end of the century Russia was still the least urbanized, the least industrialized, and the most conservative of all the Great Powers. As the 19th century drew to a close, the czars had opted for the most traditional of policies, and the most brutal repression against popular movements.

Bahá'u'lláh's words to Alexander II bore bitter fruit in 1917, when the Bolsheviks under Lenin overthrew the provisional liberal government of Kerensky. In 1918 the Bolsheviks executed Nicholas II and his entire family, bringing to an end another of the dynasties to fall to the march of history, one that had ruled Russia for more than three centuries.

> Think ye that the things ye possess shall profit you? Soon others will possess them and ye will return unto the dust with none to help or succour you. What advantage is there in a life that can be overtaken by death, or in an existence that is doomed to extinction, or in a prosperity that is subject to change? Cast away the things that ye possess and set your faces toward the favours of God which have been sent down in this wondrous Name.[9]

Before long the world would see the left emerge with even greater vigour, to leave its mark on the course of a large part of the 20th century. Withdrawing early from World War I in a separate peace with Germany, Russia would soon be submerged in an equally bloody civil war, suffering its own martyrdom under the iron fist of Stalin, the foremost spokesman of Marxist revolution for some thirty years. Stalin bears an eerie similarity and was the mirror image of Robespierre. One initiated the long 19th century, the other closed it. Each rose to power by displacing a liberal revolution in short order. Each carried out a reign of terror, arrogating to himself the authority to speak in behalf of the masses, perversely bastardizing popular power and assassinating perceived enemies in the name of the people. Each was motivated by a paranoiac fear of foreign enemies of their revolution, yet 'defended' his respective revolution by terrorizing and murdering his own people, including many of his co-revolutionaries. Yet one great difference separates Stalin from Robespierre amply and puts Stalin in a class by himself, for Stalin murdered a hundredfold more than Robespierre did – quite literally and without exaggeration, a hundredfold more.

13

Victoria and Great Britain

Lay aside thy desire, and set then thine heart towards thy
Lord, the Ancient of Days. We make mention of thee for the
sake of God, and desire that thy name may be exalted through
thy remembrance of God, the Creator of earth and heaven.[1]

Most histories of Europe in the 19th century initiate with a
consideration of Great Britain as the cradle of the Industrial
Revolution, and as the nation that dealt effectively with social
turmoil very soon thereafter. It may seem ironic that we leave
Great Britain and Queen Victoria to the last, considering the
predominant role that Britain played at many critical points.
Still, this is perhaps because nothing so dramatic happened in
Britain as in the other countries and empires that we have discussed. The monarchy did *not* fall. Britain was *not* defeated in
war with severe consequences. There were *not* bloody revolts
with thousands of casualties. Britain dealt relatively success-
fully with the crises that shook other countries, and was able to
maintain a gradual process of social transformation. Yet Britain
was a key player, not least due to its role in the final defeat of
Napoleon at Waterloo, thus putting Britain at the forefront of
forces in defence of the old order – one can say, in spite of its
own successful process of evolutionary change.

Britain also represents the extreme and opposite pole from

Russia, both in geography and in almost every other aspect that one can imagine, and yet in a sense they played similar roles in relation to the rest of Europe. It merits highlighting just how contrasting these two nations were, and yet how their roles were comparable. Sitting at the extremes of Europe, Britain on the west and Russia on the east, each was in some degree isolated from the maelstrom of wars that engulfed Europe in the 19th century and even before. The fact of being an island afforded Britain natural protection, bolstered by her development of naval power, and celebrated in the 19th century as 'splendid isolation'. While Russia did not enjoy protection of the sea, the very fact of vast distances represented some degree of protection at its heartland of Muscovy, as witnessed at how those distances and the accompanying vicissitudes conquered Napoleon far more than did the Russian army per se. Even when Napoleon won his objective of taking Moscow, the vastness of Russia took its toll and reduced his Grand Army to effective defeat. As two Great Powers on the margins of Europe, each was able to exert influence from afar, seeking to support the status quo and repressing revolution, with Russia of course exercising its power on the eastern limits of the continent. While investing much energy on the colonial front, Britain had traditionally entered into the fray of continental conflicts with much reticence, preferring to sit on the sidelines but bankrolling one or another of the combatants. However, like Russia, the Napoleonic wars would force Britain to take a more hands-on role, sitting at the table in the Congress of Vienna and subsequently playing the part of a Great Power in the Concert of Europe.

Still, the contrasts of Britain and Russia far outweigh the similarities. Britain had a long history of social evolution since the days of the Magna Carta; Russia at best flirted with liberal principles under some progressively minded czars while others rolled back reforms and secluded the nation in obscurantism.

Britain pioneered the Industrial Revolution in the mid-18th century, with its attendant urbanization, while Russia was still struggling with the early stages of industrialization 150 years later, and with an overwhelmingly rural and uneducated population. Britain confronted the challenges of social transformation over the length of the 1800s, extending education and social reforms gradually to most sectors of the population. In Russia these benefits were limited to the nobility and government bureaucrats. As the French Revolution advanced on the back of Enlightenment thought, an opposing philosophy was articulated by Edmund Burke which eventually took the name of Conservatism, still firmly rooted in a vision of a society dominated by an elite but arguing in favour of gradual social change as opposed to revolution. While the commitment of that social elite to change would often be less than evident in future years, this in essence would be the long-term approach of Britain.

Nonetheless, as the Napoleonic wars ended and each nation turned back to cultivating a settled life, the British crown was in crisis. The line of monarchical succession seemed doomed by fate to lose almost every candidate. King George III had fifteen children including nine sons, yet succession was no easy matter due to the early deaths of several of the elder sons. George IV succeeded his father as king until his death in 1830 but Charlotte, his only offspring and the heiress-apparent, died in 1817 ending that line of succession. George IV's brothers Frederick and William IV had no surviving legitimate children, and a sister (also named Charlotte) died childless. Thus, against all odds did Victoria – daughter of George III's fifth child and fourth son Edward – inherit the throne in 1837 at eighteen years of age, to reign for 61 years, the longest in the history of Britain until Elizabeth II.

The Britain that Victoria inherited was already well on the path it would follow for the length of her reign. Industrialization and urbanization were by then the rule rather than the exception. In this period reform movements were promoting laws to mitigate the worst abuses of the industrial system and to gradually expand the franchise. Parliamentary government, while still elected by a tiny fraction of the population, was poised to become more democratic. The Great Reform law of 1832 doubled the electorate, and while even then only one male in seven was allowed to vote, what was important was that many of the newly enfranchised voters were drawn from the emerging industrial middle class, thus prying the door open on the wider participation of this social group as opposed to the traditional landed class. While progress was often obtained only against the fierce opposition of social elites whose traditional disdain of the masses was complemented by fear of revolution and the memory of the French Terror – still, progress there was. Thus, Britain more than any other Great Power was positioned in the 'middle way' within the context of the times, between radical revolution and obstinate reactionary repression.

When Bahá'u'lláh addressed Victoria, He appeared to attribute actions to her for which she was not directly responsible. For example, Bahá'u'lláh states, 'We have been informed that thou hast forbidden the trading in slaves, both men and women.'[2] The slave trade was abolished in 1807, although Victoria was only born in 1819, and slavery was eliminated in the British Empire in 1832, five years before she ascended to the throne. Similarly, Bahá'u'lláh commends her because she has 'entrusted the reins of counsel into the hands of the representatives of the people',[3] although the parliamentary tradition was centuries-old. It appears that Bahá'u'lláh addresses her as personifying the entire British royal house, and beyond that, the British government and its system. This is not the only example in the Tablets of Bahá'u'lláh of employing the sovereign as representative or emblematic of a broader system or lineage. When He addresses Kaiser William I, He appears to be predicting the downfall of William I himself, although the disasters that befell the House of Hohenzollern were to come two generations later. As noted in Chapter 1, the Tablets to the Kings should be taken not only as admonitions to individuals but also to those kings in their role as heads of state, and to their entire lineage and the governments and States that they represented. This gives these letters a much wider social significance and invites a broader view in understanding their import.

In particular, the Tablet to Queen Victoria, among all of the Tablets to the Kings, is of great significance in the realm of government and social relations. The Tablet is remarkable when taken in the context of the liberal experiment of the mid-19th century and the process of nation building that was advancing on the continent with its attendant aspirations fuelled by nationalism and the desire for independent States. Regarding the British system over which Victoria presided, Bahá'u'lláh states that by entrusting

> the reins of counsel into the hands of the representatives of the people . . . thereby the foundations of the edifice of thine affairs will be strengthened, and the hearts of all that are beneath thy shadow, whether high or low, will be tranquillized. It behoveth them, however, to be trustworthy among His servants, and to regard themselves as the representatives of all that dwell on earth.[4]

The issue of form of government was indeed a vital one in mid-19th-century Europe, scarcely more than a generation removed from the uproar created by Napoleon Bonaparte, and well within memory of the revolutions of 1848. This is a message for all of Europe in this period, for at mid-century there was still relatively little tranquillity in Europe, as States sought frenetically to find forms of government that would assure a peaceful and equitable balance between tradition and progress, between workers and industrialists, between rural and urban. Indeed, far from limiting His comments to the British system, in the Tablet to Queen Victoria Bahá'u'lláh explicitly broadens His audience to the parliaments in all the world:

> O ye the elected representatives of the people in every land! Take ye counsel together, and let your concern be only for that which profiteth mankind and bettereth the condition thereof, if ye be of them that scan heedfully.[5]

'Abdu'l-Bahá repeats this theme in *The Secret of Divine Civilization*, only a few years later in 1875, both stressing the importance of 'assemblies of consultation' as the 'bedrock of government' and highlighting the need for the utmost integrity on the part of their members.

> For it has been directly witnessed in certain foreign countries that following on the establishment of parliaments those bodies actually distressed and confused the people and their well-meant reforms produced maleficent results. While the setting up of parliaments, the organizing of assemblies of consultation, constitutes the very foundation and bedrock of government, there are several essential requirements which these institutions must fulfill. First, the elected members must be righteous, God-fearing, high-minded, incorruptible. Second, they must be fully cognizant, in every particular, of the laws of God, informed as to the highest principles of law, versed in the rules which govern the management of internal affairs and the conduct of foreign relations, skilled in the useful arts of civilization, and content with their lawful emoluments.[6]

The topic of representative government was one over which

Europe had agonized since the French Revolution, and its importance cannot be overestimated at this point in the history of the continent. The Congress of Vienna had tended to throw the baby out with the bathwater, quashing republican ideals with little space for consultative assemblies, a stance that was largely though not totally validated by the repressions following 1848. France still struggled to establish a stable and sustainable form of government after deposing three kings, after Napoleon Bonaparte destroyed the First Republic, and after Napoleon III overthrew the Second Republic, soon to be deposed himself with consequences of more violent upheaval. Italy had been born as a State less than a decade before, and when Bahá'u'lláh wrote to Queen Victoria, Italy was still to complete its process of unification while liberal democracy led an uphill battle against the Church and a divided population. Germany was consolidating its own unification with an elected assembly that would struggle with Bismarck for leadership of the German masses. Alexander II sought to confront modernization and toyed with the idea of creating a representative assembly, but we have seen that those ideas floundered under later czars, until Nicholas II established and then dismissed the Duma in the 20th century. Yet Britain led the way, and was commended by Bahá'u'lláh.

Elsewhere Bahá'u'lláh comments on what could be the optimal form of government, and what can be interpreted as constitutional monarchy.

> Although a republican form of government profiteth all the peoples of the world, yet the majesty of kingship is one of the signs of God. We do not wish that the countries of the world should remain deprived thereof. If the sagacious combine the two forms into one, great will be their reward in the presence of God.[7]

The United Kingdom may well have been the best model available at that moment of the 'sagacious' combination of monarchy and republicanism, winning the favourable comments directed to Victoria. Indeed, Bahá'u'lláh later reflected in the *Lawḥ-i-Dunyá* that 'The system of government which the British people have adopted in London appeareth to be good, for it is adorned with the light of both kingship and of the consultation of the people.'[8]

Bahá'u'lláh likewise comments on the nature of the relationship between government and governed. This had also been a central issue of the Enlightenment as to the manner that governments are constituted, but here Bahá'u'lláh refers rather to the attitude of those who govern, in a passage once again addressed to the kings in general that is moving in its poignancy.

> O kings of the earth! We see you increasing every year your expenditures, and laying the burden thereof on your subjects. This, verily, is wholly and grossly unjust. Fear the sighs and tears of this Wronged One, and lay not excessive burdens on your peoples. Do not rob them to rear palaces for yourselves; nay rather choose for them that which ye choose for yourselves. Thus We unfold to your eyes that which profiteth you, if ye but perceive. Your people are your treasures. Beware lest your rule violate the commandments of God, and ye deliver your wards to the hands of the robber. By them ye rule, by their means ye subsist, by their aid ye conquer. Yet, how disdainfully ye look upon them! How strange, how very strange![9]

We referred to similar passages in the *Súriy-i-Mulúk* where Bahá'u'lláh warned the kings against betraying the trust of God in their neglect of the poor, but here in the Tablet to Victoria He adds a personal note of His own sadness at the suffering of the masses.

Britain was blessed not only by a stable parliamentary system but also by statesmen who promoted laws of reform and progress, such that over the reach of the 19th century the situation of the masses improved gradually. The names of Disraeli and Gladstone emerge as giants of the late 19th century. What Bismarck achieved in social programmes in Germany in short order, but by force of his own will and largely to preempt the socialists, in Britain was achieved through institutional process and gradual advancement.

As to Victoria, she also distinguished herself by her family life. Her marriage to Albert, a German prince, was famously romantic in an age in which royal marriages were still occasionally used to cement national alliances, leaving sovereigns to seek accompaniment in extramarital affairs. Victoria and Albert, far from being estranged, had nine children. Albert died prematurely, and sadly, this emblematic sovereign of her age spent the last forty years of her life in mourning.

14

The United States

Hearken ye, O Rulers of America and the Presidents of the Republics therein, unto that which the Dove is warbling on the Branch of Eternity: 'There is none other God but Me, the Ever-Abiding, the Forgiving, the All-Bountiful.' Adorn ye the temple of dominion with the ornament of justice and of the fear of God, and its head with the crown of the remembrance of your Lord, the Creator of the heavens. Thus counselleth you He Who is the Dayspring of Names, as bidden by Him Who is the All-Knowing, the All-Wise. The Promised One hath appeared in this glorified Station, whereat all beings, both seen and unseen, have rejoiced. Take ye advantage of the Day of God. Verily, to meet Him is better for you than all that whereon the sun shineth, could ye but know it. O concourse of rulers! Give ear unto that which hath been raised from the Dayspring of Grandeur: 'Verily, there is none other God but Me, the Lord of Utterance, the All-Knowing.' Bind ye the broken with the hands of justice, and crush the oppressor who flourisheth with the rod of the commandments of your Lord, the Ordainer, the All-Wise.[1]

Although the focus of this study is Europe and the Tablets and verses of the *Kitáb-i-Aqdas* that Bahá'u'lláh directed to the monarchs thereof, it is necessary to include the republics of the western hemisphere and especially the United States in these reflections, for several reasons. First, Bahá'u'lláh specifically directed a verse in the *Kitáb-i-Aqdas,* quoted above, to the leaders and presidents of the western hemisphere. Although the Báb had called upon the people of the West to accept His Cause, the verses of the Aqdas are perhaps the most explicit such address to the western hemisphere set down by the Most Great Pen, and its inclusion in the Most Holy Book gives it special significance. The Tablets of the Divine Plan reaffirmed the role to be played by the republics of the Western hemisphere and the United States and Canada in particular. Secondly, the United States was born of Europe and the Enlightenment project. Its founding fathers were admirers of the Enlightenment, many of them as Freemasons. As a product of Europe, of its traditions and of its philosophy, the United States also shares that western civilization upon which Bahá'u'lláh commented. Finally, the young United States was a participant, albeit in much lesser degree, in the events unfolding in Europe at the outset of the 19th century, and its own early history was formed in large part by those distant events.

In fact, the participation of the United States in the Enlightenment project predated the French Revolution, and was an inspiration to the French revolutionaries. Culminating in 1776 in the Declaration of Independence, the principles of 'life, liberty and the pursuit of happiness' were set forth as basic human rights – or natural rights as they were known in Enlightenment vocabulary. Another common formulation could have been 'life, liberty and property', and the right to property was similarly part of the founders' philosophy. In 1789 and beyond, the French would look to the United States as proof that a republican form of government was workable and should be the model to be pursued as France evolved from absolute monarchy to constitutional monarchy to a fully republican State and beyond.

Still, beyond a philosophical relationship, the fate of the nascent United States was intimately intertwined with Europe's and with events there, and especially with the centuries-long competition and warfare between Britain and France. As these two European giants competed in almost continual warfare during the 18th century, North America was one of the foremost battlefields, and the American colonies participated in the Seven Years War that eventually excluded France. Nor did the effects of the war end in 1763 with the peace treaty. The tensions which eventually led to the American War of Independence were born of the efforts of the English Parliament and King George III to impose taxes to cover the debts incurred in the war. France would reappear on the scene when Louis XVI supported the American Revolution in hopes of avenging his defeat by the British. In doing so, Louis bankrupted his government and brought on his own demise. Ironically, both the American Revolution and the French Revolution had their roots in debts incurred in the Anglo-French rivalry.

Later, as the French Revolution unfolded, Americans were sharply divided into pro-French and pro-British camps. George Washington wisely sought to steer a neutral course, but the intensity of emotions surrounding the conflict were reflected in the emerging differences in political philosophy as Adams and Jefferson succeeded Washington. The Federalists favoured a strong central government and tended to admire the accomplishments of Britain and its constitutional monarchy. At the other extreme of the spectrum were the Democratic Republicans (often simply known as Republicans) who stood for more decentralized government and the principles of individual liberty that the French Revolution espoused. Thus the European conflict which contrasted the British and French systems augmented the intensity of the domestic political debate in the young American republic.

As the Napoleonic wars spread across Europe, Bonaparte dreamed of reestablishing the French empire in North America, but his budding aspirations in the western hemisphere were dashed when Haiti, his base of operations, was lost to a slave revolt. Strapped for cash and with little use for a vast and distant wilderness, Napoleon sold off his patrimony on the American continent. In a strange twist of fate, Jefferson – himself a slaveholder – was able to purchase the Louisiana Territory for four cents an acre, thanks to the initiative of Haitian slaves seeking their own freedom. The Napoleonic wars also engendered the War of 1812 which was the first major external conflict of the new republic, when Britain would stop American ships on the high seas to search for deserters from the British navy – a practice that infuriated the Americans and that led to a declaration of war. Ending with a treaty signed in London, the war was a virtual draw but Andrew Jackson's last-minute victory in the battle of New Orleans left the flavour of having beaten the British – a battle that actually occurred after the signing of the peace treaty due to the slow communications of the day.

Thus, the early history of the nascent United States was intimately intertwined with Europe, both philosophically and practically. However, there were essential differences between the experience of Europe and that of the thirteen American colonies that would have long-term effects. Europe was shackled with the medieval social structure of three Estates, with its attendant parasitic class of nobles and a dominant Church, and even Britain with its parliamentary tradition had an ingrained system of class structure. Land in Europe was scarce and a significant proportion was in the hands of nobles and of the Church, while the rural poor lived on the edge between uncertain harvests and heavy taxes. Most European peasants enjoyed minimal mobility, spending their lives within a few miles of where they were born, and having no education whatsoever. These were barriers against which European revolutionaries struggled – barriers that slowed the longed-for social changes.

In contrast to Europe, the colonies had a relatively flat social structure with greater social mobility. Although class differences certainly did exist and created tension in the colonies, these were far less acute than in France, England and the rest of Europe. The American colonies had access to vast unexplored territory west of the Appalachians that were open to those with the initiative to take possession of it, contributing to the social mobility and the potential of the 'self-made man'. Americans by their history had left their homeland, and immigration of more Europeans to America accelerated after the formation of the United States. Mobility – both social and physical – was part of the American spirit.

The Puritan tradition of theology and ethics derived from Calvinism played a prominent role in early American thought, together with the moral philosophers of the Scottish Enlightenment, where non-Anglican intellectual leadership was concentrated in the British Isles. Religious education to assure access to the Bible made basic literacy common in America, especially in New England. America's most traditional universities that would give intellectual mentorship to many of its leaders, Harvard and Yale, were created in the very early years of English colonization for the training of clergy, symptomatic of the influence of Puritan philosophy.

While the American revolutionaries and their European counterparts were inspired by common principles and some of the same Enlightenment thinkers such as Locke and Montesquieu, the Americans had a long tradition of reflection on republican government, with special interest in the Roman Republic – not only with its functioning but in particular with its downfall. What were the causes, they asked, that led to the failure of republican governments? And how could such failures be avoided? Having inherited the parliamentary tradition from Britain that was manifested in their colonial legislatures, the founders of the American republic were avid readers of political theory and careful students of history, seeking to understand government in its applied state. Whereas the French Revolution would be both political and social, the American Revolution was essentially political.

With these differences, America's experiment with republican government had a significantly different course than in the Old Continent. These differences would bear contrasting fruit on each side of the Atlantic in the first half of the 19th century. While on the surface Europe had settled into its more traditional mode after the Congress of Vienna in 1815, in retrospect this period – the Age of Revolution – experienced intense unrest and ferment on the continent that led up to crises at mid-century. In the United States this first half-century presented its own brand of ferment that consolidated many of the tendencies of the American Revolution. Now less dominated by events in Europe, America could turn its attention to its own internal development as the 19th century advanced. This was a particularly complex period in American history that would see cultural patterns consolidated and a transformation in the participation of the 'common man'.

Originally, the founders of the republic, both Federalists and Democratic Republicans, had serious reservations about permitting participation of the masses in the election of their representatives. Both extremes of the political spectrum viewed 'the mob' with suspicion. As such, the founding fathers and their counterparts in the several states built safeguards into their systems that buffered the power of the masses. Many of the same limitations on voting rights in Europe also existed in the United States, for example, property ownership and payment of taxes. Property was assumed to reflect the stake of an individual in society, and those with property were deemed the most appropriate to decide on the fate of the nation.

In its original form the federal government was created by common consent among the states, and the Constitution originally left the determination of the voting franchise to each individual state, so it is difficult to generalize about voting rights. But the reticence to trust the nation to the masses is reflected in the mode of election of the national offices. The case of the presidential election is widely recognized even today as the 'electoral vote' is tallied on election night. The electors – summing to the combined number of senators and representatives – were originally expected to cast independent votes as determined by their own free will and best judgement. This reflected the philosophy of indirect democracy, but even the mechanism to choose the members of the electoral college was left to state legislatures and was not at first the result of direct popular vote. Neither were senators elected by popular vote, but rather state legislatures designated the persons to serve in this capacity – a clause that endured until 1913 with the adoption of the 17th amendment that established direct election of senators. The degree to which the conformation of the federal government was placed in the hands of the states was a critical factor in the conceptualization of the constitution, and indeed, only members of the House of Representatives were directly elected in the original scheme of the federal government.

However, if in Europe universal white male suffrage came about only at mid-century or much later, it evolved early on in the United States. By 1828 most states had eliminated property ownership as a requirement for enfranchisement, and within scarcely a generation of the adoption of the constitution nearly all white males were able to vote. The masses were poised to exercise popular power in the political realm. Andrew Jackson played both a real and a symbolic role in this democratization process. He famously invited the public to attend his inaugural ball, and the White House filled to overflowing with 'the common people', thronging to catch a glimpse of the wartime hero. He was the first president from west of the Appalachians (all previous presidents came from either Virginia or Massachusetts), and represented in his personality, and in his policies, the freewheeling and 'anti-establishment' attitudes of the west. During the 1820s and leading up to the election of Jackson, universal white male suffrage was established under the growing influence of the supporters of Jackson in the several states. Known to history as Jacksonian democracy, this tendency to promote wide participation of the common man in the political process would be a milestone in the empowerment of the masses. Jackson is also remembered for his brutal policy of the removal of Native Americans to lands in the far west, to the extent of disregarding the Supreme Court's decision in favour of the Choctaw tribe, but this policy likewise reflected the reality on the ground as white settlers invaded Native American lands – the dark side of popular power expressed in government policy.

We are fortunate to have an especially insightful account of this period in the work of one ardent proponent of democracy, Alexis de Tocqueville, a young Frenchman who travelled to the United States in 1831. As an educated aristocrat born shortly after the French Revolution, and who was acutely concerned with the political development of France, de Tocqueville believed firmly that democracy was the wave of the future for all countries. His journey to America was ostensibly to study reform of the prison system, but his real intention was to study the American culture and political system as a contribution to improving democracy in France. His observations were published in two volumes in 1835 and 1840 titled *Democracy in America*, a work that has become a classic of political analysis of the period.

De Tocqueville saw democracy in a much more fundamental context than that of the voting franchise. Many of his observations were on a local level, and while he did consider the normal standards of democracy such as freedom of speech and press, he went beyond what we would normally think of as the political sphere. He saw participation in the public realm in all its dimensions as contributing to a democratic attitude and creating the necessary capacities for democracy. For example, he considered the jury system to be a pillar of democracy, as it involves ordinary citizens in the application of law, serving as a school in public participation and broadening their sense of responsibility. He also was extremely concerned with what we call the tyranny of the majority, and he saw freedom of speech limited not by formal legal restrictions, but by the tendency of the majority to ostracize the unconventional thinker. His work carries many reflections on the idiosyncrasies of the American public. He found Americans to be the least interested in philosophy among all 'civilized' peoples, rather drawing their guiding principles from religion. (Contrast this with the French Revolution!) He saw Americans even in that early period as preoccupied with personal economic advancement, which, combined with a characteristic individualism, could threaten to become an overbearing materialism if not moderated by religion. Like subsequent authors and historians, he saw an important role of the frontier in creating this unique mindset.

De Toqueville made extensive comments on associations in America. A brief review of civil society has been presented earlier in this book, mentioning the widespread multiplication of associations in both America and in Europe in the 19th century. While this reached its peak at mid-century around the 1860s, de Tocqueville found it already well developed in the American republic in the 1830s, to the extent that he saw these associations as a cornerstone of democracy. Some associations had explicitly political agendas, while others such as the temperance movement had essentially moral or spiritual ends. In one of his particularly insightful observations he noted how associations with a specific purpose such as temperance could draw together people of very different viewpoints on broad issues, but who could agree on one central, narrow issue. This, he said, was healthy insomuch as it generated communication among people who otherwise would never speak to each other, this being another requisite for democracy. Furthermore, in comparing the United States with France, he saw associations in America as being more action-oriented. If the associational movement in Europe was also taking off, Tocqueville considered it to be more purposeful and advanced in the United States, and a pillar in the exercise of popular participation.

Most significantly, toward the end of his extensive commentary on the American phenomenon, he offers a surprise conclusion. Reflecting on American women, he finds them both worldly wise and virtuous, well-educated in their youth, and subsequently the guardians of domestic virtue in the home where children are educated. At one point he comments that compared to Europe where women would spend their time at the theatre, American women might be more disposed to create their own association for some social cause. He concludes saying that among all the causes contributing to the success of democracy in America, its women were the most important single factor – an amazing conclusion for that period in history.

Nonetheless, while much of his commentary was directed toward the political system and the American psyche, the aspect of American culture that impressed him most profoundly and offended his deepest sense of decency was slavery. The list of horrors associated with this perversion is long. Human beings kidnapped and shipped by the millions in cramped, fetid slave ships, where many died en route. Whippings and chains. Sale in auctions, splitting up families forever. Yet one detail in particular turned his stomach, for many female slaves bore children to their white masters – children who themselves were also slaves and were likewise subject to sale and mistreatment at their master's will.

Slavery was incoherent with everything that a nation founded on liberty stood for – a festering sore that gnawed at the moral fibre of America. At a distance of a hundred and fifty years, it is easy to reduce the issue of slavery to one of moral principle versus immoral practice, but at the time it was far more complex, with added dimensions of constitutionality, property rights, states' rights, economics, historical precedent, political expediency, and – not least of all – racism. Many in America who opposed slavery as a moral offence despaired at finding the means to end it by peaceful legal means. The ferment that had festered for wellnigh four generations and that could have continued much longer finally came to a head in 1861 when open warfare broke out between the federal government and the southern states.

Shoghi Effendi, in citing the future trials of the world that would result in the unification of the entire planet, set the example of the United States whereby national unity was only attained by this bloody war.

> How confident were the assertions made in the days preceding the unification of the states of the North American continent regarding the insuperable barriers that stood in the way of their ultimate federation! Was it not widely and emphatically declared that the conflicting interests, the mutual distrust, the differences of government and habit that divided the states were such as no force, whether spiritual or temporal, could ever hope to harmonize or control? . . . Could anything less than the fire of a civil war with all its violence and vicissitudes

– a war that nearly rent the great American Republic – have welded the states, not only into a Union of independent units, but into a Nation, in spite of all the ethnic differences that characterized its component parts?[2]

Behind this statement is a little publicized dimension of American history, that of its first eighty years in which the preservation of the union was many times in doubt. As the words of Shoghi Effendi suggest, the early years of the United States were decidedly turbulent and marked by divisiveness along fundamental fault lines of political philosophy, economics and culture.

Causes of divisions dated to the earliest days of the Revolutionary War when small states like Delaware and Rhode Island were wary of being overwhelmed by larger states in any political union. In the earliest days of the republic, contrasting economic visions took on a regional tone. Within the administration of George Washington, Alexander Hamilton presented a plan of national development and industrialization backed up by a national banking system, reflecting the commercial perspective of the northeast, while southerner Jefferson visualized an agrarian republic of independent and virtuous yeoman farmers. When in the midst of the Napoleonic wars Jefferson imposed an embargo on trade with the European belligerents – a policy that hit the commercial northeast especially hard – a powerful and radical segment of the Federalist Party, the Essex Junto of Massachusetts, threatened to secede, so tenuous was the commitment to the Union. As the young nation advanced into the 19th century, further regionalism emerged as the lands beyond the Appalachians were settled and new states were admitted to the Union. The frontier states with their agrarian focus often found themselves allied with the southern contingent and against the commercial banking interests of the northeast – opposition that was personified in Andrew Jackson.

Of greater long-term significance, the framers of the constitution had struggled with the balance of power between the states and the central government. Distrust of authority was the inheritance of the colonial period's experience with the British crown. To moderate the power of the central government, a system of checks and balances was built into the design of the executive, legislative and judicial branches – whereby no individual branch could attain to dictatorial power that would threaten the independence of the states. In the minds of many, the states were viewed as bulwarks of liberty against an imperious federal government. Even after the new republic was launched under the constitution, debates around the distribution of power between states and the federal government continued. Contrasting philosophies soon consolidated into the Federalist Party favouring strong central government, and the Democratic Republican Party emphasizing the sovereignty and relative independence of states. No less a figure than Thomas Jefferson argued that states had the right to nullify acts of the federal government – a stance that surfaced again in South Carolina in the 1830s. So impassioned was the issue of states' rights in this period that matters that today we take for granted were the cause of heated debate. For example, national projects of public works such as road building were often opposed by the southern states and their allies as placing excessive power in the hands of the federal government.

Still, the underlying issue that was implicit in almost every debate about states' rights was that of slavery. These were two sides of the same coin, like theory and practice. If 'states' rights' was the expressed principle, slavery was its operational reality. Slavery had cast a shadow over the national debate since the Constitutional Convention. Under the necessity to assure the support of the southern states in the ratification of the constitution, no direct mention of slavery was made there (nor earlier in the Declaration of Independence), outside of eliminating the importation of slaves after 1808. Furthermore, in the constitution a concession to the south permitted counting three-fifths of slaves as population for the calculation of representation in Congress and therefore in the electoral college. This was an especially pernicious clause, much hated by the opponents of slavery, whereby the power of the oppressors was augmented by the greater numbers of the oppressed, thereby perpetuating the agony of the slaves. Historians calculate that this added political weight gave the south a significant advantage and tipped the scales of more than one election in the first eight decades of the United States. Indeed, ten presidents prior to Abraham Lincoln had been slave owners, and only five were not.

For the first half of the century, managing the issue of slavery would be so central to maintaining the Union that the admission of new states was regulated by the Missouri compromise of 1820, whereby Missouri was admitted as slave and Maine as free. Subsequent entry of new states would be negotiated with painstaking care and great difficulty. Until 1861 the nation would walk a tightrope, held captive by the threat of breakup over the issue of slavery, with many northern politicians hesitant to confront the south and put the Union at risk. Stephen Douglas, senator from Illinois and long-term nemesis of Lincoln, had defended the rights of new territories and states to declare for slavery under the banner of popular sovereignty. In Congress, John Quincy Adams deserves our respect as the most strident and principled voice raised consistently against the tyranny of enslavement. Slavery was the biggest single issue that stood between the fundamental principle of the nation that 'all men are created equal', and its fulfilment in the empowerment of the masses.

Enter upon the scene Abraham Lincoln – self-educated, insightful, highly principled, an iconic figure that emerged from the agricultural America that Jefferson had envisioned. Born in the slave state of Kentucky and married to another native Kentuckian, his earliest years passed in that border zone between the slave and the free, at one time travelling down the Mississippi to New Orleans where he would have witnessed slave labour in its home territory. Never reconciled to slavery, he pondered the issue for many years, thoughtfully considering the position of southerners in defending the economic system that they had constructed. In his formative years he was not a radical abolitionist, and like many other northerners he viewed the abolitionist movement as endangering the very existence of the Union. But in his famous speech declaring that 'a house divided against itself cannot stand', he also saw that resolution of the issue was necessary and inevitable, by one means or another. The issue was not *if* but *how* to bring slavery to an end. Eventually it would be South Carolina that would push the question by seceding in December 1860 and in attacking Fort Sumter in April of the following year.

Abraham Lincoln could also see slavery in the context of other essential issues in the mid-1800s, even as Europe continued to struggle with its internal matters of form of government. In his Gettysburg Address, delivered in November 1863 – seven months after Bahá'u'lláh's Riḍván Declaration – he reminded his audience of its Enlightenment principles, that the United States was a 'nation conceived in liberty and dedicated to the proposition that all men are created equal'. He refers to the 'great civil war' as 'testing whether that nation or any nation, so conceived and so dedicated, can long endure'. To a mind as sharp as Lincoln's, it would not have escaped him that in the recent history of Europe, several governments 'so conceived and so dedicated' had indeed not endured more than a few years or even a few months, either due to violent reactionary opposition or to fractious internal politics. Is Lincoln asking if the enemies of liberty and equality are destined to arise in the defence of old privileges? Or is he asking, as some founding fathers did, if disorder and violence were inherent in a system with liberty and equality at its foundation, and were destined to emerge at critical moments of crisis? Does liberty carry within it the seeds of its own destruction? If society's multiple components exercise liberty and are not suppressed by a strong central authority, are they mature enough to resolve their crises without resorting to violence? The question of slavery was just such a crisis that violated those sacrosanct founding principles and that was destined to test the mettle of the nation.

Lincoln saw slavery both as a moral issue and as a case of a more generic issue of social relations and governance. In this sense, Stephen Douglas had argued in essence that the majority in a state had the right to decide to enslave a minority, and Lincoln had seen and heard southerners defend slavery as an institution supported by the principles of private property and the liberty inherent in states' rights under the constitution. 'We all declare for Liberty; but in using the same word we do not all mean the same thing,' mused Lincoln in a speech in 1864. 'With some the word liberty may mean for each man to do as he pleased with himself, and the product of his labour; while with others the same word may mean for some men to do as they please with other men, and the product of other men's labour.'[3] Lincoln recognized that governments based on liberty and equality face special challenges.

We do not know everything that was on Lincoln's mind when he penned those words in the Gettysburg Address about nations 'conceived in liberty', but the question that he posed was equally relevant for Europe. It is perhaps not a coincidence that Lincoln hit two of the three buttons of the French Revolution: liberty and equality. Lincoln hoped that the response to his question about the durability of a nation 'conceived in liberty' would be 'yes'. In contrast, the answer that the Congress of Vienna had given some fifty years earlier in 1815, was a resounding 'NO'. The United States, to remain united, would sacrifice nearly three-quarters of a million lives to find the answer.

The Gettysburg Address suggests deep reflections about human society. How can a society find a healthy balance between liberty and equality on the one hand, and on the other the necessary authority of institutions that organize, guide and coordinate the component parts of society – all with due regard for moral principles? This issue came to the forefront violently in the French Revolution and persistently throughout Europe in the 19th century as its nations struggled through a period of transition from the old order to the modern world. More than a century after Lincoln's address, the Universal House of Justice would reflect on the role of liberty within a stable social structure, as considered in Chapter 5 of this book.

The end of slavery with the 13th amendment in 1865 was a milestone in American history, resolving after nearly a century an essential contradiction in the very soul of the nation. It terminated the forced and inhumane servitude of some three million African Americans – a segment of the masses that would initiate its road to empowerment. The emancipation of the slaves culminated that bloody war of rebellion that played out as Bahá'u'lláh announced His Divine Mission in the Garden of Riḍván. The war ended as the Faith of God dealt with the rebellion of Mirza Yaḥyá in Adrianople – a test of rebellion that resolved its own unique character more clearly. Fifty years later 'Abdu'l-Bahá would comment on the wider significance of the end of slavery in the United States:

The great proclamation of liberty and emancipation from slavery was made upon this continent. A long bloody war was fought by white men for the sake of coloured people. These white men forfeited their possessions and sacrificed their lives by thousands in order that coloured men might be freed from bondage. The coloured population of the United States of America are possibly not fully informed of the wide-reaching effect of this freedom and emancipation upon their coloured brethren in Asia and Africa where even more terrible conditions of slavery existed. Influenced and impelled by the example of the United States, the European powers proclaimed universal liberty to the coloured race and slavery ceased to exist.[4]

In summary, the United States enjoyed a unique history, founded by thoughtful, erudite and virtuous men; dedicated to noble principles of government that would serve the goals of 'life, liberty and the pursuit of happiness'; with a government 'of the people, by the people, for the people' with ample opportunity for the masses of humanity for self-improvement, self-determination, and participation in public administration. One could well imagine that such a history that permitted the masses to emerge so vigorously would give that nation a head start on the road to spiritual self-determination as well, once the issue of slavery was resolved. However, the Civil War cost the young nation even more than countless lives and treasure. The generation that lived through that holocaust was scarred for life, having witnessed the butchery in what some consider to be the world's first manifestation of industrialized warfare. Lincoln's dictum in his second inaugural address as the war drew to a close, of acting 'with malice toward none, with charity toward all' gave way to bitter infighting around policies to reincorporate the southern states into the Union, in the end leaving African Americans to face ingrained prejudice and discrimination for generations to come. The demands that the war had placed for an invigorated productive capacity opened the door on a new expression of the Industrial Revolution, marked by the so-called robber barons in the budding industries of steel, railroads, oil and others. Political corruption waxed unconstrained. Materialism ruled. The relative innocence and virtue of the frontier yeoman farmer ceded to the crass reality of the modern industrial State.

The American Civil War and its immediate consequences occurred within those two fateful decades at mid-century that saw the consolidation of nation States in Italy and Germany, the retreat of the papacy, and the rise and eventually the fall of Napoleon III. The revelation of the *Kitáb-i-Aqdas* in 1873 came at the end of these years of change in Europe and the United States. It closed the series of epistles and proclamations that the Lord of the Age directed to the temporal leaders of mankind. Having insistently called upon the kings and presidents collectively to establish justice in His first major epistle to world leaders, the *Súriy-i-Mulúk*, His address to the presidents of the West repeated this urgent command:

> Adorn ye the temple of dominion with the ornament of justice and of the fear of God, and its head with the crown of the remembrance of your Lord, the Creator of the heavens... Give ear unto that which hath been raised from the Dayspring of Grandeur: 'Verily, there is none other God but Me, the Lord of Utterance, the All-Knowing.' Bind ye the broken with the hands of justice, and crush the oppressor who flourisheth with the rod of the commandments of your Lord, the Ordainer, the All-Wise.[5]

In 1938 Shoghi Effendi directed his own epistle, now known as *The Advent of Divine Justice*, to the Bahá'ís of the United States and Canada, explaining the role of those countries in the establishment of the Administrative Order, key instrument of divine justice, and the motive for which this role had been bestowed upon North America. He compared the United States to darkest Persia where God chose to kindle the first light of the nascent faith, whereby its light would shine brighter through contrast. Citing 'those virtues and qualities [of the American nation] of high intelligence, of youthfulness, of unbounded initiative, and enterprise which the nation as a whole so conspicuously displays' – qualities that its unique history most certainly served to engender – he nonetheless stated that it is not

> for some mysterious purpose or by any reason of inherent excellence or special merit Bahá'u'lláh has chosen to confer upon their country and people so great and lasting a distinction. It is precisely by reason of the patent evils which, notwithstanding its other admittedly great characteristics and achievements, an excessive and binding materialism has unfortunately engendered within it that the Author of their Faith and the Centre of His Covenant have singled it out to become the standard-bearer of the New World Order envisaged in their writings.[6]

Indeed, the United States did not escape that judgement of Bahá'u'lláh that 'the peoples of the West' have pursued 'that which is vain and trivial'.[7] However, it is precisely among a people 'immersed in a sea of materialism, a prey to one of the most virulent and long-standing forms of racial prejudice, and notorious for its political corruption, lawlessness and laxity in moral standards' that God will raise up 'men and women who, as time goes by, will increasingly exemplify those essential virtues of self-renunciation, of moral rectitude, of chastity, of indiscriminating fellowship, of holy discipline, and of spiritual insight . . .'[8] However far and however rapidly the population of the United States had progressed along the path of self-determination of the masses in its first decades, it would fall prey to its own vices. The residual effects of the age of slavery – racial prejudice, 'the most vital and challenging issue confronting the Bahá'í community'⁹ – would plague the nation. Materialism, the roots of which Alexis de Tocqueville had detected a generation before, took on new proportions in the aftermath of the Civil War. Industrialization would consume its attention. Americans would have other obstacles to overcome in their designated path of service to the Lord of the Age.

15

The Great War

The outbreak of World War I in midsummer 1914 caught many by surprise, and none took it seriously at the outset. Both the Germans and the French thought that they would be victorious in a matter of months. Much to the contrary, a fratricidal struggle awaited them that would leave more than ten million dead and countless more injured, maimed, disfigured or deranged by toxic gases. Life in the trenches was like no previous experience of warfare, with men constrained for months on end in mud-filled labyrinths, freezing cold, and surrounded by cadavers and the rats that devoured them. So unequalled in human memory was the carnage that in its aftermath it was called the war to end all wars. No one, it was thought, would ever again dream of war after such an experience.

The decades immediately preceding the war had been relatively uneventful in the Western world in the sense of wars and international tensions. Some positive signs could be noted. An international peace movement had taken root and flourished across Europe and the United States, the proponents of which assured each other of the impossibility of war. The movement for women's rights was gaining momentum among various groups, though with varying degrees of forcefulness in demanding equal rights. However, in the larger picture the end of the century – the *fin de siècle* – was a period in which the West coasted along the path set at mid-century. Industrialization gathered momentum and the accompanying materialism gained respectability as the standard of the good life. In the United States a generation scarred by the Civil War soon became even more disillusioned by political corruption that paralleled the unbridled advance of robber barons. The industrial working class responded with strikes that were often repressed violently. In Europe liberal democracy bumped along. Bismarck kept German society on a short leash, in Italy the government receded into a mode of arbitrator among conflicting social forces, Russia reverted to czarist absolutism, while one French politician commented symptomatically that a republican form of government was the one that divided France the least. With a failing vision of mission and principle, with society sinking ever further into sterile materialism, and having neglected the clarion call of Bahá'u'lláh in His proclamation to the crowned heads and peoples, Europe drifted along the path of national competition and militarism.

No one could foresee the coming apocalypse, much less the intensity of the suffering – except for 'Abdu'l-Bahá. He struggled in His own way to warn against the impending destruction. The last months of His journey through the West were spent in the heart of Europe. It was the only winter that He spent in the north in the three years of travel, and in spite of His own ill health and hardship He made this one last heroic effort to awaken the victims to the impending danger, and to accompany however briefly those stalwart Bahá'ís who would experience the disaster first hand. And when it came, He suffered at a distance, voicing His distress with words such as these:

O God, my God! Thou seest how black darkness is enshrouding all regions, how all countries are burning with the flame of dissension, and the fire of war and carnage is blazing throughout the East and the West. Blood is flowing, corpses bestrew the ground, and severed heads are fallen on the dust of the battlefield.

O Lord! Have pity on these ignorant ones, and look upon them with the eye of forgiveness and pardon. Extinguish this fire, so that these dense clouds which obscure the horizon may be scattered, the Sun of Reality shine forth with the rays of conciliation, this intense gloom be dispelled and the resplendent light of peace shed its radiance upon all countries.[1]

What went wrong?

In a century that held so much promise, that inaugurated the age of maturity, that was marked by exuberant optimism, that set Europe on the path of liberal thought and participatory democracy, that spread public education and saw legislation of social protection – how could this happen? In the simplest of terms, when the crowned heads ignored the summons of Bahá'u'lláh they condemned themselves and their subjects to the consequences. Early in His proclamation He called upon the kings to reduce their armaments, and when they rejected the Most Great Peace, He urged them to pursue the Lesser Peace. But not even the Lesser Peace was to be their lot: 'Bahá'u'lláh's Tablets to the kings and rulers of the world [are] a propitious reminder of the dire consequences of ignoring His warnings against injustice, tyranny and corruption.'[2]

'Abdu'l-Bahá could foresee the impending disaster and alluded to its outbreak while travelling in Europe and the United States: 'We are on the eve of the Battle of Armageddon referred to in the sixteenth chapter of Revelation. The time is two years hence, when only a spark will set aflame the whole of Europe.'[3] He could also see the limitations of Europe burdened down with the baggage of centuries-old conflict when He said that the United States was better positioned to establish universal peace:

I find the United States of America an exceedingly progressive nation . . .Therefore it is my hope that inasmuch as the standard of international peace must be upraised it may be upraised upon this continent . . . If other nations should attempt to do this the motive will be misunderstood. For instance, if Great Britain should declare for international peace it will be said that it has been done to insure the safety of her colonies. If France should hoist the standard other nations will declare some hidden diplomatic policy underlies the action; Russia would be suspected of national designs if the first step were taken by that people, and so on with all the European and eastern governments.[4]

His was a daunting mission, assumed with unswerving commitment and unmoved by the overwhelming odds that argued against the success of His message of peace.

Uncompromising in defence of the truth, yet infinitely gentle in manner, He brought the universal divine principles to bear on the exigencies of the age. To all without distinction – officials, scientists, workers, children, parents, exiles, activists, clerics, sceptics – He imparted love, wisdom, comfort, whatever the particular need. While elevating their souls, He challenged their assumptions, reoriented their perspectives, expanded their consciousness, and focused their energies.[5]

Many of the talks that 'Abdu'l-Bahá gave throughout His three-year journey in the West can be viewed in the light of commentaries on the 19th century, as subtle admonishments on the shortcomings of society and its leaders. A number of topics were especially pertinent to the impending disaster, or were cited repeatedly as critical issues of a just society. At a fundamental level, the materialist philosophy – confident of explaining all existence through natural law and penetrating into the lifestyle of entire populations – was at the heart of the crisis, contributing to and paralleled by a decline in the fortunes of religion. When 'Abdu'l-Bahá arrived in the United States, in His first few days there He commented several times on His experience in Europe:

> A few days ago I arrived in New York . . . On a former trip I travelled to Europe, visiting Paris and London. Paris is most beautiful in outward appearance . . . I found the people of that city submerged and drowning in a sea of materialism. Their conversations and discussions were limited to natural and physical phenomena, without mention of God. I was greatly astonished. Most of the scholars, professors and learned men proved to be materialists.[6]

> During my visit to London and Paris last year I had many talks with the materialistic philosophers of Europe. The basis of all their conclusions is that the acquisition of knowledge of phenomena is according to a fixed, invariable law – a law mathematically exact in its operation through the senses.[7]

The term 'materialism' is used in two different ways. In common usage materialism refers to consumerism and the pursuit of material goods. On the other hand, in the quotations above 'Abdu'l-Bahá refers to philosophical materialism which is the belief system that posits that all reality has its origins in material or physical reality. Atheism is an expression of materialism. Thomas Hobbes was an early materialist who went head to head with Descartes in the 17th century, but philosophical materialism gained ground throughout the Enlightenment as science appeared to explain natural phenomena without the need of religion. Materialism would extend its influence far beyond the confines of Europe, as Bahá'u'lláh comments: 'When the eyes of the people of the East were captivated by the arts and wonders of the West, they roved distraught in the wilderness of material causes, oblivious of the One Who is the Causer of Causes, and the Sustainer thereof . . .'[8]

Many Enlightenment thinkers viewed religion with suspicion as essentially superstitious and contrary to logic. When in Paris, at the very heart of much Enlightenment thought, 'Abdu'l-Bahá stated: 'There is no contradiction between true religion and science. When a religion is opposed to science it becomes mere superstition: that which is contrary to knowledge is ignorance.'[9] He alluded to the commonly held Enlightenment dichotomy when He said:

> We are familiar with the phrases "Light and Darkness", "Religion and Science". But the religion which does not walk hand in hand with science is itself in the darkness of superstition and ignorance . . . When religion, shorn of its superstitions, traditions, and unintelligent dogmas, shows its conformity with science, then will there be a great unifying, cleansing force in the world which will sweep before it all wars, disagreements, discords and struggles – and then will mankind be united in the power of the Love of God.[10]

Thus, in one brief talk, 'Abdu'l-Bahá debunked one of the central debates of the Enlightenment as a non-issue and a false dichotomy. It is no coincidence that these comments were made in Paris where He found so much stifling materialism among the intellectual leaders of society, and where Enlightenment thought had flowered. Neither should we underestimate the degree to which His comments flew in the face of then-current dogma.

Far from a benign intellectual movement that condescendingly permitted religion to function in its private and personal realm, materialism led to the conclusion that, like the movement of the planets, society was also governed by the unbending laws of nature and the physical world. Modern science had been discovering the laws of nature since the time of Galileo and Isaac Newton but this tendency gathered momentum in subsequent years and was extended to the social sciences. Schools of thought were emerging that claimed to have discovered immutable laws, spawning an attitude of hubris on the part of those who believed themselves to be uniquely in possession of truth. Charles Darwin discovered the laws of evolution which were quickly misappropriated as social Darwinism, assuming that the principles of the physical origin of species applied equally to human society, and justifying the abuse of the weak and powerless. The Industrial Revolution did not require philosophical materialism to have come into being, but its dark side was facilitated by social Darwinism and its own immutable laws of social relations. Building on the laws of economics of Adam Smith, David Ricardo added arguments as to why the poor are destined to remain poor. Such laws led to the conclusion that government was powerless to influence social welfare and should follow the policy of *laissez faire*. The master of immutable social laws was Karl Marx who with Friedrich Engels claimed to have found the laws of history and social evolution in so-called 'scientific materialism'. The means of production defined social classes and drove the processes of history, and class conflict would produce the next higher level of society. These immutable laws would become mental straitjackets for those who used them to arm revolutions, formulate social structures, spread persecution, or rationalize economic injustice.

Another point that 'Abdu'l-Bahá emphasized repeatedly and in no uncertain terms was the issue of equal rights for women, both as an issue of social justice and as a requisite for the progress of society as a whole. Time and again He posed the issue of equality in the context of gender equity:

> To accept and observe a distinction which God has not intended in creation is ignorance and superstition. The fact which is to be considered, however, is that woman, having formerly been deprived, must now be allowed equal opportunities with man for education and training. There must be no difference in their education. Until the reality of equality between man and woman is fully established and attained, the highest social development of mankind is not possible . . . The only remedy is education, opportunity; for equality means equal qualification . . . And let it be known once more that until woman and man recognize and realize equality, social and political progress here or anywhere will not be possible.[11]

It is telling that in spite of the fact that equality was a core value of the Enlightenment and of the French Revolution, the inferior status of women was and continues to be a shortcoming of societies the world around. This was typified by the fact that in no country of the world were women permitted to vote until the 20th century, although obtaining the franchise is only a milestone and not a solution. Gender equality remains a challenge to attaining integral social development.

'Abdu'l-Bahá made especially pointed and forceful comments on the injustice of the economic system and the need for reform. Economic exploitation that developed under the Industrial Revolution had been bolstered and justified by old class prejudices, by capitalism that glorified the creation of wealth, and by social Darwinism. That perverse dynamic of action and reaction that dominated the 19th century characterized much of labour relations, as workers protested the model of factory production and the hideous working and living conditions of industrial centres, and as governments suppressed protests violently. If the ideals of the French Revolution were attractive to middle and working classes alike, the Industrial Revolution was the more immediate influence on the masses and created an ugly environment both physically and socially that would dominate the daily lives and eventually the social outlook of the working classes. By the time 'Abdu'l-Bahá spoke during His extensive travels in the West, the Industrial Revolution was far beyond the stage of revolution and was the mainspring of the western economies. The masses had begun to experience the benefits of trickledown economics, and their lot was gradually improving. Still, 'Abdu'l-Bahá could speak in the following terms to His American audience: 'Between 1860 and 1865 you did a wonderful thing; you abolished chattel slavery; but today you must do a much more wonderful thing: you must abolish industrial slavery.'[12]

In recent years restive workers had joined the socialist movement that had grown powerful over previous decades, and at the end of the 19th century the rural sector was likewise stirring with discontent in some countries. Social tensions were coming to a head and set the context for some of the most far-reaching and socially significant comments of 'Abdu'l-Bahá: 'One must therefore enact such laws and regulations as will moderate the excessive fortunes of the few and meet the basic needs of the myriad millions of the poor, that a degree of moderation may be achieved.'[13] In Boston He cited the overarching spiritual implications of the issue for society:

The Bahá'í Cause covers all economic and social questions under the heading and ruling of its laws. The essence of the Bahá'í spirit is that, in order to establish a better social order and economic condition, there must be allegiance to the laws and principles of government. Under the laws which are to govern the world, the socialists may justly demand human rights but without resort to force and violence . . . Today the method of demand is the strike and resort to force, which is manifestly wrong and destructive of human foundations. Rightful privilege and demand must be set forth in laws and regulations.

While thousands are considering these questions, we have more essential purposes. The fundamentals of the whole economic condition are divine in nature and are associated with the world of the heart and spirit. This is fully explained in the Bahá'í teaching, and without knowledge of its principles no improvement in the economic state can be realized.[14]

In an especially lengthy discourse to the socialists in Montreal, 'Abdu'l-Bahá gave a wide-ranging address on social equity both in rural communities and in an industrial society. He promoted then-novel ideas of profit sharing among workers and factory owners.

Also, every factory that has ten thousand shares will give two thousand shares of these ten thousand to its employees and will write the shares in their names, so that they may have them, and the rest will belong to the capitalists. Then at the end of the month or year whatever they may earn after the expenses and wages are paid, according to the number of shares, should be divided among both.[15]

These were very practical solutions to address the abuses of the Industrial Revolution and the industrial culture that developed in the 19th century, insisting on a balanced approach to resolving the economic problem. 'Abdu'l-Bahá stated that laws should be structured 'so that neither the capitalist suffer from enormous losses nor the labourers become needy'.[16] However, by the time any degree of relief had come to the masses at the turn of the century, the resentments of the working classes had been consolidated. The popular classes found a voice in socialism, and increasingly in Marxism – movements that were fuelled by principles that had animated the French Revolution, but that took a new form dictated by the Industrial Revolution and grounded in socialist economic theory. And if the French Revolution had initiated in relative calm but degraded into barbarism, Marxism took violence as its point of departure. We saw how class tensions at mid-century wracked France after the fall of Napoleon III, how a similar situation occurred in Germany at the end of World War I, and how Lenin and Stalin would authorize mass murder in the name of socialist revolution. These memories overshadow lesser but similar events that gripped several other countries of Europe in the aftermath of the Great War, such that 'Abdu'l-Bahá foresaw the growth of the influence of the left. Without an equitable solution, He warned ominously that 'the labour problem will lead to much destruction, especially in Europe. Terrible things will take place.'[17]

Furthermore, in *The Secret of Divine Civilization*, 'Abdu'l-Bahá makes a brief statement about the western model of progress that is especially pertinent both for its content and for its timing. Written as an open letter to the Iranians, 'Abdu'l-Bahá analyzes both the benefits of western civilization and its shortcomings. The House of Justice notes the far-reaching implications of this letter, observing, 'What the letter prophetically laid out was the challenge of modernity.'

The meaning of modernity and the features of that rising flood of cultural revolution were explicitly identified in the Master's message: constitutional and democratic government, the rule of law, universal education, the protection of human rights, economic development, religious tolerance, the promotion of useful sciences and technologies and programmes of public welfare. In praising the achievements of what He termed this 'temporal and material apparatus of civilization', the Master made it clear that He was not proposing simply a credulous imitation of the West. On the contrary. In uncompromising language, He portrayed European society as drowning 'in the sea of passion and desire', trapped in a materialistic perception of reality that could bring in its wake nothing but disillusionment: 'Be just: can this nominal civilization, unsupported by a genuine civilization of character, bring about the peace and well-being of the people or win the good pleasure of God? Does it not, rather, connote the destruction of man's estate and pull down the pillars of happiness and peace?'[18]

Furthermore, *The Secret of Divine Civilization* takes on even greater significance considering the period in which 'Abdu'l-Bahá made this analysis. He was writing in 1875 soon after the most dramatic changes in European society had taken place. The popular uprisings of 1848 that revealed the frustrations and unfulfilled expectations of the French Revolution had come and gone, and popular power was seeking wider expression either in political processes or in even more violent revolution. In the 1860s Bahá'u'lláh had written His epistles to the kings, and in 1870 Napoleon III had fallen and the Pope had lost the last vestiges of his temporal power over the city of Rome. In 1873, only two years before 'Abdu'l-Bahá's commentary, Bahá'u'lláh had revealed the *Kitáb-i-Aqdas* with its warnings and final judgements on the crowned heads of Europe. By 1875 Bismarck was firmly in control in Germany and was setting the pace for the rest of the continent. As such, when 'Abdu'l-Bahá wrote His analysis, the violent upheavals that had changed the face of Europe had passed, Europe was entering on a period of relative calm, and the directions for the next thirty years were established and were being consolidated. Thus He was able to comment on the respective processes, and the results or failings of which could then be discerned.

As noted above, 'Abdu'l-Bahá cites those advances of western civilization which He viewed as potentially beneficial to the Iranian nation.

> Would the extension of education, the development of useful arts and sciences, the promotion of industry and technology, be harmful things? . . . Would the setting up of just legislation, in accord with the Divine laws which guarantee the happiness of society and protect the rights of all mankind and are an impregnable proof against assault – would such laws, insuring the integrity of the members of society and their equality before the law, inhibit their prosperity and success?
>
> Would it spell perdition for our subjects if the provincial and district governors were relieved of their present absolute authority, whereby they function exactly as they please, and were instead limited to equity and truth . . .?[19]

Interestingly, 'Abdu'l-Bahá refers to a number of issues that were central to the Enlightenment project, including education, science, the happiness of society, equitable government, and equality before the law. His comments also align with the Industrial Revolution in His call for 'the promotion of industry and technology'. These were the social realities of the previous hundred years in Great Britain and the European continent, with which Europe had struggled at the threshold of the modern age. After citing the technological and social advances of the West, 'Abdu'l-Bahá notes that some of His readers might question the success of the western model in creating a just and prosperous society. If this model has not been fully successful, He says, this is due principally to two causes: the corruption of its leaders, and the lack of education and consensus among the masses.

Should anyone object that the above-mentioned reforms have never yet been fully effected, he should consider the matter impartially and know that these deficiencies have resulted from the total absence of a unified public opinion, and the lack of zeal and resolve and devotion in the country's leaders. It is obvious that not until the people are educated, not until public opinion is rightly focused, not until government officials, even minor ones, are free from even the least remnant of corruption, can the country be properly administered.[20]

As applied to the West and to the corruption of its leaders, Bahá'u'lláh's own Tablets are sufficient testimony. There He admonishes the kings for their pursuit of luxury, their pride, their aggressive ambition, and their disregard for their subjects. Having urged them repeatedly in the *Súriy-i-Mulúk* to rule with justice, He reminded them that their peoples were the trust that God had placed in their hands. Subsequently in His judgement of them, He implies that they had betrayed their trust. Referring to one of the pillars of the liberal experiment, 'Abdu'l-Bahá extends this critique of the country's leaders, in particular to the elected representatives who serve in legislative bodies.

First, the elected members must be righteous, God-fearing, high-minded, incorruptible. Second, they must be fully cognizant, in every particular, of the laws of God, informed as to the highest principles of law, versed in the rules which govern the management of internal affairs and the conduct of foreign relations, skilled in the useful arts of civilization, and content with their lawful emoluments.[21]

It is unquestionable that the object in establishing parliaments is to bring about justice and righteousness, but everything hinges on the efforts of the elected representatives. If their intention is sincere, desirable results and unforeseen improvements will be forthcoming; if not, it is certain that the whole thing will be meaningless, the country will come to a standstill and public affairs will continuously deteriorate.[22]

Most countries in the West had, by the turn of the century, experimented with some form of representative government including a legislative branch. However, years later 'Abdu'l-Bahá would comment on the sad state of parliamentary democracy in His own time.

In France I was present at a session of the senate, but the experience was not impressive. Parliamentary procedure should have for its object the attainment of the light of truth upon questions presented and not furnish a battleground for opposition and self-opinion. Antagonism and contradiction are unfortunate and always destructive to truth. In the parliamentary meeting mentioned, altercation and useless quibbling were frequent; the result, mostly confusion and turmoil; even in one instance a physical encounter took place between two members. It was not consultation but comedy.[23]

The issue of the lack of education of the masses merits even deeper reflection. 'Abdu'l-Bahá notes:

Close investigation will show that the primary cause of oppression and injustice, of unrighteousness, irregularity and disorder, is the people's lack of religious faith and the fact that they are uneducated . . . At present, however, because of their inadequate schooling, most of the population lack even the vocabulary to explain what they want.[24]

The steady progress of the Bahá'í Faith since the days of

Bahá'u'lláh and 'Abdu'l-Bahá, and especially in the last two decades, has permitted a vision to emerge, however embryonically, of what this education entails. This is education in a much broader sense, a sense that is reflected in the goal of the Bahá'í Faith to raise up a new race of men. Education is both a right and a necessary requirement to fulfil each one's role in society, as the Universal House of Justice has written: 'Access to knowledge is the right of every human being, and participation in its generation, application and diffusion a responsibility that all must shoulder in the great enterprise of building a prosperous world civilization . . .'[25] This is a right that the Enlightenment thinkers might well have considered a 'natural right', being born of that innate capacity in man's inner being to learn, to imagine, to analyze, to create.

True education is closely allied with the concept of spiritual empowerment of the individual for a life of service within a social context, within which the individual forms a part of a new structure of society, with new relations between individuals and institutions. It implies a systematic process to prepare each one as a worthy participant, ready to play his or her part in that tripartite society composed of the individual, the institutions, and the community, as defined by the Universal House of Justice. It posits a new understanding of a mode of life in which worship and service are balanced in dynamic equilibrium. It is an education that unfolds in a social context, but that initiates at the most fundamental level of the human soul, as we will explore in the next chapter.

16

Identity and Social Transformation

The 19th century saw transformations on virtually every front of human endeavour, with changing concepts about society and the way people relate to each other, about governance structures, and about self-understanding of entire populations. In the mid-20th century, as World War II was raging in Europe, Shoghi Effendi identified three ideologies that contributed to these transformations, that had displaced religion in the hearts of men, and that he referred to as 'three false gods':

> The chief idols in the desecrated temple of mankind are none other than the triple gods of Nationalism, Racialism and Communism, at whose altars governments and peoples, whether democratic or totalitarian, at peace or at war, of the East or of the West, Christian or Islamic, are, in various forms and in different degrees, now worshipping.[1]

These false ideologies had captured the imagination of governments and entire peoples – three 'war-engendering, world-convulsing doctrines' propagated by 'the politicians and the worldly-wise, the so-called sages of the age' who in their new false religions had sacrificed 'the flesh and blood of the slaughtered multitudes'.[2] These doctrines were among what the Universal House of Justice would categorize in a later age as 'spiritually bankrupt and moribund ways of an old social order that so often seeks to harness human energy through domination, through greed, through guilt or through manipulation'.[3] Shoghi Effendi wrote his critique of these ideologies in 1941, although these false religions had their roots in the 19th century. These are not exhaustive of the ideologies that emerged from that century, but they do reflect some of the most important, and reflect the dynamism of that period that was misdirected toward destructive power.

Nationalism was latent in the ethnic differences inherent in Europe, and had many diverse expressions. It was energized by the French Revolution and the sense of liberty that accompanied that epoch-making event and that generated visions and expectations of nationhood free of external domination. It gathered momentum for the length of the century, contributing to the unification of Germany and Italy, and to the unrest of the Austro-Hungarian Empire. It yielded its bitterest fruits in the Great War when a Serbian nationalist set off the tinderbox and felled the heir to the Hapsburg throne.

Racial prejudice has taken many forms and with different degrees of intensity. Slavery as practised in the United States had a clear racist dimension that was accentuated in defence of that institution as it came under attack from abolitionists. Blacks, it was argued, had no capacity to fend for themselves, and required the 'benevolent' oversight of a white master. However, racialism as an ideology went beyond prejudice and was consolidated in the 19th century through multiple pseudo-intellectual mechanisms such as measurements of physical features to establish the 'scientific' basis of racial superiority. Social Darwinism in turn assumed that the world dominance of the white race had been won through its inherently superior mental capacity and survival ability, which by nature endowed it with rights of dominion. While permeating the attitudes of many countries and cultures, racialism reached its most perverse political expression in the Nazi regime and its fiction of a superior Aryan race, destined to dominate all others.

The most concrete and discrete of the three ideologies was Communism that traces to Marx, while having intellectual roots in earlier socialist thinkers and even in the French Revolution. We have referred briefly to its development from the publication of the *Communist Manifesto* in 1848, its growth in Europe and in Germany in particular, and its thrust upon the international scene with the Bolshevik Revolution and the leadership of Joseph Stalin. Among these three false gods, Communism explicitly rejected religion, consciously and systematically seeking to extirpate it from the life of the masses.

Such were the tragedies that these three false gods brought upon humanity. But an ideology is most powerful when it can move the masses. To capture the imagination of an entire people, each of these isms needed to create an identity to which individuals and communities could subscribe. Each created a mental construct about the essential nature of a human being and the respective community that is derived from that conception. Each of these false gods inspired the masses with their ideologies, convincing them that a particular identity represented their own reality that satisfied their need for self-understanding, and leading them to worship at their altars with catastrophic circumstances.

Nationalism taught that an individual was described and defined essentially by his or her association with a homeland and an ethnic tradition. Individuals and entire populations understood themselves first and foremost as pertaining to a nation – as Croats, as Czechs, as French or English or Scots. Furthermore, that nationalistic identity was often defined in the context of opposition to the other, especially where a dominant power was perceived to have a different national identity, as in the Austro-Hungarian empire. Nationalism was brewing across Europe, fuelling aspirations for independent statehood among ethnicities, and it was nationalist fervour that stoked the fires of war on both sides of the trenches. While 'Abdu'l-Bahá did not criticize directly the intense nationalism that was building since the latter decades of the 19th century, He offered a long-term vision whereby the destructive force of nationalism would be displaced by universal solidarity.

> The oneness of the kingdom of humanity will supplant the banner of conquest, and all communities of the earth will gather under its protection . . . When the people of the future are asked, 'To which nationality do you belong?' the answer will be, 'To the nationality of humanity. I am living under the shadow of Bahá'u'lláh. I am the servant of Bahá'u'lláh. I belong to the army of the Most Great Peace.' The people of the future will not say, 'I belong to the nation of England, France or Persia'; for all of them will be citizens of a universal nationality – the one family, the one country, the one world of humanity – and then these wars, hatreds and strifes will pass away.[4]

Here 'Abdu'l-Bahá alluded to the aspect of identity in nationalism when He said that in the future, man would not say 'I belong to the nation of England, France or Persia'. The 'I belong . . .' in that declaration reflects the identity felt by that hypothetical Englishman or Frenchman or Persian – an identity that in the future would be altered under the influence of Bahá'u'lláh's teachings.

Racism has been a blight on many societies in the modern age, and the self-understanding of one race as superior to others has influenced social relations to the degree of justifying genocides. Racialism built on those racial prejudices and took many forms, but drew much of its energy from emphasizing differences to create a sense of self, defining a higher self by its relation to a perceived lower race. Colonialism was tinged with racialism in many cases. However, Nazi ideology bastardized the Aryan or Indo-European racial classification that was popular in the 19th century and created a fictitious Aryan race to which its adherents imagined themselves to belong – a perverse identity that swept over much of a population and that permitted untold horrors.

As Communism gathered momentum in mid-late century, social class was promoted as the defining criterion of identity. The foundation of social coherence was class, and class consciousness was invoked to ingrain an identity whereby workers would understand themselves first and foremost as members of the proletariat. Millions would sacrifice their own lives and those of others for this ideology under the banner of class conflict, convinced of the justness of their cause and the truth of its theory. Here, too, as with nationalism, the opposition to the other fortified the identity of the proletariat.

These are especially dramatic examples of identities that emerged in the modern world, but they are not the only ones. In particular, the current identity to which many subscribe, consciously or otherwise, is that of a consumer of material goods – an identity that drives much of the current economic system. However, these three false gods emphasized by Shoghi Effendi leave us with at least two conclusions about identity and society. First, they illustrate the power of an identity in eliciting the active support of the masses of a society, albeit for destructive purposes. Secondly, they highlight the need to radically alter the way people understand their own nature, their own purpose, their own existence, and their place in the scheme of things – in short their identity – and on a large scale, if society is to be reformed. Any attempt to transform society must address the issue of identity, and must address it systematically, if it is to be successful.

In Chapter 6 we referred to a passage from the *Tablets of the Divine Plan* in which 'Abdu'l-Bahá spoke of collective centres, and we suggested that in those limited collective centres each enjoyed some identity that united its adherents. 'Abdu'l-Bahá concluded that 'the Collective Center of the Kingdom, embodying the Institutes and Divine Teachings, is the eternal Collective Center',[5] which is to say, the Revelation of Bahá'u'lláh, within which each individual responds to the insistent call to the 'court of the Presence of the Generous One',[6] and finds his or her 'most exalted home beneath the canopy of [God's] majesty and within the precincts of [God's] mercy'.[7] Rather than a foreign dogma that is imposed upon the soul and twists it to a mold, the magnet that draws the soul to the Collective Centre of the Kingdom is a feeling of fulfilment of the purpose of one's existence, a homecoming with one's own reality, a sense of calling and discovery of one's relationship to being. This is the essence of identity.

While countless souls over the ages have discovered this identity in every religion revealed to mankind, the challenge of social transformation is to systematically bring this spiritual realization to the masses of humanity, which is to say, to educate millions upon millions about their true self. True education must find a way to bring this sense of identity to the hungering masses.

In this context we consider the role of the Bahá'í institute process, and the first book of the Ruhi Institute programme, *Reflections on the Life of the Spirit*, widely known as 'Book 1'. An introduction to this book reads:

> The first book in this sequence of courses is largely concerned with the question of identity. What is the real identity of the 'I' in the sentence 'I walk a path of service'? Three aspects of

identity from a Bahá'í perspective are explored in the book: 'The reality of my existence is my soul which passes through this world to acquire the attributes it needs for an eternal and glorious journey towards God. My most cherished moments are those spent in communion with God, for prayer is the daily nourishment that my soul must receive if it is to accomplish its exalted purpose. One of my principal concerns in this life is to study the Writings of Bahá'u'lláh, strive to increase my understanding of His teachings, and learn to apply them to my own daily life and to the life of the community.[8]

Book 1 consists of three units. Unit 1, 'Understanding the Bahá'í Writings', is intended to assist the participant in engaging with the revealed Word, and to put that Word at the centre of one's thoughts as the point of departure in any endeavour.

To read the sacred word is to drink from the ocean of Divine Revelation. It leads to true spiritual understanding and generates forces that are necessary for the progress of the soul. To read the sacred word is to drink from the ocean of Divine Revelation. It leads to true spiritual understanding and generates forces that are necessary for the progress of the soul.[9]

In this unit and others the participant is led progressively through

three levels of comprehension. The first is a basic understanding of the meaning of words and sentences . . . The second level of comprehension is concerned with applying some of the concepts in the quotations in one's daily life. The third level of understanding requires the participants to think about the implications of the quotations for situations with no apparent or immediate connection with the theme of quotation. [10]

Applying the revealed Word to one's life and environment is the first step in developing the analytical capacity of reading reality in light of the Teachings of Bahá'u'lláh and the principles that He inculcated.

Unit 2 on 'Prayer' touches the spiritual fibre of the human being. Communication with God through prayer positions man in relation to his Creator, and thus plants the seed of a conception of man as a spiritual being subservient to his Creator. Its three principal objectives are 'to clarify the concept of prayer itself and to help the participants understand its great importance as one of the laws of this Dispensation'; 'to awaken in participants the desire to "converse with God" and to feel the joy of being near to Him'; and to cultivate 'the attitudes with which prayer should be approached'.[11] This section invites the participant to live and experience that spiritual identity that Book 1 seeks to cultivate.

Unit 3, 'Life after Death'' explores the Bahá'í Writings on the afterlife, and thus looks at the relationship between life in the earthly plane and an eternal spiritual existence.

> Service in this world has to be understood in the fullest context of life which extends beyond our earthly existence and continues forever as our souls progress through the worlds of God. In a process of education in contrast to the mere acquisition of simple skills, it is essential that participants become increasingly conscious of the meaning and significance of what they are doing.[12]

For a soul that is in the earliest days of exploring its relationship to God, this section sets the overarching context of that journey, within which one's identity is anchored.

When viewed as a whole, *Reflections on the Life of the Spirit* has the objective of setting in motion an educational process that starts by cultivating a spiritual identity in each individual, positioning the individual in relation to God and within the context of an eternal process of drawing near to Him. This identity is reinforced throughout the Writings of Bahá'u'lláh, for example in the Hidden Words: 'O Son of Being! With the hands of power I made thee and with the fingers of strength I created thee; and within thee have I placed the essence of my light.'[13] In contrast to those identities that supported nationalism, racialism and Communism that drew their energy from differences with others, and were exclusive of large parts of humanity, a spiritual identity can be shared by all and leads to uplifting and noble results. Furthermore, an identity born of prayer and devotion engenders worship which leads to service – a dynamic that is at the heart of the institute process. Prayer places man in the role of subservience before God, within which servitude is the spontaneous response. Worship and service are 'two essential, inseparable aspects of Bahá'í life'.[14]

Book 1 is the prelude to the following volumes that prepare the participant for specific acts of service such as teaching children's classes, or serving as an animator of a junior youth group. Book 1 is the first step in a path of service – defining the human being as a soul created by God to know Him and to worship Him, and setting that soul on its path of service as the direct consequence of that consciousness. In the words of the Universal House of Justice:

Central to the pattern of action ... is the individual and collective transformation effected through the agency of the Word of God. From the beginning of the sequence of courses, a participant encounters Bahá'u'lláh's Revelation in considering such weighty themes as worship, service to humanity, the life of the soul, and the education of children and youth.[15]

These simple acts of service, each within reach of a person whose purpose is to serve God and man, jointly have the potential to empower communities in a process that is only beginning to express its potential, and that opens new and exciting horizons. When considered at the level of community and its progress through successive levels of increasing complexity, these represent a collective awakening of the masses through spiritual empowerment and an appropriation of their future in ways for which the masses were not otherwise prepared over the past two centuries. This is a historical process that responds to the frustrations and blighted hopes engendered in the 19th century but betrayed by 'the politicians and the worldly-wise'. In the next chapter we will consider this historical perspective and the remarkable process of community building that is unfolding before our eyes.

17

The 21st Century

When Bahá'u'lláh declared that power had been taken away from two ranks of men, kings and ecclesiastics, a vacuum was created that was filled by what was known in pre-revolutionary France as the Third Estate and that emerged with great force in the course of the 19th century. Even in revolutionary France this Estate soon separated into social groups that would eventually be consolidated as the middle class or the so-called bourgeoisie, and the working class – classes that would surge with greater force as the century advanced. While the French Revolution began relatively peacefully, a perverse cycle of action and reaction emerged early on from the medieval structure of society that pitted the Third Estate against the Church and the nobles, with émigrés of the noble class plotting against the Revolution in the exterior, and members of the clergy resisting in the hinterland. The Jacobins rapidly claimed leadership in the name of the masses, and popular power boiled over into violence, generating opposition and repression and putting in motion the Great Terror. As the Terror exhausted revolutionary fervour, the middle class asserted its new-found power, later confirmed by Napoleon Bonaparte.

This was soon followed by the expansion of the Industrial Revolution, already firmly established in Great Britain, which brought the middle class to the forefront of the economy. The middle classes had existed long before, but principally as merchants, artisans or landed gentry. The emergence of industrial production created a relatively new context for an expanding middle class and a new social context of labour relationships. Education came to the working classes in mid-late century, and economic relief came even later. By this time religion was losing its firm hold on the conscience of the masses. The Church offered little support, as Pope Pius IX focused on resisting perceived incursions of the State into its ancient domains, withdrawing in protest into the Vatican until late in the 19th century. Thus, alienated by the economic system, scorned by social elites, manipulated by despots driven by militarism, and finding little support in religion, the working class was increasingly influenced and politicized by the left.

Popular power failed to develop as a moral force that could influence the direction of events, with potential to avert disaster. Women continued to be suppressed, and their options to exercise any effective influence were extremely limited. The development of civil society at mid-century offered the greatest hope for positive action by the masses, although this also became more politicized as the century advanced. If the masses did not contribute to causing the tragedy of the First World War, neither were they able to do anything to prevent it. Those who could have taken effective action to avert war were those kings to whom Bahá'u'lláh directed His Tablets, on whom He laid the responsibility to propagate His Cause, and who neglected His warnings and failed to take the necessary steps to protect and defend the poor. Indeed, the power to support the healthy development of the masses was in the hands of the kings, but these neglected the working classes, distracting them from nobler ends with calls to nationalism. Bahá'u'lláh's warning to 'betray not' the poor can well be viewed in a much more profound sense than a simple call to charity, for the kings denied the poor the means to develop their capacities for their own benefit and that of all society. Moreover, the poor were denied the opportunity to know their very Saviour, for 'what "oppression" is more grievous than that a soul seeking the truth, and wishing to attain unto the knowledge of God, should know not where to go for it and from whom to seek it?'[1]

Far from being limited to the 19th century, the effects of the oppression of the working class formed much of the 20th century. With the social turmoil induced by World War I, the popular classes reverted to an aggressive revolutionary mode, and – as foreseen by 'Abdu'l-Bahá – the left grew in influence and gained the upper hand in Russia and eventually in all of eastern Europe and China. Fascism likewise fed on the frustrations of the working class, and was greatly bolstered by the fear of Communist revolution, attracting many who otherwise would have rejected Fascism's perverse philosophy – still another expression of action and reaction. The tension of the Cold War that molded much of the 20th century was born of the blighted development of the masses in the 19th century, first brutally repressed, and then misguided by scientific materialism. With the much touted fall of Communism in the late 20th century, symbolized so graphically by the razing of the Berlin wall, this chapter in the destiny of the masses came to an abrupt end.

Nor was this model limited to Europe. Through the mechanism of the colonial system that was extended and consolidated in the 19th century, Africa and parts of Asia would, on the one hand, follow the lead of western liberal democracy, and on the other hand, would be drawn into the tensions of the Cold War. Yet more lasting is the western economic model as India, China and other countries advance precipitously along the road to industrialization and urbanization, with their attendant evils of displaced populations, urban slums and poverty. The underlying precepts of liberal democracy and western capitalism are now taken as 'givens'. The role of the masses of humanity now seems to be defined as occasional participation through the ballot box, and to gradual incorporation into the middle class through social mobility available to a fortunate few. To what extent are we still under the influence of the 19th century and the Enlightenment that engendered it? We benefit from its positive aspects, and are still dealing with its shortcomings.

Human rights: The Enlightenment could see the value of the individual in the humanist tradition, and individual rights found expression in documents like the Declaration of the Rights of Man promulgated by the French Revolution and the American Bill of Rights. It is no exaggeration that the Universal Declaration of Human Rights adopted in 1948 by the United Nations and without a single dissenting vote drew its inspiration from these pioneering and visionary efforts. It is a milestone of human advancement that the nations of the world could agree on this fundamental statement as a minimum requirement of a civilized people. It is equally true that it remains aspirational in many lands and that 'the victims of injustice today number in countless millions. Each year, the agendas of the human rights organizations are overwhelmed by appeals from spokespersons for oppressed minorities of every type – religious, ethnic, social and national.'[2] Not least among those oppressed are the champions of the Cause of Bahá'u'lláh in the land of His birth.

Individualism and rebellion: Western culture is marked by an endemic and vigorous individualism, not infrequently linked to a rebellious nature. We live 'in a period of history dominated by the surging energy, the rebellious spirit and frenetic activity of adolescence . . .' The Universal House of Justice notes that 'The models of the old world order' were a product of the Enlightenment thinkers and 'were, in many instances, conceived in rebellion and retain the characteristics of the revolutions peculiar to an adolescent, albeit necessary, period in the evolution of human society'.[3] While that energy has undoubtedly contributed to the dynamism and material growth of the West and the United States in particular, it is a cultural characteristic that must be carefully channelled and buffered by a sense of commitment to the common weal.

Liberal democracy: The arbitrary autocracy that generated protest and revolution in the 18th and 19th centuries is recognized as an anachronism, although authoritarian regimes continue to exist in several countries. Liberal democracy was able to relieve humanity of one of its greatest burdens. However, lacking the spiritual discipline and integrity that 'Abdu'l-Bahá highlighted in *The Secret of Divine Civilization* as requisite qualities, leaders have often failed to uphold the highest interests of their electors.

> In many nations the electoral process has become discredited because of endemic corruption. Contributing to the widening distrust of so vital a process are the influence on the outcome from vested interests having access to lavish funds, the restrictions on freedom of choice inherent in the party system, and the distortion in public perception of the candidates by the bias expressed in the media. Apathy, alienation, and disillusionment are a consequence, too, as is a growing sense of despair of the unlikelihood that the most capable citizens will emerge to deal with the manifold problems of a defective social order. Evident everywhere is a yearning for institutions which will dispense justice, dispel oppression, and foster an enduring unity between the disparate elements of society.[4]

Industrial production and technology: Industrialization is now the mainstream of materially prosperous societies and a primary measure of the success of an economy. It has brought material well-being to millions of persons who as recently as two generations ago would never have dreamed it possible. Consumer goods as diverse as automobiles, computers, clothing, kitchen appliances, cellphones and televisions are readily available to a growing middle class and even to the working class, including in countries like China and India that scarcely four decades earlier were considered to be on the brink of disastrous overpopulation and starvation. We no longer can even visualize a world without the benefits of industry. Those countries of the West that saw the dawn of the Industrial Revolution have largely put the uglier side of industrialization behind them, and have even dealt with many of the problems of environmental pollution, while other so-called developing countries that are in the midst of industrialization often serve as sources of cheap labour for the globalized international market, experiencing some of the same problems as Europe and the United States in the 19th century. Indeed, globalization was initially hailed as a vast step toward the unification of the world, but now reveals symptoms of a marketplace driven by unbridled competition, in which the social good, the threat of climate change, and the economic stability of the planet have yet to receive their due priority. Indeed, the Industrial Revolution opened the door on 'industrial slavery' and gave a perverse turn to the 'economic life of humanity, where injustice is tolerated with indifference and disproportionate gain is regarded as the emblem of success'.[5]

Scepticism about religion, especially organized religion: Many Enlightenment philosophers were explicitly critical of the abuses of organized religion, and typically were sceptical about its mystical dimensions. Scepticism was institutionalized in the French Revolution in its attacks on the Catholic Church, and was expressed as atheism in Marxism. At mid-century Pius IX could see the ocean of anticlerical feeling surging around him, and struggled futilely to resist it.

We live the failures of the social systems and modes of authority that grew out of the 19th century – systems that claimed to speak on behalf the masses, who today are marked by the 'lethargy imposed on them by society . . . Passivity is bred by the forces of society today.'[6] Even when large segments of society arise in protest against some clear danger or social injustice, their persistence is tested by the intransigence of a system that lumbers on under its own inertia, impervious to principles of societal ethics, wise economic management, scientific fact, or common sense. Ironically, this reality is the diametric opposite of those aspirational attempts to transform society and that engendered such idealistic optimism at the dawn of the 19th century.

We have referred to the 20th century only in passing – 'a century that deserves to be reflected upon by any Bahá'í who wishes to understand the tumultuous forces that influenced the life of the planet and the processes of the Cause itself at a crucial time in humanity's social and spiritual evolution'[7] – that Century of Light, so precious as the years that challenged the young Guardian and saw him mature into the lonesome pillar of the Cause of God on whose shoulders the fate of mankind rested. In 1941 Shoghi Effendi wrote his far-reaching letter that we know as *The Promised Day Is Come*, in which he explicitly linked the tragic breakdown of society in the 20th century to those events surrounding the crowned heads of Europe and Asia, and their rejection of the call of God raised by the Supreme Manifestation of God and His Precursor, issuing in the dawn of a new era in the spiritual realm. Thus, the 19th century witnessed the emergence of both the material and the spiritual forces that have shaped the modern era. Furthermore, we saw that in His Tablets and Writings, Bahá'u'lláh engaged with some of the most critical social issues of His day, and together with the commentaries of 'Abdu'l-Bahá, these represent highly relevant sources for a critique of the origins and current state of society.

The one especially pertinent issue that has remained unresolved during these two hundred odd years – indeed, one of the essential questions of the new age – is the role of the masses of humanity. How would this fundamental issue of the 19th century be addressed by a nascent and proscribed faith? As the 20th century advanced and the nations of the world struggled with implementing the political and economic models of the modern era, Shoghi Effendi was establishing the Bahá'í Administrative Order, until . . .

> With the successful establishment in 1963 of the Universal House of Justice, the Bahá'ís of the world set out on the first stage of a mission of long duration: the spiritual empowerment of the whole body of humankind as the protagonists of their own advancement.[8]

Thirty years would pass in which the Faith would expand and would experience its early stages of rapid growth, designated 'entry by troops' in countries as distant and diverse as Uganda, India, Bolivia and the United States. Still, the numerical growth of the Faith was not matched by a qualitative change on the same scale. Rather, experience was accumulated gradually and was summed from distant communities to be refocused on a coherent approach, both to build on past experience and to systematize a process for future learning.

In 1995 a Four Year Plan was announced to the Continental Counsellors, highlighting 'a global enterprise aimed at one major accomplishment: a significant advance in the process of entry by troops,'[9] implying a renewed and wider approach to the masses of humanity – a goal that would continue in subsequent plans. This in turn was supported by a landmark call to develop training institutes systematically around the world, to create the capacity needed to serve the Cause and to reach the masses.

In many regions, it has become imperative to create institutes as organizational structures dedicated to systematic training. The purpose of such training is to endow ever-growing contingents of believers with the spiritual insights, the knowledge, and the skills needed to carry out the many tasks of accelerated expansion and consolidation, including the teaching and deepening of a large number of people – adults, youth and children.[10]

With this announcement was launched a worldwide effort to consolidate and expand an educational mode that would come to be known as the institute process. Within only three years the House of Justice was able to announce the existence of 344 such institutions of learning around the world.[11] So enthusiastic was the response of the Bahá'í community, and so dramatic was the qualitative effect on attitudes and comprehension of the process of growth, that in 2001 the House of Justice announced the entry upon the Fifth Epoch of the Formative Age of the Faith – a testimony to the long-term significance of the institute process focused on the expansion of spiritual capacity, and a prophetic vision of the implications of this change that would unfold in the next decades.[12]

In its letters referring to the essence of the institute process, the Universal House of Justice refers repeatedly to spiritual empowerment, especially of youth. Spiritual empowerment liberates

the powers of the human spirit that the Bahá'í Faith – for that matter, every great religious tradition that has appeared throughout the ages – hopes to tap: the power of unity, of love, of humble service, of pure deeds. Associated with power in this sense are words such as 'release', 'encourage', 'channel', 'guide' and 'enable'. Power is not a finite entity which is to be 'seized' and 'jealously guarded'; it constitutes a limit-less capacity to transform that resides in the human race as a body.[13]

True education seeks to empower the individual for his or her role in a model of transformation, in the acquisition of qualities that contribute to 'an ever-advancing civilization'. It is an education that begins with Bahá'í classes for children and spiritual empowerment groups for 'junior youth', that continues with adult deepening and capacity building, that extends to the day-to-day experience of community life, and that seeks to promote 'the spiritual empowerment of individuals, who will come to see themselves as active agents of their own learning, as protagonists of a constant effort to apply knowledge to effect individual and collective transformation'.[14] It entails a sharpened analytical capacity to read reality based on spiritual principles, both in the outer world and in one's own soul. Underlying this spiritual capacity is a strengthened bond with the Word of God, nurturing 'the love for Bahá'u'lláh held in the heart of a committed believer . . . all activity begins with this simple strand of love. It is the vital thread from which is woven a pattern of patient and concentrated effort . . .'[15]

As concepts of an educational process took form through-out the Bahá'í world, a major educational milestone emerged in the form of a programme for junior youth. In words of the Universal House of Justice praising the spiritual capacities of this age group (about 11 to 14), and describing the junior youth programme, one can visualize the foundation of a future civilization that exceeds the expectations of past generations:

> While global trends project an image of this age group as problematic, lost in the throes of tumultuous physical and emotional change, unresponsive and self-consumed, the

Bahá'í community – in the language it employs and the approaches it adopts – is moving decidedly in the opposite direction, seeing in junior youth instead altruism, an acute sense of justice, eagerness to learn about the universe and a desire to contribute to the construction of a better world . . . There is every indication that the programme engages their expanding consciousness in an exploration of reality that helps them to analyse the constructive and destructive forces operating in society and to recognize the influence these forces exert on their thoughts and actions, sharpening their spiritual perception, enhancing their powers of expression and rein- forcing moral structures that will serve them throughout their lives. At an age when burgeoning intellectual, spiritual and physical powers become accessible to them, they are being given the tools needed to combat the forces that would rob them of their true identity as noble beings and to work for the common good.[16]

Furthermore, while focused on the process of growth and col- lective development of communities inspired by the vision of Bahá'u'lláh, these capacities are the essential substance of pro- gress in any endeavour. Parallel to this expanding process and also in 1995, the Bahá'í International Community issued a chal- lenging declaration, *The Prosperity of Humankind*, that mirrored many of the concepts of the institute process and the funda- mental purpose of spiritual empowerment, extending these to efforts in socio-economic development. The House of Justice states that 'As you continue to labour in your clusters, you will be drawn further and further into the life of the society around you and will be challenged to extend the process of systematic learning in which you are engaged to encompass a growing range of human endeavours.'[17] The declaration highlights the indispensable role of the masses of humanity in confronting the challenges of advancing civilization, and touches on the issue of an evolving identity of the masses:

> The transformation in the way that great numbers of ordinary people are coming to see themselves – a change that is dramatically abrupt in the perspective of the history of civilization – raises fundamental questions about the role assigned to the general body of humanity in the planning of our planet's future.
>
> Future generations, however, will find almost incomprehensible the circumstance that, in an age paying tribute to an egalitarian philosophy and related democratic principles, development planning should view the masses of humanity as essentially recipients of benefits from aid and training.[18]

A central challenge, therefore – and an enormous one – is the expansion of scientific and technological activity. Instruments of social and economic change so powerful must cease to be the patrimony of advantaged segments of society, and must be so organized as to permit people everywhere to participate in such activity on the basis of capacity . . . such reorganization will require the establishment of viable centres of learning throughout the world, institutions that will enhance the capability of the world's peoples to participate in the generation and application of knowledge.[19]

In *The Prosperity of Humankind* analytical capacities comparable to those engendered by the institute process are cited as derived from a scientific viewpoint:

> People need, for example, to learn how to separate fact from conjecture – indeed to distinguish between subjective views and objective reality; the extent to which individuals and

institutions so equipped can contribute to human progress, however, will be determined by their devotion to truth and their detachment from the promptings of their own interests and passions. Another capacity that science must cultivate in all people is that of thinking in terms of process, including historical process . . .[20]

In this parallel between the institute process and the perspective of the Faith on socio-economic development, one can foresee the glimmerings of a vision articulated in subsequent years calling for coherence among all lines of activity: teaching and consolidation, social action, and influencing public discourse. Empowerment reaches all domains of human endeavour, but clearly, the context of empowerment that receives the most attention in the Bahá'í Faith today, within which individuals and institutions develop their capacity inherent in their nature, is the field of teaching and consolidation, and it is in this field that the institute process is focused.

Parallel to the process of raising the capacity within a population to assume the direction of its own destiny is the maturation of the institutions that nurture this process. Empowerment of individuals and indeed, of groups of like-minded individuals, does not alone lead to a future civilization. Rather, within the reality that we know as the 'community', individuals and institutions interact in a dynamic relationship whereby capacity is both created and channelled into collective action. Indeed, 'the [Local] Assembly's proper involvement with the Plan becomes crucial to every attempt to embrace large numbers – itself a requisite for the manifestation of the full range of its powers and capacities'.[21] Furthermore, with the advance of the institute process, another dimension is observed. Members of those institutions that are charged with promoting a process of capacity building – institutions which at this point are undergoing their own process of capacity development – those members are themselves products of the institute process. Rising through the ranks, as it were, and gaining the maturity that comes with service, they have come to understand the capacity building process through their own liberating experience, and thus have a vision born of practice to bring to bear on guiding others in their path of service. Thus closes the circle of a self-perpetuating process that grows in ever-expanding waves, as Assemblies, Regional Councils, and institute boards find their realization in nurturing this process.

The capacities so developed within the context of the principles of the Faith, with a spiritual identity fostered by the institute process, and under the guidance of its institutions, engender a desire to render service to community and to mankind. This is the foundation of 'a process that seeks to raise capacity within a population to take charge of its own spiritual, social and intellectual development'.[22] Such concepts might sound futuristic or even utopian but for the results that are already emerging in different continents and cultures around the world. It is no longer unusual to hear youth of humble origins and often from rural settings expounding on processes of community development that have evaded theoreticians in socio-economic progress for decades. The institute process carries the words of Shoghi Effendi to a level previously unseen in the history of the Faith.

> If only the friends could realize it, the glory of our Faith is not that people with unique abilities do the work of the Cause, but that it is done by the sacrifice of loving and devoted souls who arise selflessly to undertake work they feel themselves incompetent, sometimes, to achieve. God works through them and endows them with gifts they did not dream they could ever possess.[23]

As wider experience was garnered with the institute process, this found expression in an operative strategy on the level of community. After a decade and a half of systematic experience in capacity building, in its Riḍván Message of 2010 the House of Justice called upon the Bahá'ís to focus on

> smaller pockets of the population, each of which should become a centre of intense activity . . . A rhythm of community life should gradually emerge, then, commensurate with the capacity of an expanding nucleus of individuals committed to Bahá'u'lláh's vision of a new World Order . . . The work advancing in every corner of the globe today represents the latest stage of the ongoing Bahá'í endeavour to create the nucleus of the glorious civilization enshrined in His teachings, the building of which is an enterprise of infinite complexity and scale, one that will demand centuries of exertion by humanity to bring to fruition.[24]

The vision of a world-embracing civilization is thus cultivated in smaller geographic areas that permit a learning process of qualitative change and the realization of their potential.

In its Riḍván Message of 2012 the House of Justice hinted at the relationship between current activities and the evolution of a future civilization: 'In the spirit animating the activities of any Bahá'í community . . . can be perceived an indication of how a society founded upon divine teachings might develop,'[25] and in 2013, it offered a remarkable and far-reaching overview of progress in an ongoing process that can only be understood in the context of the long-term empowerment of the masses of humanity, sowing the seeds of a new culture among both adherents of the Faith and the surrounding public at large, and destined to grow out of local focal points of intensive activity and learning:

From this landscape of thriving activity, one prospect deserves particular mention. In the message addressed to you three years ago, we expressed the hope that, in clusters with an intensive programme of growth in operation, the friends would endeavour to learn more about the ways of community building by developing centres of intense activity in neighbourhoods and villages . . . In essence, this approach centres on the response to Bahá'u'lláh's teachings on the part of populations who are ready for the spiritual transformation His Revelation fosters. Through participation in the educational process promoted by the training institute, they are motivated to reject the torpor and indifference inculcated by the forces of society and pursue, instead, patterns of action which prove life altering . . . Youth are empowered to take responsibility for the development of those around them younger than themselves. Older generations welcome the contribution of the youth to meaningful discussions about the affairs of the whole community. For young and old alike, the discipline cultivated through the community's educational process builds capacity for consultation, and new spaces emerge for purposeful conversation. Yet change is not confined merely to the Bahá'ís and those who are involved in the core activities called for by the Plan, who might reasonably be expected to adopt new ways of thinking over time. The very spirit of the place is affected. A devotional attitude takes shape within a broad sweep of the population. Expressions of the equality of men and women become more pronounced. The education of children, both boys and girls, commands greater attention. The character of relationships within families – moulded by assumptions centuries old – alters perceptibly. A sense of duty towards one's immediate community and physical environment becomes prevalent. Even the scourge of prejudice, which casts its baleful shadow on every society, begins to yield to the compelling force of unity. In short, the community-building work in which the friends are engaged influences aspects of culture.[26]

Continuing with this theme in 2014, the House of Justice noted that the Bahá'í community was beginning to influence the surrounding community at large. Increasingly reports are received of gatherings of hundreds of enthusiastic supporters, both declared believers and friends of the Faith, who are attracted by its sublime Message carried to action with children, junior youth, youth and adults, and 'the movement of an entire population becomes discernible', for 'when the elements of the Plan's framework for action are combined into a coherent whole, the impact on a population can be profound'.[27] Though as yet insignificant in terms of total numbers, this is perhaps the first time in its short history that entire populations are responding to the call of the Faith, presaging a remarkable and long-awaited phase in its unfolding destiny – and as a result of systematic efforts that can and will be replicated many times over.

We who live in this age and witness such processes unfolding before our eyes cannot appreciate their long-term significance. In 1998, as the institute process was taking shape throughout the Bahá'í world, the House of Justice impressed upon the followers of the Faith that they were 'involved in a vast historic process the like of which has not ever before been experienced by any people'.[28] We can well consider that this historic process was initiated by the advent of Bahá'u'lláh and the spiritual forces that were released even as His appearance in this world was approaching, and as He declared His Mission and proclaimed His Cause. Indeed the 19th century was pregnant with the stirrings of the modern age, as the Day in which God's Supreme Manifestation walked the earth.

Invested though each day may be with its pre-ordained share of God's wondrous grace, the Days immediately associated with the Manifestation of God possess a unique distinction and occupy a station which no mind can ever comprehend.[29]

It is evident that every age in which a Manifestation of God hath lived is divinely ordained, and may, in a sense, be characterized as God's appointed Day. This Day, however, is unique, and is to be distinguished from those that have preceded it.[30]

There is little doubt that the spiritual influence released by the Twin Manifestations of God gave an impetus to those transformations that so distinguished the 19th century and that formed the modern world.

At the centre of these transformations is the concept of power as shared by every single human being – a power that was infused into every human frame in this age. Nearly a hundred years would pass from the birth of Bahá'u'lláh to the day when 'Abdu'l-Bahá would proclaim to a London public that we live in a new cycle of human power. While that power has found expression in revolutions and political processes, the mechanisms and social structures that were forged in the 19th century and that evolved throughout the 20th century have proved incapable of channelling its potential toward an ever-advancing civilization. Rather, today we can understand that human power in terms of human empowerment, and more specifically spiritual empowerment. The manifestation of that new cycle of human power proclaimed by 'Abdu'l-Bahá is long overdue.

From the revolutions that were inspired in the Enlightenment, to liberal democracy, to the economic system that accompanied the Industrial Revolution – all drew their energy from the spirit of the modern age, all began with great optimism in their potential to create a better world, yet all failed to meet the expectations engendered at the dawn of the 19th century, and have left the masses of humanity largely alienated, marginalized and disillusioned. It is the institute process which is emerging that fills the breach left by the revolutionary movements, the educational models, and the political processes of the modern age, and that lays that groundwork for an entirely new social structure that is worthy of the age of maturity. In the future, these days and this simple yet subtly profound process will be viewed as a critical phase and an inflection point in that process set in motion by the advent of Bahá'u'lláh Himself, and meeting the hopes of that turbulent century that was stirred by the first breezes of divine inspiration.

Epilogue

The Revelation of Bahá'u'lláh impacts upon every aspect of life and society. As such, there are many ways that one can attempt to contextualize the Teachings of God for this day. For Christians His Dispensation may be posed as the Kingdom of God on earth. For the activist His Teachings represent the answer to the social ills of the world. For the mystically inclined His Writings are the path to a higher consciousness. The perspective offered in this book is that of the history of the masses of humanity in the modern age, and the significance of Bahá'u'lláh's Revelation for their emerging self-determination.

Though a perspective of social history is by no means unique to this treatise, this is nonetheless not the typical approach to history to which we have been exposed and that often focuses on leaders, on battles and wars, and on the rise and fall of nations. Those indeed have been forces that have driven the destiny of the masses, and so should not be isolated from this topic. We are, however, entering upon a new phase in the history of mankind in which the masses are becoming the protagonists of history instead of passive victims.

We are familiar with the declaration that the Revelation of Bahá'u'lláh is destined to create an ever-advancing civilization, and in presentations of the Faith the point is often made that every revealed religion has, in its own day and epoch, created a unique civilization reflecting the values and qualities of that religion. We are, however, in a unique position in this regard; we are aware of this mission and the potential of Bahá'u'lláh's Revelation to bring about this transformation. Never before in the history of the world has a religion, its leaders and its followers addressed this mission so consciously and systematically, in an explicit process of learning.

How will this come about? To say that the institute process is at the centre of this ambitious endeavour must sound pretentious. It could be informative to consider this question in a broader context of the three thematic areas of effort of the Faith in the present era.

The area which occupies the greatest number of Bahá'ís the world around is the *growth and consolidation* of the Faith, and the institute process is the cornerstone of this effort, as the vehicle of consolidation and the driver of capacity building for the processes of growth. The Bahá'í community has learned to view teaching and consolidation as two inseparable components of a single process. Perhaps a review on how we understand consolidation and the institute process is useful.

We are familiar with these words of Bahá'u'lláh: 'The Great Being saith: Regard man as a mine rich in gems of inestimable value. Education can, alone, cause it to reveal its treasures, and enable mankind to benefit therefrom.'[1] Here Bahá'u'lláh highlights the role of education, and states that its purpose is to put those gems inherent in man's soul at the service of mankind. Far beyond a training exercise in the execution of basic activities, the institute process is one of developing an educational system capable of creating the capacity to put into practice an expanding comprehension of the Revelation.

In this context the term 'capacity' takes on a deeper meaning at the level of the human soul. The current institute process as we know it, while deceptively simple, has developed through a systematic process of learning, and touches and fortifies the essential spiritual fibre of the human soul, strengthening the inherent spiritual 'instincts' within the soul: the desire to help and serve others; the search to find one's identity and to understand one's place in life; the urge to admire beauty and to draw close to and worship the ultimate Cause of Being; the sense of justice that permits one to see with one's 'own eyes and not through the eyes of others'.[2] In the course of this educational process one's capacities of expression are enhanced, one's commitment to justice is fortified, one's power of discernment is sharpened, and one's ability to distinguish between truth and falsehood is reinforced. These dimensions emerge forcefully in the junior youth programme, addressing the needs and potential of an age group that has won the praise of the Universal House of Justice for its 'altruism, an acute sense of justice, eagerness to learn about the universe and a desire to contribute to the construction of a better world'.[3]

More than a programme focused on deepening, a cornerstone of this educational system is that this fundamental transformation can only take place and be fully rooted in the interior being of each person when these capacities find expression and are exercised in the field of meaningful service. Indeed, the institute process develops capacities with implications far beyond the immediate tasks at hand. If at its inception the institute was designed to respond to specific needs of children's classes, junior youth groups and the formation of teachers of the Faith, this was due to the immediate circumstances of the moment. And even within this context, it is impressive to see communities and populations being moved to action by these activities of this incipient educational process.

A second thematic area of Bahá'í endeavour is that of *social action* – through projects and programmes to bring the teachings of Bahá'u'lláh into practice for the benefit of the Bahá'í community and any or all of those who come into contact with it. Social action bridges both the Bahá'í community and the surrounding population, which is to say, society at large. Linking social action to education and capacity building, the House of Justice notes:

> Access to knowledge is the right of every human being, and participation in its generation, application and diffusion a responsibility that all must shoulder in the great enterprise of building a prosperous world civilization – each individual according to his or her talents and abilities. Justice demands universal participation. Thus, while social action may involve the provision of goods and services in some form, its primary concern must be to build capacity within a given population to participate in creating a better world.[4]

The third area that occupies the Bahá'í community is *influencing the public discourse* on topics of broad social importance that find relevance in the Writings of Bahá'u'lláh. Topics that have been the object of comment by the Bahá'í community cover a wide range of current issues: human rights, the environment, the role of women, poverty, social justice, among others. While Bahá'ís may well find the declarations emitted by the Bahá'í International Community and its office in the United Nations to be of interest and to be useful in teaching efforts, the target of these efforts is explicitly a broad population beyond the limits of the Bahá'í community, whereby the principles of the Revelation are brought to bear on current events and societal needs.

Arguably, the process of growth and consolidation is the foundation of the other two processes. The numerical growth of Bahá'í communities opens the possibility for these to work together in unison toward the goals of social action as per the specific needs of their community, and the institute process promulgates the common spiritual values and qualities of service and sacrifice that facilitate joint action. A community that has attained to such a level of service and sacrifice can progress visibly and be an example for the society at large, and its learning experience can be articulated within the public discourse. Moreover, the expression of spiritual principle, the effectiveness of social action and its sustainability, and the lessons that emerge are all the more powerful when participation is universal and when the community at large is the protagonist. Hence, the Writings of the Faith pose this process in the context of the masses of humanity taking the reins of their destiny into their own hands under the guidance of the Sacred Word of God and encouraged and empowered by the Bahá'í institutions.

Evidence of recent progress in all three areas is cited by the Universal House of Justice in its Riḍván Message of 2018 in its review of the Bicentenary of the Birth of Bahá'u'lláh. The House of Justice notes that 'the number of intensive programmes of growth in the world is approaching half the five thousand contemplated in the current global endeavour, and the rate at which this number is rising has been steadily increasing'. Not limited to its internal development, 'the friends are using the new capacities they have developed to improve conditions in the society around them, their enthusiasm kindled by their study of the divine teachings'. Moreover, the influence on leaders of thought was visible:

> One telling indicator of progress was the numerous places where it became clear that the Faith had emerged from obscurity at the national level. There were government leaders and leaders of thought who stated publicly – and sometimes emphasized privately – that the world stands in need of Bahá'u'lláh's vision and that the Bahá'ís' endeavours are admired and should be expanded. [5]

Returning to the question of how a civilization can emerge from the current efforts of the Bahá'í community, the long-term implications of these reflections for the future civilization should not be underestimated. While the answer is clearly hidden in future centuries, and the establishment of the Lesser Peace as a prior step to a world civilization rests not with the Bahá'ís but with peoples and leaders of the world, one can suggest that increasingly these three processes and possibly others must come together and reinforce each other in what the current vocabulary of the Faith describes in terms of 'coherence'. Again in the Riḍván 2018 Message, the House notes that 'From the resulting transformation visible in the individual and collective lives of peoples may be discerned the unmistakable stirrings of the society-building power of the Cause of Bahá'u'lláh.'

And again, we return to the issue of the role of the masses of humanity.

While the first experiences of entry by troops extended from country to country in the 1960s and 70s, the issue of participation of new recruits to the Faith came to the forefront. Universal participation was mentioned in the very first message of the House of Justice to the Bahá'í world after its election in 1963, and in April of 1964 the House launched a Nine Year Plan with two central objectives: expansion and universal participation.[6] The significance of universal participation can now be understood more clearly, as the mobilization of those troops, and as the first glimmer of the activation of the masses of humanity. Thus, the emergence of the masses is not a new theme; it has been with us for all of our lives.

As noted in the first paragraph of this chapter, the emergence of the masses of humanity to play their rightful role in their self-determination is only one dimension of the Revelation of Bahá'u'lláh. At the end of the day, does this perspective bring anything to our efforts to further the fortunes of the Faith? Does it matter that we are conscious of this perspective?

We tend to be results-oriented, and sometimes we focus on statistics, but without denying the importance of results, the process of involving an increasing number of inspired and motivated individuals is in itself a topic that demands attention. With this perspective, might we not reflect on the degree of participation in the Nineteen Day Feast, and the quality of the consultation that occurs there? Would attendance at reflection meetings and the contribution of each participant take on greater importance? Would participation in Bahá'í elections not have a wider significance? Would we give greater attention to the promotion of localized nuclei of individuals who seek to find their field of service? Would this put the active promotion of basic activities of the Faith in another light, as vehicles to give expression to the spiritual potential of the masses?

At the end of the day, even in our most modest contributions, we are part of history.

Bibliography

'Abdu'l-Bahá. *'Abdu'l-Bahá in London* (1912, 1921). London: Bahá'í Publishing Trust, 1982.

— *Foundations of World Unity*. Wilmette, IL: Bahá'í Publishing Trust, 1968.

— *Paris Talks: Addresses given by 'Abdu'l-Bahá in 1911* (1912). London: Bahá'í Publishing Trust, 12th ed. 1995.

— *The Promulgation of Universal Peace: Talks Delivered by 'Abdu'l-Bahá During His Visit to the United States and Canada in 1912* (1922, 1925). Comp. H. MacNutt. Wilmette, IL: Bahá'í Publishing Trust, rev. ed. 2007.

— *The Secret of Divine Civilization*. Trans. M. Gail. Wilmette, IL: Bahá'í Publishing Trust, 1957, 1990.

— *Selections from the Writings of 'Abdu'l-Bahá*. Trans. by a Committee at the Bahá'í World Centre and by Marzieh Gail. Haifa: Bahá'í World Centre, 1982.

— *Some Answered Questions* (1908). Comp. and trans. Laura Clifford Barney. Haifa: Bahá'í World Centre, rev. ed. 2014.

— *Tablets of the Divine Plan*. Wilmette, IL: Bahá'í Publishing Trust, rev. ed. 1993.

— *A Traveler's Narrative Written to Illustrate the Episode of the Báb* (1891). Trans. E. G. Browne. Wilmette, IL: Bahá'í Publishing Trust, rev. ed. 1988.

Bahá'í International Community, Office of Public Information. *The Prosperity of Humankind* (1995). http://www.bahai.org/library/other-literature/official-statements-commentaries/prosperity-humankind/#r=prh_en-title

Bahá'í Prayers: A Selection of Prayers Revealed by Bahá'u'lláh, the Báb, and 'Abdu'l-Bahá. Wilmette, IL: Bahá'í Publishing Trust, 2002.

Bahá'í Reference Library. Authoritative online source of Bahá'í writings. https://www.bahai.org/library/

Bahá'í World Centre. *Century of Light.* Commissioned by The Universal House of Justice. Haifa: Bahá'í World Centre, 2001.

Bahá'u'lláh. *Epistle to the Son of the Wolf.* Trans. Shoghi Effendi. Wilmette, IL: Bahá'í Publishing Trust, rev. ed. 1988.

— *Gleanings from the Writings of Bahá'u'lláh.* Trans. Shoghi Effendi. Wilmette, IL: Bahá'í Publishing Trust, 1983.

— *The Hidden Words of Bahá'u'lláh.* Trans. Shoghi Effendi. Wilmette, IL: Bahá'í Publishing Trust, 1985.

— *The Kitáb-i-Aqdas: The Most Holy Book.* Haifa: Bahá'í World Centre, 1992.

— *Kitáb-i-Íqán: The Book of Certitude.* Trans. Shoghi Effendi. Wilmette, IL: Bahá'í Publishing Trust, 1983.

— *Prayers and Meditations by Bahá'u'lláh.* Trans. Shoghi Effendi. Wilmette, IL: Bahá'í Publishing Trust, 1938, 1987.

— *The Summons of the Lord of Hosts: Tablets of Bahá'u'lláh.* Haifa: Bahá'í World Centre, 2002.

— *Tablets of Bahá'u'lláh Revealed after the Kitáb-i-Aqdas.* Translated by Habib Taherzadeh with assistance of a committee at the Bahá'í World Centre. Haifa: Bahá'í World Centre, 1978.

Bairoch, P.; Goertz, G. 'Factors of urbanisation in the nineteenth century developed countries: A descriptive and econometric analysis', in *Urban Studies*, vol. 23 (1986), pp. 285–305.

Balyuzi, H. M. *Bahá'u'lláh, the King of Glory*, Oxford: George Ronald, 1980.

Bartolini, S. 1996. *Enfranchisement, Equality and Turnout in the European Democratisation Process: A Preliminary Comparative Analysis*, Working Paper No. 121. Florence: European University Institute, 1996.

The Dawn-Breakers: Nabíl's Narrative of the Early Days of the Bahá'í Revelation. Trans. and ed. Shoghi Effendi. Wilmette, IL: Bahá'í Publishing Trust, 1932, 1999.

Engelstein, L. 'The dream of civil society in tsarist Russia: Law, state and religion', in N. Bermeo and P. Nord (eds): *Civil Society Before Democracy*. Oxford: Rowman and Littlefield, 2000.

Esslemont, J. E. *Bahá'u'lláh and the New Era*. Wilmette, IL: Bahá'í Publishing Trust, 1980.

Furútan, 'Alí-Akbar. *Stories of Bahá'u'lláh*. Oxford: George Ronald, 1986.

Goodman, J. 'Class and religion: Great Britain and Ireland', in J. C. Albisetti, J. Goodman and R. Rogers (eds): *Girls' Secondary Education in the Western World: From the 18th to the 20th Century*. New York: Palgrave McMillan, 2010.

Gubin, E. 'Politics and anticlericalism: Belgium', in J. C. Albisetti, J. Goodman and R. Rogers (eds): *Girls' Secondary Education in the Western World: From the 18th to the 20th Century*. New York: Palgrave McMillan, 2010.

Hobsbawm, E. J. *The Age of Revolution, 1789–1848*. New York: Random House, 1996.

— *Industry and Empire: The Birth of the Industrial Revolution*. New York: New Press, 1999.

Hoffmann, S. *Civil Society and Democracy in Nineteenth Century Europe: Entanglements, Variations, Conflicts*, Discussion Paper No. SP IV 2005-405. Berlin: Social Science Research Center, 2005. Revised version of the article "Democracy and associations: Towards a transnational perspective', in *Journal of Modern History*, vol. 75 (2003), pp. 269–99.

Holy Bible. King James version. London: Eyre and Spottiswoode, various dates.

Huard, R. 'Political association in nineteenth-century France: Legislation and practice'. in N. Bermeo and P. Nord (eds): *Civil Society Before Democracy*. Oxford: Rowman and Littlefield, 2000.

Lights of Guidance: A Bahá'í Reference File. Comp. H. Hornby. New Delhi: Bahá'í Publishing Trust, 5th ed. 1997.

Morris, R. 'Civil society, subscriber democracies, and parliamentary government in Great Britain', in: N. Bermeo and P. Nord (eds): *Civil Society Before Democracy*. Oxford: Rowman and Littlefield, 2000.

Pope Pius IX. *The Syllabus of Errors*. 1864. http://www.papalencyclicals.net/Pius09/p9syll.htm.

Prochaska, F. 'Good neighbours: Associational philanthropy and civic apprenticeship in 19th Century England'. http://www.artstrategies.org/downloads/Battersea_Good_Neighbours.pdf.

Rogers, R. 'Culture and Catholicism: France', in J. C. Albisetti, J. Goodman and R. Rogers (eds): *Girls' Secondary Education in the Western World: From the 18th to the 20th Century*. New York: Palgrave McMillan, 2010.

Ruhi Institute. *Reflections on the Life of the Spirit*. West Palm Beach: Palabra Publications, various dates. http://www.ruhi.org/institute/path.php

Shoghi Effendi. *The Advent of Divine Justice* (1939). Wilmette, IL: Bahá'í Publishing Trust, 1990.

— *God Passes By* (1944). Wilmette, IL: Bahá'í Publishing Trust, rev. ed. 1974.

— *The Promised Day Is Come* (1941). Wilmette, IL: Bahá'í Publishing Trust, rev. ed. 1980.

— *The World Order of Bahá'u'lláh: Selected Letters by Shoghi Effendi* (1938). Wilmette, IL: Bahá'í Publishing Trust, 1982.

— *Victory Promises*. From a letter dated 12 December 1943 written to an individual believer. National Spiritual Assembly of the Bahá'ís of the Hawaiian Islands, 1978.

Smith, A. *An Inquiry into the Nature and Causes of the Wealth of Nations*. 1776.

Soldani, S. 'Chequered routes to secondary education: Italy', in J. C. Albisetti, J. Goodman and R. Rogers (eds): *Girls' Secondary Education in the Western World: From the 18th to the 20th Century*. New York: Palgrave McMillan, 2010.

Star of the West: The Bahai Magazine. Periodical, 25 vols. 1910–1935. Vols. 1–14 RP Oxford: George Ronald, 1978. Complete CD-ROM version: Talisman Educational Software/Special Ideas, 2001.

The Universal House of Justice. *Individual Rights and Freedoms in the World Order of Bahá'u'lláh: A Statement by the Universal House of Justice*. Letter to the Followers of Bahá'u'lláh in the United States of America, 29 December 1988. Wilmette, IL: Bahá'í Publishing Trust, 1989.

— *Messages from the Universal House of Justice 1963–1986: The Third Epoch of the Formative Age*. Comp. Geoffry W. Marks. Wilmette, IL: Bahá'í Publishing Trust, 1996.

— Message to the conference of the Continental Counsellors. 1995. http://www.bahai.org/library/authoritative-texts/the-universal-house-of-justice/messages/#d=19951226_001&f=f1

— Message to the conference of the Continental Counsellors, 29 December 2015. http://www.bahai.org/library/authoritative-texts/the-universal-house-of-justice/messages/#d=20151229_001&f=f1

— Regarding 'Abdu'l-Bahá's letter to the people of Iran, titled *The Secret of Divine Civilization*, 26 November 2003. http://www.bahai.org/library/authoritative-texts/the-universal-house-of-justice/messages/#d=20031126_001&f=f1

— Regarding several issues related to the principle of non-involvement in partisan political affairs. 2013. http://www.bahai.org/library/authoritative-texts/the-universal-house-of-justice/messages/#d=20130302_001&f=f1

— Regarding some elements of the Bahá'í electoral process, 25 March 2007. http://www.bahai.org/library/authoritative-texts/the-universal-house-of-justice/messages/#d=20070325_001&f=f1

— Riḍván Message. 1998. http://www.bahai.org/library/authoritative-texts/the-universal-house-of-justice/messages/#d=19980421_001&f=f1

— Riḍván Message. 1999. http://www.bahai.org/library/authoritative-texts/the-universal-house-of-justice/messages/#d=19990421_001&f=f1

— Riḍván Message. 2001. http://www.bahai.org/library/authoritative-texts/the-universal-house-of-justice/messages/#d=20010421_001&f=f1

— Riḍván Message, 2002. http://www.bahai.org/library/authoritative-texts/the-universal-house-of-justice/messages/#d=20020421_001&f=f1

— Riḍván Message. 2008. http://www.bahai.org/library/authoritative-texts/the-universal-house-of-justice/messages/#d=20080421_001&f=f1

— Riḍván Message. 2010. http://www.bahai.org/library/authoritative-texts/the-universal-house-of-justice/messages/#d=20100421_001&f=f1

— Riḍván Message, 2011. http://www.bahai.org/library/authoritative-texts/the-universal-house-of-justice/messages/#d=20110421_001&f=f1

— Riḍván Message 2012. http://www.bahai.org/library/authoritative-texts/the-universal-house-of-justice/messages/#d=20120421_001&f=f1

— Riḍván Message. 2013. http://www.bahai.org/library/authoritative-texts/the-universal-house-of-justice/messages/#d=20130421_001&f=f1

— Riḍván Message. 2014. http://www.bahai.org/library/authoritative-texts/the-universal-house-of-justice/messages/#d=20140421_001&f=f1

— Riḍván Message. 2015. http://www.bahai.org/library/authoritative-texts/the-universal-house-of-justice/messages/#d=20150421_001&f=f1

— Riḍván Message. 2018. http://www.bahai.org/library/authoritative-texts/the-universal-house-of-justice/messages/#d=20180421_001&f=f1

— *Selected Six Year Plan Messages*. Prepared by the Research Department of the Universal House of Justice. Haifa: Bahá'í World Centre, 1986.

White, R. *A. Lincoln, a Biography*. New York: Random House, 2009.

Notes and References

Prologue

1 Bahá'u'lláh, *Epistle to the Son of the Wolf*, p. 22.
2 ibid. p. 21.
3 Bahá'u'lláh, *The Summons of the Lord of Hosts*, p. 98.

1. Why Europe?

1 Shoghi Effendi, *The Promised Day Is Come*, p. 28.
2 ibid. p. 11.
3 Shoghi Effendi, quoting Bahá'u'lláh, ibid. pp. 11–12.
4 'Abdu'l-Bahá, *'Abdu'l-Bahá in London*, p. 19.
5 *The Dawn-Breakers*, p. 213.
6 Shoghi Effendi, *The Promised Day Is Come*, p. 18.
7 Bahá'u'lláh, *Gleanings from the Writings of Bahá'u'lláh*, CII, p. 207.
8 Bahá'u'lláh, *The Summons of the Lord of Hosts*, p. 191.
9 Bahá'u'lláh, *Gleanings from the Writings of Bahá'u'lláh*, XCVI, p. 196.
10 Bahá'u'lláh, *Tablets of Bahá'u'lláh Revealed After the Kitáb-i-Aqdas*, p. 69.
11 ibid. p. 144.
12 Bahá'u'lláh, *Gleanings from the Writings of Bahá'u'lláh*, CLXIV, pp. 342–3.
13 Shoghi Effendi, *The Promised Day Is Come*, p. 15.
14 ibid. p. 19.
15 ibid. p. 48.

2. The Enlightenment

1 'Abdu'l-Bahá, *Paris Talks*, no. 11, p. 32.

3. The French Revolution

1 'Abdu'l-Bahá, *The Secret of Divine Civilization*, p. 72.

4. The Industrial Revolution

1 Adapted from Bairoch and Goertz, 'Factors of urbanisation in the nineteenth century developed countries . . .'
2 Hobsbaum, *Industry and Empire*, p. 46.
3 Smith, *An Inquiry into the Nature and Causes of the Wealth of Nations*, Chapter 8: 'Of the wages of labour'.
4 Bahá'u'lláh, *The Summons of the Lord of Hosts*, p. 189.
5 ibid. p. 75.
6 ibid. p. 78.
7 ibid. p. 79.
8 Bahá'u'lláh, *Gleanings from the Writings of Bahá'u'lláh*, C, p. 102.
9 ibid. CXLV, pp. 314–15.
10 King James Bible, John 12:8.
11 Hobsbaum, *Industry and Empire*, p. 142.
12 Bahá'í World Centre, *Century of Light*, p. 30.
13 *The Dawn-Breakers*, p. 131.

5. Basic Principles and Processes

1 Bahá'í World Centre, *Century of Light*, p. 30.
2 'Abdu'l-Bahá, *A Traveller's Narrative*, p. 91.
3 The Universal House of Justice, *Individual Rights and Freedoms in the World Order of Bahá'u'lláh*, p. 21.
4 ibid. pp. 7–8.
5 Bahá'u'lláh, *Gleanings from the Writings of Bahá'u'lláh*, CX, p. 216.
6 'Abdu'l-Bahá, *'Abdu'l-Bahá in London*, p. 29.
7 Bahá'u'lláh, *Gleanings from the Writings of Bahá'u'lláh*, V, p. 8.
8 'Abdu'l-Bahá, *The Promulgation of Universal Peace*, p. 302.
9 ibid. p. 303.
10 'Abdu'l-Bahá, *Paris Talks*, no. 40, p. 135.
11 Bahá'u'lláh, *Hidden Words*, Persian no. 5.
12 'Abdu'l-Bahá, *Star of the West*, vol. IV, no. 7 (13 July 1913), p. 120; also in *Lights of Guidance*, p. 239.
13 Bahá'u'lláh, *Hidden Words*, Persian no. 6.
14 The Universal House of Justice, Regarding some elements of the Bahá'í electoral process, 25 March 2007.
15 'Abdu'l-Bahá, *Paris Talks*, no. 40, p. 134.
16 Shoghi Effendi, *The World Order of Bahá'u'lláh*, p. 43.
17 'Abdu'l-Bahá, *The Promulgation of Universal Peace*, p. 550.
18 ibid. pp. 197–8.
19 Bahá'u'lláh, *Hidden Words*, Arabic no. 1.
20 The Universal House of Justice, *Individual Rights and Freedoms in the World Order of Bahá'u'lláh*, pp. 10–11.
21 ibid. pp. 5–6, quoting Shoghi Effendi.
22 The Universal House of Justice, Riḍván Message 2012.
23 The Universal House of Justice, *Individual Rights and Freedoms in the World Order of Bahá'u'lláh*, p. 10.

24 ibid. p. 7.
25 ibid. p. 9.
26 Bahá'í International Community, *The Prosperity of Humankind*, p. 3.
27 'Abdu'l-Bahá, quoted in The Universal House of Justice, *Individual Rights and Freedoms in the World Order of Bahá'u'lláh*, p. 9.
28 The Universal House of Justice, *Selected Six Year Plan Messages*, p. 57.

6. Voting Rights, Education and Civil Society

1 Bartolini, *Enfranchisement, Equality and Turnout in the European Democratisation Process: A Preliminary Comparative Analysis*.
2 See Rogers, 'Culture and Catholicism: France'.
3 See Goodman, 'Class and religion: Great Britain and Ireland'.
4 See Soldani, 'Chequered routes to secondary education: Italy'.
5 See Gubin, 'Politics and anticlericalism: Belgium'.
6 Rousseau, as quoted in Rogers, 'Culture and Catholicism: France'.
7 Goodman, 'Class and religion: Great Britain and Ireland'.
8 'Abdu'l-Bahá, *Selections from the Writings of 'Abdu'l-Bahá*, no. 103, p. 129.
9 'Abdu'l-Bahá, *The Promulgation of Universal Peace*, p. 243.
10 'Abdu'l-Bahá, *Paris Talks*, no. 50, p. 170.
11 'Abdu'l-Bahá, *The Promulgation of Universal Peace*, p. 451.
12 Bahá'u'lláh, *Tablets of Bahá'u'lláh Revealed After the Kitáb-i-Aqdas*, p. 22.
13 Bahá'u'lláh, *Gleanings from the Writings of Bahá'u'lláh*, XCII, p. 184.
14 ibid. CXI, p. 217.
15 See Morris, 'Civil society, subscriber democracies, and parliamentary government in Great Britain'.
16 See Huard, 'Political association in nineteenth-century France: Legislation and practice'.
17 Prochaska, 'Good neighbours: Associational philanthropy and civic apprenticeship in 19th century England'.
18 De Tocqueville, quoted in Hoffmann, *Civil society and democracy in nineteenth century Europe: Entanglements, variations, conflicts*.
19 'Abdu'l-Bahá, *The Promulgation of Universal Peace*, pp. 435–444.
20 'Abdu'l-Bahá, *Tablets of the Divine Plan*, pp. 101–02.
21 The Universal House of Justice, *Selected Six Year Plan Messages*, pp. 56–7.

7. Dawn of a New Day

1 *The Dawn-Breakers*, p. 17.
2 ibid. p. 34.
3 Bahá'u'lláh, *The Summons of the Lord of Hosts*, p. 188.
4 ibid. pp. 93–4.
5 Shoghi Effendi, *The World Order of Bahá'u'lláh*, pp. 42–3.
6 See Hobsbawm, *The Age of Revolution, 1789–1848*, pp. 123–4.

8. Napoleon III and France

1 Bahá'u'lláh, *The Summons of the Lord of Hosts*, p. 72.

2 Shoghi Effendi, *The Promised Day Is Come*, p. 50.
3 Bahá'u'lláh, *The Summons of the Lord of Hosts*, p. 71.
4 ibid. p. 72.
5 ibid. pp. 72–3.
6 'Abdu'l-Bahá, quoted in Notes to the Kitáb-i-Aqdas, no. 121, in Bahá'u'lláh, *The Kitáb-i-Aqdas*. p. 217.
7 Bahá'u'lláh, *The Kitáb-i-Aqdas*, para. 90, p. 53.
8 Shoghi Effendi, *The Promised Day Is Come*, p. 4.
9 Bahá'u'lláh, *The Summons of the Lord of Hosts*, p. 72.
10 Shoghi Effendi, *The Promised Day Is Come*, p. 50.
11 'Abdu'l-Bahá, *The Promulgation of Universal Peace*, pp. 37–8.

9. Kaiser William I and Germany
1 Bahá'u'lláh, *The Kitáb-i-Aqdas*, para. 86, p. 51.
2 Shoghi Effendi, *The Promised Day Is Come*, p. 58.
3 Bahá'u'lláh, *The Summons of the Lord of Hosts*, p. 188.
4 ibid. p. 93.
5 Bahá'u'lláh, *The Kitáb-i-Aqdas*, para. 86, p. 51.
6 Shoghi Effendi, *The Promised Day Is Come*, pp. 58–9.
7 ibid.
8 'Abdu'l-Bahá, *The Secret of Divine Civilization*, p 32.
9 Shoghi Effendi, *The Promised Day Is Come*, p. 59.
10 Bahá'u'lláh, *The Kitáb-i-Aqdas*, para. 90, p. 53.
11 Shoghi Effendi, *God Passes By*, p. 287.
12 Shoghi Effendi, *The Advent of Divine Justice*, pp. 2–3.

10. The Papacy and Italy
1 Bahá'u'lláh, *The Summons of the Lord of Hosts*, p. 61.
2 Shoghi Effendi, *The Promised Day Is Come*, p. 54.
3 ibid.
4 Pope Pius IX, *The Syllabus of Errors*, available at: http://www.papalencyclicals.net/Pius09/p9syll.htm.
5 Bahá'u'lláh, *The Summons of the Lord of Hosts*, p. 56.
6 ibid. p. 70.

11. Francis Joseph and Austria
1 Bahá'u'lláh, *The Kitáb-i-Aqdas*, para. 85, pp. 50–51.
2 Shoghi Effendi, *The Promised Day Is Come*, p. 108.
3 See Shoghi Effendi, *God Passes By*, pp. 13–16.
4 Balyuzi, *Bahá'u'lláh, the King of Glory*, p. 225.
5 Shoghi Effendi, *God Passes By*, pp. 179–80.
6 Bahá'u'lláh, *The Kitáb-i-Aqdas*, para. 36, p. 31.
7 Shoghi Effendi, *The Promised Day Is Come*, p. 60.
8 ibid.

12. Alexander II and Russia

1 Bahá'u'lláh, *The Summons of the Lord of Hosts*, p. 83.
2 Engelstein, 'The dream of civil society in tsarist Russia: Law, state and religion', p. 34.
3 Bahá'u'lláh, *The Summons of the Lord of Hosts*, p. 83.
4 Furútan, *Stories of Bahá'u'lláh*, pp. 48–9.
5 Bahá'u'lláh, *The Summons of the Lord of Hosts*, p. 84.
6 Shoghi Effendi, *The Promised Day Is Come*, p. 57.
7 Engelstein, 'The dream of civil society in tsarist Russia: Law, state and religion', p. 28.
8 Shoghi Effendi, *The Promised Day Is Come*, p. 57.
9 Bahá'u'lláh, *The Summons of the Lord of Hosts*, p. 87.

13. Victoria and Great Britain

1 Bahá'u'lláh, *The Summons of the Lord of Hosts*, p. 89.
2 ibid. p. 89.
3 ibid. p. 90.
4 ibid.
5 ibid.
6 'Abdu'l-Bahá, *The Secret of Divine Civilization*, p. 17.
7 Bahá'u'lláh, *Tablets of Bahá'u'lláh Revealed After the Kitáb-i-Aqdas*, p. 28.
8 ibid. p. 93.
9 Bahá'u'lláh, *The Summons of the Lord of Hosts*, p. 93.

14. The United States

1 Bahá'u'lláh, *The Kitáb-i-Aqdas*, para. 88, p. 52.
2 Shoghi Effendi, *The World Order of Bahá'u'lláh*, p. 45.
3 Quoted in White, *A. Lincoln, a Biography*, p. 627.
4 'Abdu'l-Bahá, *Foundations of World Unity*, p. 35.
5 Bahá'u'lláh, *The Kitáb-i-Aqdas*, para. 88, p. 52.
6 Shoghi Effendi, *The Advent of Divine Justice*, p. 14.
7 Bahá'u'lláh, *Gleanings from the Writings of Bahá'u'lláh*, XCVI, p. 196.
8 Shoghi Effendi, *The Advent of Divine Justice*, p. 14.
9 ibid. p. 28.

15. The Great War

1 'Abdu'l-Bahá, in *Bahá'í Prayers*, p. 181.
2 The Universal House of Justice, Riḍván Message, 2002.
3 'Abdu'l-Bahá, quoted in Esslemont, *Bahá'u'lláh and the New Era*, p. 243.
4 'Abdu'l-Bahá, *The Promulgation of Universal Peace*, p. 168.
5 The Universal House of Justice, Riḍván Message, 2011.
6 'Abdu'l-Bahá, *The Promulgation of Universal Peace*, p. 22.
7 ibid. p. 27.
8 Bahá'u'lláh, *Tablets of Bahá'u'lláh Revealed After the Kitáb-i-Aqdas*, p. 144.

9 'Abdu'l-Bahá, *Paris Talks*, no. 44, p. 145.
10 ibid. pp. 148, 150.
11 'Abdu'l-Bahá, *The Promulgation of Universal Peace*, p. 105.
12 'Abdu'l-Bahá, quoted in Esslemont, *Baha'u'lláh and the New Era*, p. 144.
13 'Abdu'l-Bahá, *Some Answered Questions*, no. 78, p. 274.
14 'Abdu'l-Bahá, *The Promulgation of Universal Peace*, pp. 333–4.
15 ibid. p. 443.
16 ibid. p. 442.
17 ibid. p. 443.
18 The Universal House of Justice, 'Regarding 'Abdu'l-Bahá's letter to the people of Iran, titled *The Secret of Divine Civilization*', 26 November 2003.
19 'Abdu'l-Bahá, *The Secret of Divine Civilization*, pp. 14–15.
20 ibid. p. 16.
21 ibid. p. 17.
22 ibid. p. 23.
23 'Abdu'l-Bahá, *The Promulgation of Universal Peace*, p. 99.
24 'Abdu'l-Bahá, *The Secret of Divine Civilization*, p. 18.
25 The Universal House of Justice, Riḍván Message, 2010.

16. Identity and Social Transformation

1 Shoghi Effendi, *The Promised Day Is Come*, p. 117.
2 ibid. p. 118.
3 The Universal House of Justice, Riḍván Message, 2010.
4 'Abdu'l-Bahá, *The Promulgation of Universal Peace*, p. 25.
5 'Abdu'l-Bahá, *Tablets of the Divine Plan*, p. 102.
6 Bahá'u'lláh, *Bahá'í Prayers*, p. 209.
7 Bahá'u'lláh, *Prayers and Meditations*, CLXXXIII, p. 319.
8 See http://www.ruhi.org/institute/path.php.
9 Ruhi Institute, *Reflections on the Life of the Spirit*, 'To the collaborators'.
10 ibid.
11 ibid.
12 ibid.
13 Bahá'u'lláh, Hidden Words, Arabic no. 12.
14 The Universal House of Justice, Riḍván Message, 2012.
15 The Universal House of Justice, Message to the conference of the Continental Counsellors, 29 December 2015.

17. The 21st Century

1 Bahá'u'lláh, *Kitáb-i-Íqán*, para. 29, p. 31.
2 The Universal House of Justice, Regarding 'Abdu'l-Bahá's letter to the people of Iran, titled *The Secret of Divine Civilization*, 26 November 2003.
3 The Universal House of Justice. *Individual Rights and Freedoms in the World Order of Bahá'u'lláh*, pp. 10–11.
4 The Universal House of Justice, Regarding some elements of the Bahá'í electoral process, 2007.

5 The Universal House of Justice, Riḍván Message, 2012.
6 The Universal House of Justice, Riḍván Message, 2010.
7 The Universal House of Justice, Riḍván Message, 2001.
8 Bahá'í World Centre, *Century of Light*, pp. 139–40.
9 The Universal House of Justice, Message to the conference of the Continental Counsellors, 1995.
10 ibid.
11 The Universal House of Justice, Riḍván Message, 1999.
12 The Universal House of Justice, Riḍván Message, 2001.
13 The Universal House of Justice, Regarding several issues related to the principle of non-involvement in partisan political affairs, 2013.
14 The Universal House of Justice, Riḍván Message, 2010.
15 The Universal House of Justice, Riḍván Message, 2015.
16 The Universal House of Justice, Riḍván Message, 2010.
17 The Universal House of Justice, Riḍván Message, 2008.
18 Bahá'í International Community, Office of Public Information, *The Prosperity of Humankind*, p. 2.
19 ibid. p. 7.
20 ibid. pp. 8–9.
21 The Universal House of Justice, Riḍván Message, 2010.
22 ibid.
23 From a letter written by Shoghi Effendi to an individual, 12 December 1943, in *Victory Promises*, p. 17.
24 The Universal House of Justice, Riḍván Message, 2010.
25 The Universal House of Justice, Riḍván Message, 2012.
26 The Universal House of Justice, Riḍván Message, 2013.
27 The Universal House of Justice, Riḍván Message, 2014.
28 The Universal House of Justice, Riḍván Message, 1998.
29 Bahá'u'lláh, *Gleanings from the Writings of Bahá'u'lláh*, CXXIV, p. 263.
30 ibid. XXV, p. 60.

Epilogue

1 Bahá'u'lláh, *Gleanings from the Writings of Bahá'u'lláh*, CXXII, p. 260.
2 Bahá'u'lláh, Hidden Words, Arabic no. 2.
3 The Universal House of Justice, Riḍván Message, 2010.
4 ibid.
5 The Universal House of Justice, Riḍván Message, 2018.
6 See The Universal House of Justice, Message to National Conventions 1963, para. 2.11, in *Messages from the Universal House of Justice, 1963–1986*, p. 10; Launching of the Nine Year Plan, April 1964, section 14, ibid. pp. 31–4.

About the Author

Stephen Beebe grew up on a farm in Iowa in the 1950s, and received a Ph.D. in Plant Breeding and Genetics from the University of Wisconsin. He has spent his professional life in Latin America working on crop improvement with a cadre of agricultural scientists for the benefit of small farmers in the tropics of Central and South America and Eastern-southern Africa. He has served in Bahá'í administrative bodies, both Local and National Spiritual Assemblies, in Guatemala and in Colombia where he lives with his wife and family.

He is the author of two books on the nexus between early Christianity and the Bahá'í Writings. *Between the Menorah and the Cross: Jesus, the Jews, and the Battle for the Early Church* shows how the historical context of early Christianity as a persecuted minority religion coloured the presentation of the Gospel writers, with spiritual modes of expression that 'Abdu'l-Bahá would explain many years later. *The Logic of the Apocalypse* argues that consistent internal patterns in the New Testament's most mysterious and controversial book reveal its intentions when placed under the lens of the Bahá'í Writings.

www.ingramcontent.com/pod-product-compliance
Lightning Source LLC
Chambersburg PA
CBHW021220090426
42740CB00006B/311